THE IRWIN SERIES IN ECONOMICS

CONSULTING EDITOR

LLOYD G. REYNOLDS
YALE UNIVERSITY

BOOKS IN THE IRWIN SERIES IN ECONOMICS

SOVIET ECONOMIC PROCESSES

SOVIET ECONOMIC PROCESSES

BY

EDWARD AMES

Professor of Economics
Purdue University

1965

RICHARD D. IRWIN, INC.

HOMEWOOD, ILLINOIS

to Debbie

ACKNOWLEDGMENTS

A writer is lucky to have any readers; thrice lucky is the writer who has readers of his manuscript. J. R. T. Hughes, Holland Hunter, and Morton Kamien ferreted out errors, blunders, and omissions in my draft with such zeal that hardly a paragraph emerged intact. Chapter 4 is much tidier as a result of suggestions by Francis Seton. J. Michael Montias, by expressing grave doubts about portions of Chapters 2 and 3, led me to clarify my thoughts (and I hope my exposition) not only here, but also in Chapters 6, 10, and 11 as well. Michael Kaser and Alfred Zauberman allowed me to try out parts of the book on their seminars, with edifying (to me) results. Finally, Paul Gekker and Leon Herman have made a number of useful suggestions. In expressing my gratitude to all these friends for their efforts, I must simultaneously absolve them of responsibility for defects remaining in the finished product and for the opinions I have expressed in it.

At quite a different level of explanation this book was written because the London School of Economics, and more particularly its Director, Sir Sydney Caine, and Professor Ely Devons of its Economics Department asked me to give a series of lectures at L.S.E. I should not, moreover, have been in London in the first place without the support of a grant from the Rockefeller Foundation and a grant of sabbatical leave from Purdue University.

EDWARD AMES

Lafayette, Indiana
March, 1965

TABLE OF CONTENTS

Chapter 1

INTRODUCTION

This book presents a theory of the Soviet economy, to provide an explanation of the behavior of Soviet producing enterprises and of the nature of general economic equilibrium in the Soviet system. It sets forth in macroeconomic terms the three main dichotomies which characterize this system: that between agriculture and industry, that between current production and capital formation, and that between the Soviet state on the one hand and producing enterprises and households on the other.

Two general economic theories now exist. The first is based on the pure competition hypothesis, the second on the pure monopoly hypothesis. Although both of these present difficulties, both provide relatively unified ways of treating the economic processes of a country.[1] Neither of these general approaches is at all appealing to anyone who has looked at what goes on in the Soviet economy, but Sovietologists have so far had no practical theoretical alternatives. Since Soviet methods (for good or ill) dominate a large part of human economic activity, economists are effectively prevented from plying their trade in studying the extremely interesting group of problems in the Communist world.[2]

To fill this great gap, it is necessary to construct an entire system; for it is not clear that any of the ordinary theoretical con-

---

[1] I omit the theory of monopolistic competition from my list, because it needs integration with game theory to become a system in the sense that the other theories are systems.

[2] When I speak of economists, I naturally refer to economists in the various western traditions. Marxist economists are a different category. As theorists, they are not concerned with the problems which interest us, but with problems we would class as "political economy," sociology and historiography. Soviet economists, as government officials, must deal with economic problems in the western sense. It is my belief (strictly irrelevant to this book) that they have even less explicit theory about their own economy than western Sovietologists.

1

structs of economics are valid if applied to Soviet conditions. On the other hand, economics has (as a profession) thought seriously about a certain class of economic processes. It is natural to try to make as much use of existing economic methods as possible and to make theoretical innovations as few and as explicit as is possible. In particular, it is desirable to maintain the theoretical unity of the profession by treating the Soviet economy in terms of maximization hypotheses, since such hypotheses underly all the rest of economics.

Thus, if the following treatment is successful it will provide economics in general with a third system, to supplement the purely competitive and monopolistic systems. It will, in particular, provide a theoretical basis for Sovietologists who have been forced into an "institutionalist mold" by the lack of a relevant theoretical schema. Obviously, it is highly improbable that such a first treatment will be definitive. In this case, its argument, if stated explicitly enough, may stimulate economic theorists to make the needed corrections. If this is its consequence, it will have achieved one of its purposes: to interest theorists in the numerous challenging problems which are posed by the workings of the Soviet system.

Sooner or later, every student of economics learns to recite that economics is concerned with the application of scarce means to given ends. Every academic economist, moreover, has probably had occasion to say that all economies plan: in some the plans are centralized and in the hands of the state, while in others they are decentralized and in the hands of private firms. It is a point of pride among economists that whenever useful things are scarce (that is, where there are prices), economics should be able to say something about the utilization of these useful things. That is, economics should be able to analyze the Soviet economy and its planning processes.

Scientific method, which economists are also fond of talking about, consists of making formal hypotheses, drawing from them verifiable conclusions, testing these conclusions, and revising the hypotheses as needed. In particular, if one is to believe the preceding paragraph, economic hypotheses should specify both the given ends and the scarcity of the means. That is, they should ultimately be derivable from constrained maximum hypotheses of one kind or another.

Since 1945 very large amounts of economic research about the

U.S.S.R. have been carried on in the United States and (to a lesser extent) Britain. If this work followed the clichés of the profession, as set forth in the foregoing two paragraphs, there should by now be a body of theory presenting Soviet economic problems in terms of constrained maxima and demonstrating the validity (if any) of models based on these hypotheses; but one will look in vain for such analysis. The bulk of the research has been concerned with the reconstruction of a historical record of events. (There are good reasons why this should have been the case.) The work has, in the main, been historical rather than economic and has used economics as a source of accounting devices rather than as a source of hypotheses. Thus national income accounting has been much used, but national income theory has been little used.

It would be nice to have a proper economic theory of the Soviet type of economy. As long as such a theory does not exist, nobody knows whether it is possible to construct one; consequently, the validity of the statement made above (that whenever useful things are scarce, economics should be able to say something about their utilization) is in doubt, and empiricists can sneer at the theorists for not having done their homework.

As long as no theory exists, it is difficult for the Sovietologist to be an economist, although he may perform computations resembling those performed by economists. Such computations are usually justified on the grounds that if pure competition existed, they would have a theoretical meaning. It is hard enough to talk about any real private enterprise economy as if it conformed to the purely competitive model; surely it is more difficult to talk about the U.S.S.R. as if it were a purely competitive private economy. As long as there is no theory appropriate to Soviet circumstances, however, this is precisely what happens when one makes production indices or national income accounts for the U.S.S.R.

Two simple illustrations will show why such a work as this is needed. It is known that in the U.S.S.R. plans are made as to what output is to be. Suppose that in 1964 T tons of catnip were produced and that in 1965 the government plans to produce $1.15T$ tons. Actually, 1965 output will not ordinarily be $1.15T$ tons but some figure close to it. Suppose the figure turns out to be $1.17T$. There is now no economic explanation of why a change in plan should bring about a change in output. Assuming that a change in plan does produce a change in output, there is no economic explanation of why the change in output should be either less than or greater than the change in the plan.

Second, very detailed statistical analysis (which we accept for the present purpose) has shown that in the successive periods 1945–50, 1950–55, and 1955–60 the rate of increase of Soviet industrial output showed a steady decline. Thus, although output grew, it tended over time to grow less rapidly. Consider the problem of estimating in 1965 the growth rate from 1965–70. Such an analysis requires a hypothesis of the general form: the index of industrial output at time t, $I(t)$ is a function of variables $y_1(t)$, . . . , $y_m(t)$ which are given from outside and of variables $z_1(t)$, . . . , $z_n(t)$ which depend on Soviet government action. Output in 1970 depends upon the state of affairs in 1965, uncontrollable events occurring in 1966–70, and what the government does in 1966–70. In order to assert that the rate of growth will continue to slow down, it is necessary to assert that $I(1970)$ has some maximum value, given y_1 (1965) . . . y_m (1965), whatever be the pattern of z_1 . . . z_n over the following years, and that this maximum is less than the level of output that would have prevailed if there had been a constant rate of growth. Clearly such a theory does not now exist. There is now no hypothesis about the level of output, such as the function $I(t)$.

Of course, this second example is "difficult." It is doubtful whether adequate five-year hypotheses exist for private enterprise economies either. One must not reproach the Sovietologists for not having better theories than other economists. As a practical matter, however, they are called on to make forecasts. In the absence of explicit theories about what determines (and limits) the rate of Soviet industrial growth, they are forced to use rules of thumb which would repel any other kind of economist.

In the absence of theory, the Sovietologist interested in economic phenomena must rely on his intuition, and make informed guesses. Such guesswork can be a powerful tool, because some people have excellent intuition. My Sovietologist friend X told me that he had been dissatisfied with some estimates by my friend Y. These estimates were explained in about ten pages in Y's book. After three years' hard work X had written an entire book on the subject and at the end had a result which was within 10 percent of Y's figure. The accuracy of any estimate in this area is subject to a margin of error of at least 10 percent. Obviously Y has a valuable intuition. Unfortunately, he cannot transmit it to anyone else, and his secret must die with him.

If one hesitates to rely on informed guesswork, one must follow the rules of model-building. There are risks to model-building. There may be internal errors in the derivation of the properties of the model; these errors are within the area of theory proper. Or the model may lead to wrong predictions. In an ideal world, theorists would not make mistakes, and untested theories would never be published. No comment about the first possibility is needed. The second deserves the comment that some division of labor between theoretical and empirical work is inevitable as long as the tastes and talents of economists differ.

Economic theory is generally divided into microeconomics and macroeconomics along an imaginary line separating "big" from "small" economic entities. Precepts about "scarce means and given ends" in private enterprise economies are taken to refer to individual consumers and firms. In general, however, economists are interested in aggregations of consumers and firms. Why, then, need one worry at all about microeconomics?

The answer which is relevant for private enterprise economies is that macroeconomic hypotheses must be constructed from microeconomic theories. One describes the behavior of an individual and assumes that the group behaves as if it were an individual.[3] The macroeconomic hypothesis states that there are several groups[4] with assumed different kinds of behavior and considers the behavior of an economy consisting of such groups.

In the case of the U.S.S.R., it is natural to inquire whether it is necessary to divide the economy into more than three macroeconomic sectors: households, collective farms, and the state, since almost all nonagricultural activity (and a growing share of agriculture) takes place in state-owned facilities. A curious preoccupation in the literature with legal forms of ownership makes it necessary to discuss this question in some detail. As a matter of reality, it is important to distinguish between the state and the enterprises it owns, for two reasons. First, enterprises do not usually do exactly what they are told to do, although they usually do more or less

---

[3] Or, perhaps, that the group behavior is an "expected value" for a population of randomly differing individuals.

[4] In elementary courses households, businesses, banks, and government are the usual breakdown.

as they are told. Consequently there must be a theory which will explain why they do "more or less" but not "exactly" what they are told. Second, the actions of the state do not affect all enterprises in the same way; differences in treatment of various kinds of enterprises form an important aspect of Soviet economic policy.

The discussion of enterprises is thus a useful preliminary, even for economists whose main interests are in macroeconomic phenomena. This discussion is in part a description of Soviet business practices. These turn out to have some resemblance to those of private enterprise economies. Thus consumers earn money wages and use these for the purchase of consumer goods, for paying taxes, and for personal savings. Enterprises sell their output, using the proceeds to pay for inputs. Money is either in the form of bank notes or of checking accounts; in either case money is a liability of the banking system. The assets of the banking system mainly consist of loans to enterprises. The state has a budget—taxes are collected and the proceeds spent. The country has a balance of payments, including invisible items such as shipping and capital movements, as well as changes in gold and foreign reserves.

The economist, confronted with these numerous similarities, may wonder why a special theory is necessary to make Soviet economic processes intelligible. To answer this question we return to the microeconomic level and observe that the prices at which almost all transactions take place are fixed and sometimes may remain unchanged for a decade or more. When they do change, there is no evidence that they change in any systematic response to changes in demand or supply. Indeed, it is not clear what demand or supply might mean in the Soviet context. Whatever their meaning, it should be different from the private enterprise meaning; for the demand for factors and the supply of products are based, respectively, on the marginal productivity curves and marginal cost curves of firms. This is because the firms are assumed to be maximizing profits. Soviet enterprises certainly do not try to maximize profits, and there is no reason why their demand for inputs and supply of output should follow the same principles as those of private firms.

Thus, to clarify the theory of Soviet enterprises, it is necessary to state precisely what the enterprise is seeking to achieve (what it is maximizing) and what the constraints upon it may be. Prices are presumably one set of constraints; however, because of their invariance, prices in general do not have the same role in the U.S.S.R. as in private enterprise economies. Plans, however, do change often, and they do affect enterprises' actions. Hence an economic theory of Soviet enterprises must show that enterprises are affected by plans. These questions may be dealt with in more or less abstract ways. Since the U.S.S.R. is the main object of the theory, however, it is apposite to start from a description of Soviet practices, so that the theory, in addition to being internally consistent, should if possible use a defensible statement of initial conditions which reflects an intelligent estimate of Soviet reality.

Finally, economic theorists would need to know whether the analysis of single enterprises is consistent with the existence of equilibrium for the economy as a whole. Suppose that individual enterprises seek to maximize output; given production functions, a set of (fixed) prices, and a plan, is there a uniquely determined set of outputs for the economy in the sense that everything produced for sale is purchased, and the amounts desired by purchasers are indeed available? It is now possible to state the problem with some precision and to sketch a rather informal proof.

The foregoing is essentially a preparation for Chapters 2–6. These in turn lay a foundation for the later chapters, in which macroeconomic analysis is presented. It seems expedient to present an outline of the macroeconomic analysis in Chapter 7, in context, rather than at this point. Several points remain to be discussed in this introduction.

This book is intended to be a theoretical work. It relates, however, to a real country and, moreover, a country which has greatly changed over the past generation and will no doubt continue to change. Since the theoretical structure of the book is closely related to particular business practices, the reader must wonder (as the author has wondered) to what extent the theory applies specifically to one particular period of Soviet history and to what extent it is likely to be valid over the entire period from 1930 (when most of the features discussed were formalized) to some date after 1964, when the book was written. For instance, the discussion of agriculture in Chapter 8 could not have been written before 1941; it would have been very different if it had been written before 1952. The implications of collective farming for monetary stability did not become clear until the second world war; and the two proposed remedies we know of originated, respectively, in 1952 and in the late 1950's. In 1964 agriculture continued to be an object of government attention; no doubt other policies will sooner or later be adopted. From a theoretical point of view, it is useful to compare the measures so far adopted or considered, but it is dangerous to speak with any pretense of finality on an area of public policy which has been bothersome for a generation (to go no farther back). It is impossible to predict what a Soviet government might decide to do about agriculture in (say) 1975.

It is natural to ask how many changes in the Soviet economy it would take to invalidate the analysis given here, for Stalin's economic policies in the early 1930's would have invalidated a theory based on the Soviet system of the 1920's. Many changes took place in the decade from Stalin's death to Khrushchev's removal. Others must be expected in the future. Is there any way of defining what is the difference between essential and nonessential changes, as far as economic theory is concerned? It is clear, for instance, that a decision to diversify investment is not of theoretical importance. Whether steel or chemicals is the focal point of investment policy is perhaps an important political issue within the U.S.S.R., but it is of no analytical importance. On the other hand, if enterprises were allowed to fix their own prices, a major change in the theory would be needed. If enterprises were allowed to retain most of their profits, or if profits rather than output became the measure of managerial performance, the validity of the theory would be affected. If agriculture were to be given priority over industry in development programs, or if consumer goods production were given priority over heavy industry, the formal validity of the theory would not be affected, but the entire set of constraints in the economy would be altered beyond recognition. In this case, the motive for maintaining many of the arrangements here described would disappear, and hence the arrangements might well be modified beyond recognition.

This book makes no effort to compare Soviet practices with those of the European satellites of the U.S.S.R. or with those of Communist China and such Communist Chinese satellites as Albania, North Korea, and North Viet Nam. Nor does it deal with Yugoslavia, which introduced novel and ingenious legislation in the early 1950's. The European satellites generally adopted Soviet practices, outside agriculture, in 1948–50, and finished collectivizing agriculture (except in Poland) around ten years later. The analysis given here should apply fairly well to them. They are individually small and indifferently endowed with natural resources, however, and this should make for significant practical differences in the operations of their economies. I should be interested to know how far this model applies to Communist China, concerning which I am completely ignorant.

One of Pirenne's best works[5] was written to pass away the time while he was in prison, with no reference notes to distract him. My book was written as a series of lectures given at the London School of Economics in 1964, while I was a visitor there. The L.S.E. served the role of Pirenne's prison in only one respect, but this was essential: it made me work without my notes, which I had left at home. To deliver the lectures, I had to concentrate upon those matters which did not depend upon large accumulations of factual detail. To make the lectures useful, I had to rely upon "large" facts and to show how these could be used in developing an economic theory of how the Soviet system works.

If this book is successful, its readers will be able to bypass some of the steps which I followed in arriving at my present view of Soviet economic processes; but to go from a theoretical to an empirical understanding, they must still mainly go through the same process I went through: they must learn to read the Soviet press, for this is the primary source of economic information and misinformation about the U.S.S.R. It is worthwhile to comment in some detail upon the Soviet press, because it is so important a source of data.[6]

The Soviet press differs in an important respect from that we are accustomed to. The views and the facts which it presents are the only views and facts available to Soviet citizens. Consequently, its writers have a responsibility which writers in other countries do not have. Their function is to provide the only legitimate sources of information to their readers and to do so in such a way that the readers reach conclusions which it is desired that they reach. In

[5] Henri Pirenne, *A History of Europe From the Invasions to the XV Century,* (New York: University Books, 1955), preface by Jacques Pirenne.

[6] I have also learned from non-Soviet students, academic and other. Among the latter I include Messrs. Q and L, who spent three days together in a Soviet train. Mr. Q, looking out of the window, would say, "See those happy, prosperous collective farmers!" Mr. L, looking out of the same window, would reply, "Look at those poor, miserable, downtrodden peasants."

consequence, a great deal more care is exercised in stating (and in not stating) certain facts than is used by the press of other countries. Likewise, standards of truth and falsehood must be very different.

There are those who claim to believe that the Soviet press tells the truth, the whole truth, and nothing but the truth. This point of view is certainly a naive one and should normally disappear as one reads the Soviet press systematically. There are others who claim to believe the converse proposition, that the Soviet press tells only lies. This view is also naive, because it suggests that the Soviet press does not care whether its readers believe it. Anyone who has ever told a lie (and that includes all of us) knows that ordinarily one tells a lie hoping that it will be believed.[7] Consequently, it is important to a would-be liar that as much as possible of his statement including the lie be true. If some parts of the statement are demonstrably true, the reader will be more inclined to believe the part which is false. Since Soviet readers are as intelligent as other readers, they will believe the press to the extent that what it says conforms to their own experience. Consequently, the press cannot fabricate falsehood about Soviet events without risking its control over people's beliefs. In certain cases, the press may be willing to take this risk; but it cannot always, or even usually, do so. For this reason, the Soviet government has in general found it more convenient to suppress certain kinds of information than it has to utter direct falsehoods when it is talking about internal affairs; for readers of the Soviet press do live in the Soviet Union.

Let us suppose, for example, that a given industry has been forced to reduce output because of a shortage of materials. This is a fact which will certainly be known to thousands of people in the industry. Some of these will have been working short hours; others have access to the true data as a necessary part of their jobs. If the press states (contrary to fact) that output has risen, these readers will know that a lie has been uttered, and they will be the less willing to believe other statements (which may well be true). It is much better that the press say nothing than that it make demonstrably false statements.

---

[7] In some cases one tells a lie in such a way that everyone knows it a lie, implying thereby a truth one does does not care to state explicitly. Space limitations preclude a full discussion of this interesting subject.

The western reader will frequently find it difficult to interpret statements in the Soviet press. Let me give a clear example of the problem. A few weeks before the German invasion of the U.S.S.R. in June, 1941, TASS, the official Soviet news agency, issued on behalf of the Soviet government a statement which said: *(a)* the foreign press has reported that German troop concentrations are taking place along the Soviet frontier; *(b)* these reports are designed to weaken Soviet-German relationships; *(c)* TASS has been authorized to deny these reports.

Some western observers (including Germans) have said that this denial is clear demonstration that the Soviet government was not expecting a German attack. Others, however, say that this was a clear warning to the Soviet people that war was at least possible in the near future. The former rely upon the wording of the statement. The latter say that this statement was the first direct evidence given in the Soviet press that there was any basis at all for believing that Soviet-German relations were not what they should be. It is known today that the British and American governments, and also some highly placed individuals in the German embassy in Moscow, had warned the Soviet government of the impending attack and that the Soviet government appeared not to believe such warnings. Both sources agreed that the announcement was greeted by very great interest on the part of ordinary Soviet citizens and that both of the points of view expressed above could be heard from them. It can only be guessed what the purpose of the TASS denial may have been.

There seem to be many categories of statement in the Soviet press, and various kinds of credibility may be attached to them. As indicated, I believe a statement which says, "T tons of commodity C were produced in year Y," and gives numbers. I also believe statements which say, "Output of C increased by P percent between years Y_1 and Y_2," although I do not exclude the possibility that somewhere between Y_1 and Y_2 output of C reached a peak and declined thereafter.

If I see a statement which says, "The volume of retail trade increased by P percent between years Y_1 and Y_2," I believe that there exists a method of calculating a volume index for the two years which will yield an increase of P percent. I do not conclude that the increase P is necessarily greater than some other increase P' reported for the same period by some other country; however, if P is greater than some increase P'' reported by the U.S.S.R. for some other period for the same variable (i.e., volume of retail trade), I am inclined to believe that in the first period the volume of Soviet retail trade rose more rapidly than in the second.

If I see a statement that Soviet workers are better off than other workers, or that their welfare is rising more rapidly than that of other workers, I think of Stalin. In 1931, at a time when the Soviet standard of living was declining catastrophically, he declared that Soviet workers were better off than workers in any other country, because (a) there was no unemployment in the U.S.S.R., (b) there were no capitalists or landowners in the U.S.S.R. and (c) the U.S.S.R. was run by the Communist party. No reasonable person could have disagreed with statements (a), (b), and (c). It is open to dispute, however, whether (b) and (c) are conducive to human happiness, and whether an employed Soviet worker in 1931 had a higher rate of personal consumption than an unemployed non-Soviet worker. "Everybody has his own taste," the old lady declared as she kissed the cow.

Thus there is no single answer to the question: "Can Soviet statements be believed?" Some can, and others cannot. If there is any valid mystery to Sovietology, it lies in the ability to infer from a reading of truths, half-truths, and lies what the truth may be. Scholarship about the Soviet economy is based upon a careful examination of a set of texts; these texts consist of the daily press, the periodical literature, and specialized monographs. The foreign student must form his own interpretation of statements which are sometimes concrete but more often deliberately vague at the crucial points. He must aim at an interpretation which is consistent with as much as possible of the factual data available. In this respect, his task is like that of the economic historian; but what makes it particularly frustrating is his suspicion that the full information is being concealed from him. The student of the Middle Ages, for instance, does not suspect that the English Exchequer kept its accounts according to approved modern practices and maintained the Pipe Rolls only to make things difficult for later scholars; however, the Soviet government may keep excellent records of its investment expenditures and publish most inconvenient data in order to prevent foreign (presumably hostile) sources from obtaining access to the true data. It may be, however, that Soviet records are as bad as published sources suggest.

The amount of information concerning the Soviet economy has varied greatly. Thus, in the 1920's there was a great deal of economic information published, although its technical standards were frequently low (and it was no secret that this was the case). After about 1935, the amount of information published currently declined sharply (although reporting standards should have improved). From about 1938 until about 1955 it became extremely hard to collect even the simplest kinds of data about the Soviet economy. Since 1955, there has been a noticeable improvement in the amount of published data, so that at present many Soviet statistics, while not very conveniently presented, are relatively accessible. But these fluctuations in Soviet policy about releasing information have had important repercussions upon foreign scholarship.

Foreign economic writing on the Soviet bloc has been overwhelmingly concerned with reconstructing the statistical records. It tends to assume that the Soviet government has continuously had available to it fairly adequate records, only fragments of which have been released to the press at any particular time. By a careful collation of the published fragments, foreign scholarship hopes to reassemble facsimiles of the original Soviet records. It is overwhelmingly time-consuming and tedious to do this, but it is possible. One need only examine the records of such indefatigable workers as Jasny, Nutter, and Chapman to see how much can be done along these lines.[8]

The reader who surveys this body of literature will wonder, of course, why so much effort has been devoted to the statistical problem. In part the answer is to be found in the whole trend of modern economics, which has sought to become a quantitative science. If modern economists in general use quantitative national income analysis, it is not surprising that they should wish to apply it to the Soviet economy as well as to others; and one should not wonder at writers like Bergson and Heyman, who have devoted years to the preparation of Soviet national accounts data. Indeed, in this particular example, Bergson and Heyman use western concepts of the national income, which differ considerably from Soviet

---

[8] I shall frequently have occasion to mention authors whose work forms an important part of the literature on the Soviet economy. Where this work does not immediately support a statement in the text, I shall omit a footnote. A list of such background literature is given at the end of this book.

concepts. Thus, these writers have managed to produce statistics which do not exist in the U.S.S.R. and will not exist so long as Soviet economists remain Marxists. We are grateful and regret (no doubt with these authors) only that the time used to assemble the data could not have been used for analytical purposes.

In the process of preparing these major statistical works, the entire level of foreign economic analysis of the Soviet economy has been enormously improved. One need only compare briefly the work appearing in the last fifteen years with that which appeared before 1945 to see the vast technical improvement which has taken place. Continuous series of data are now available, information is subjected to a scrutiny which was seldom if ever undertaken in earlier periods, a clarification of the critical issues in interpretation of fact has taken place. There is no longer any excuse for the English-speaking economist to rely upon his emotions as a substitute for analysis of data.

On the other hand, the preoccupation with statistics has reflected an essentially narrow preoccupation of research students. It is hardly a secret that most of the research on the Soviet economy since 1945 has been financed ultimately by United States military intelligence. The purpose of military intelligence is stated to be to determine the capability, vulnerability, and intention of a potential or real enemy. It is no secret that the United States government has considered the Soviet government to be an actual or potential enemy. In the economic sphere its capabilities and vulnerability must be defined in terms of ability to produce military goods. Under modern conditions, military output comes from all sectors of the economy. To quantify and to determine the location of economic activity must be the central objective of military intelligence.

The combined biases of the Soviet press (the supplier of data) and of the U.S. intelligence community (the user of data) have reinforced each other. Economists have been forced into thinking about plans and plan fulfillment, because the Soviet press talked about these and because the United States needed to know about them. The Soviet government has insisted that price policy simply was of no importance in a socialized economy, and the U.S. government has been interested in prices mainly *(a)* as a device to aid in the construction of output indices or *(b)* as propaganda material to illustrate the unquestionably low Soviet standard of living. The Soviet government has felt that fiscal and monetary policies were to be used mainly as controls on managerial efficiency, and the United States has felt that these policies could never reduce Soviet military potential. By common consent, as it were, problems which loom large in the analysis of other economies have simply vanished from discussions of the U.S.S.R., within the country and abroad. A discussion (such as this) which resurrects prices, fiscal policy, monetary policy, and other such will probably be offensive to both. The theorist must, therefore, don Mambrino's helmet and ride unhesitatingly on.

It is reasonable to guess that if military considerations had been less important, the preoccupation of English-speaking economists with "counting things" would have been far less important than it has actually been. It is my personal conviction that, beyond a certain point, collection of data is tedious without necessarily being particularly informative to anyone save the man who must select targets for missiles. Even he, moreover, must be guided by some theory about selecting those targets which it is most expedient to destroy. For any purposes but these rather extreme ones, rather more subtle analysis is required to make sense of Soviet economic processes.

In the absence of thermonuclear war (which would certainly alter economic processes generally), is it possible to construct an economic theory of the Soviet economy which serves the purposes of the economic theory with which we are familiar? That is, are there categories such as the theory of consumer demand, the theory of the individual firm and of the individual industry, the theory of money, and the theory of national income which apply to the Soviet system? It would be very convenient if the existing body of economics could be applied to Soviet conditions; however, as every schoolboy knows, the Soviet economy is different. It is socialist—whatever that means. Although friend and foe agree that it is not the same as ours, is it then so different that all economic analysis must be cast aside?

A certain antiseptic tone to the formal discussion which follows may distress foreign readers of the Soviet press. In part, this distress is like that which observers of private business organizations feel at any economic theory. Theory is neat, while life is messy. Second, economic theory treats the business as a mechanism which responds passively but optimally to environmental change; life suggests that some businesses affect their environment, and that even in businesses which do not, a great deal goes on which economic theory does not discuss. I sympathize with both views, but hold that they do not invalidate economic theory as an approach to those problems which economic theory seeks to answer; and I think that economic theory is concerned with important problems.

In particular, however, readers will feel that Chapters 2–13 slight the role of the Soviet bureaucracy. It is well known that the Soviet administrative system is large, cumbersome, and "Russian." It has fascinated writers as diverse as Gogol, Dostoevski, and Zoshchenko, and its doings are daily described in the Soviet press. Until Chapter 14, however, I treat this vast superstructure as a polished monolith, exerting an even and predictable (though arbitrary) pressure upon the foundation of enterprises and consumers which supports it. The internal operations of the administration are not considered in detail until the last chapter, which explains why the internal workings of Soviet administration pose an economic problem. I have used this approach partly for expository reasons: given a differentiation between enterprises and administrative agencies, it is possible to construct an economic theory which explains a main part of the Soviet system. I cannot now construct a theory of the administrative system itself. My final chapter explains the need for such a theory, and the questions such a theory must answer, even though it recognizes that this part of the Soviet system has so far defied formal treatment.

PART I

Microeconomics

Chapter 2 : PROPERTY, PLANS, AND REGULATIONS

Three words will be useful in our discussion: *property, plan,* and *regulation.* These words are used here in narrow senses, although in other contexts they have emotional and political overtones. *Property* is taken to mean any material object used in the production of goods and services. A *plan* is an order by one legally constituted body to another to produce or consume some given amount of goods and services in some stated period of time. A *regulation* is an order which is not a plan.[1]

Property means productive assets. Property is classified by Soviet law into two basic categories: private and socialist; and socialist property is divided into two subcategories, state and cooperative. In principle, private property (that is, property owned by individuals) is recognized by law; however, individuals may not employ the labor of others, so in fact the only legal private property is in firms consisting of a single person. For practical purposes, all productive assets in the Soviet Union are socialized. The property of individuals should not be confused with their *personal possessions,* which have no productive purposes.

Again, by law, certain classes of productive assets are exclusively reserved to the state. Land and mineral resources, for example, are state property. In fact, though not necessarily in principle,

---

[1] A plan is also to be distinguished from a *contract,* in which a buyer and seller, each obeying plans, agree to buy or sell some amount of goods or services. For the moment, plans are assumed to fall "from the heavens" on subordinates. This assumption is invalid, in that plans are prepared with some participation of subordinates. No particular connection is assumed to exist between the plans given different subordinates. Actually, the co-ordination of plans, in the interests of ensuring some desired macroeconomic effect, is an important theoretical and practical problem. Both of these matters will be discussed in more detail below, when the path has been cleared to them.

19

the assets of industry and transportation are almost entirely state property. In agriculture and rural trade, however, co-operative property is the most common legal form. Since agriculture naturally takes place on the land, one might wonder how co-operative agriculture is compatible with state ownership of land. Legally, the procedure is simple. The farming unit (collective farm) receives a charter from the state, which gives it the right to *use* a certain portion of land. Thus a collective farm owns its buildings, machinery, and so on, whereas a state-owned farm does not. In principle, the land is assigned to a collective farm without stipulation of time limit. In practice, when the state has wished to consolidate several collective farms into a single business unit, it has had no difficulty in doing so. Beginning in 1950, for example, the number of collective farms was reduced to about one fifth the former number by consolidations, and there is no record of any legal problem having arisen. Since there were 237,000 collective farms before the mergers, and only 45,000 in 1960, one might have expected at least a few mergers to have been opposed if there had existed a strong right to the use of land in the charters of individual collective farm organizations.

Collective farms are unique among co-operative economic units in one respect. They have no hierarchical organizational structure. That is to say, there have never been regional or national organizations of collective farms. Their situation thus contrasts strongly with the situation of other co-operative organizations. These are basically of two kinds. First, we may mention consumer co-operatives. These were of some importance in urban retail trade in the early 1930's and in the late 1940's, and they are the basic form of retail trading organization in rural areas. The individual store in the co-operative system, however, is part of a national trading organization, which establishes its basic rules of procedure, trains and appoints its managerial personnel, fixes the prices at which it sells, and so on. The philosophy behind this type of organization I shall return to later; for the moment it is sufficient to note the fact.

The second type of co-operative has been the artel, or producer co-operative. This type of organization was originally concerned with the supply of services, and to a lesser extent the manufacture of consumer goods, in urban areas. For instance, laundry, shoe repair, watch repair, manufacture of made-to-order clothing, and similar enterprises were likely to be organized as artels—although at some periods of Soviet history individuals have been able to operate private business involving this type of work. These organizations were typically united into city-wide or regional organizations under the supervision of local governmental units; and they did not ordinarily establish their own wage rates, prices, and the like. In 1958, these artels were simply transformed into state enterprises under municipal control. They are mentioned because they played an important, if marginal, role in supplying services to city dwellers.

Collective farms, however, have never formed national or even regional organizations. The reason for this fact is that there is no economic reason, in the Soviet state, for such a situation. Agriculture has been one of the central concerns of the government throughout Soviet history, and the Ministry of Agriculture has sought direct contact with individual farms, rather than the indirect contact which (say) the Ministry of Trade has with individual co-operative stores through the central co-operative organization. If one is anti-Soviet he will state the same point in a different way. The government, he will say, has never trusted individual collective farms, and even less has it trusted groups of them; it has therefore prevented the farms from forming groups.

Industry, transport, construction, urban trade, and banking have assets which are legally state property. That is, ownership of all these productive assets is vested in the state. Legally, the Ministry of Finance is treated as the owner. When a new factory is completed, for example, there is a procedure in which the plant is turned over by the construction agency to the Ministry of Finance, which then assigns it to an operating agency and gives it a charter. In principle, additions to existing factories are handled as if they were new construction which (when completed) is turned over to the management of an existing firm.

There are various practical reasons for emphasizing this somewhat obscure legal aspect of Soviet property relations. Socialists, in general, have been concerned with eliminating private ownership of the means of production. If the means of production are not private, then they belong not to "capitalists," but to someone else. It is conceivable that the factories might be the property of those individuals who are employed there. Some socialists have felt that this type of ownership was a good or admissible one. Indeed, in principle, the former Soviet artel was the property of the workers in the artel, and not of the state. The collective farm is the property of its members.

The Soviet government, however, takes the position that state property belongs to the entire nation and not to those particular workers who happen to be employed there. This view is taken to imply that if the output of that particular plant is sold at a profit, the profit does not create any claim on higher pay by those employed there. The state may, if it chooses, reward some of those employed at the plant for their efficiency. Conversely, if a plant is operated at a loss, the state may choose to subsidize that plant rather than force its personnel to accept lower wages. Decisions about what and how much should be produced at the plant are vested in the owner, the state. If we make the additional assumption that the state expresses the "popular will," actions by the personnel of a given plant that are contrary to state interest are automatically actions against the popular will and therefore undemocratic.

It takes only a simple extension of this principle to see why the individual consumer co-operative does not select its own management, fix its own prices, and so on. The individual store is only one link in an entire system. If the store sets its own desires in opposition to those of the system as a whole, then it acts as a small minority. If we make the assumption that the national organization represents the will of the entire system, we have no difficulty in seeing how it is that only centralized authorities in principle may regulate economic affairs. In practice, they may choose not to intervene in some matters, but in principle they retain the right to do so.

It is the case, therefore, that all legal forms of activity are represented by suitable organizations, some of which are part of the governmental structure and some of which are not; but the social organizations do not differ in form from the governmental organization, although there is naturally some difference in terminology. For instance, the term *council* (in Russian *sovet*) is limited to government organization; the corresponding unit in a social organization is *committee* (in Russian *komitet*). The governmental unit in charge of a city is the "city council"; the corresponding party unit is the "city committee" of the party. Since the party by virtue of its constitutional position has a unit in every organization, both state and social, its own organization presents very considerable complications, which need not in fact long detain us. It is sufficient to observe that if plant X is located in city Y, there will be attached to the plant a party committee which is associated administratively with the party committee of other plants in the same administrative system and also with the party committees of other organizations in the same city, to whatever administrative system they may belong.

Any organization has what may be termed a *legislative body*, the generic name for which is *congress* (in Russian *s'ezd*). The congress may not meet very often. For example, the Communist party had no congress between 1939 and 1952. There is, however, a standing committee of the congress which is enabled to act in the name of the congress between meetings of the major body. Thus, the governmental congress, the Supreme Soviet, which normally meets twice a year for a period of about one week, has a standing committee, the Presidium, which acts for it in the intervals. As a part of its business, the Supreme Soviet ordinarily ratifies the actions of the Presidium. The Presidium of the congress of the Communist party was, curiously enough, of rather later formation. Until 1952, two standing committees, the Political Bureau and the Organizational Bureau, were the relevant standing committees, although only the first appears to have been of major importance.

The executive of any unit is elected by the congress and is responsible to it. The executive of the state is called the Council of Ministers; that of the party is the Central Committee. (The term "central committee" is applied to many other executive units.) In practice, executives tend to contain very many members and to be inconveniently large for policy formation; therefore, smaller groups tend to be formed. In the government, for example, there are apparently many ministers of little consequence. The most important ministers are given the rank of deputy premiers and seem to form a group. We do not know, however, whether they meet as a formal body.

Naturally, the direction of all organizations by the Communist party means that there is considerable overlapping in the membership of the executives of the various organizations. Historically, most important policy statements and decrees have been issued jointly by the Council of Ministers and the Central Committee of the Communist party. When Stalin or Khrushchev spoke, it was as head of both organizations, and in some sense it is idle to try to separate the two positions.

At the lower levels of life, however, there are important distinctions between party officials and government officials. One does not find plants where the director is also secretary of the party organization; the head of the trade union committee is never the party secretary. It makes a great deal of sense that the various organizations should merge in the persons of their leaders, since otherwise there could be serious administrative differences of political significance. It also makes a good deal of sense that at the lower levels the organizations should be distinct, since the role of each organization is specialized and, in some degree at least, each serves as a check upon the others.

The members of an organization are considered to be bound by the decisions of the executive. The members of the Soviet civil service (the employees of the ministries, and so forth) are obviously bound by decisions of their superiors. The same thing is true of the trade unions, the Communist party committees, and other groups. The vehicle for selection of the leadership is, in principle, the congress (or between congresses, the standing committee). At congresses, moreover, programs are presented to the membership for approval. Needless to say, it has been a great many years since more than one candidate has been nominated for any one post or where two alternative policies were presented at a single congress of a major organization.

The Soviet constitution goes one step further. Article 126 states:

In accordance with the interests of the workers, and in order to develop organizational initiative and political activity of the masses of citizens of the U.S.S.R., there is guaranteed the right of uniting into social organizations: trade unions; co-operative units; youth organizations; sporting and defense organizations; cultural, technical and scientific societies; and the more active and conscious citizens in the ranks of the working class, working peasants and working intelligentsia are voluntarily enrolled in the Communist party of the Soviet Union, which is the leading unit of the workers in their struggle for the building of a communist society, and which is the leading nucleus of all organizations of workers, both social and state.

This statement is, of course, a legal one. Read carefully, it defines types of activities which are legal and the types of organizations which are permitted. It then states that all legal activities are ones directed by the Communist party. Political scientists will note that other political parties might legally exist, but only if their leading personnel were drawn from the Communist party. From our point of view, the important principle is that the Soviet system presupposes a centralized ownership of productive assets.

At this particular point, economists will naturally object: if, indeed, the Soviet economy is based upon such centralized ownership and control, is there any meaning in the concept of microeconomics for the Soviet economy? Surely, if the state operates its property as if it were a single unit, if both state and co-operative property are operated by organizations led by the Communist party, then "microeconomics" can apply only to individual consumers and to the (negligible) private enterprises which exist in the U.S.S.R. Conversely, if such microeconomics can be shown to be of real significance, that can only mean that the Communist party is unable to carry out those functions assigned to it by law and in fact allows enterprises an independence they should not, in law, be permitted. This objection is a natural one and indeed raises problems which are of continuing interest to the student of the Soviet economy. I shall not try to answer the question at once, but will return to it in later chapters.

The second word mentioned at the beginning of this chapter was *plan*, an order issued by one legally constituted body to another, relating to the production of goods and services. A *plan* is a statement of the form "*Do X.*" But the expression "*Do X*" means also "Do not do not-X." It is of some importance, then, to specify in individual cases what constitutes violation of the order. Thus, if the plan relates to production, the plan "Produce 1 million tons of steel" does not mean "Do not produce 1,000,001 tons of steel." It does mean "Produce at least 1 million tons of steel." On the other hand, the plan "Pay wages of 1 million rubles in January" does not mean "Pay at least 1 million rubles in wages in January," but rather "Pay at most 1 million rubles in wages in January."

All plans are orders, but not all orders are plans. I shall call orders which are not plans *regulations*. An important class of regulation is of the form "Whenever you do A do it in manner M." The two guiding words are *whenever* and *manner*. Obviously regulations are extremely important in the U.S.S.R., as they are in other countries. Regulations set forth the framework in which communications among economic (and other) agencies proceed. For instance, it would not be clear that the *plan* "Produce 1 million tons" means "Produce at least 1 million tons" rather than "Produce at most 1 million tons" unless there was a body of regulations such that plant officials knew they should interpret the plan as I have indicated. The regulations implicitly say, "When you produce, see that the amount you produce is not less than the production plan."

In a large organization, the preparation of orders is a difficult task. There are several kinds of problems. First, the person preparing the order must know what he wants; second, he must know what he will probably be able to get, and third, he must know the connection that exists between what he orders and what he gets. For example, (*a*) parents must know that they wish their sons to come to the table with clean hands; (*b*) they must know how well boys of any age are apt to wash their hands; (*c*) they must know how insistently they must clamor in order to obtain hands of a given degree of cleanliness. In any family in which the order "Go wash your hands" is given, there are regulations. In one family, the regulations may read, "Unless the old man raises his voice to a shout, go on with what you were doing." In another it may read, "If you hear a whisper from the old man, watch out."

In private business organizations, both plans and regulations exist. The order "This drop in profits must stop" means "Profits next year must be at least as large as they were this year" and is, in our terminology, a plan. The order "Whenever you make a profit, write it down in a little book, and tell the Internal Revenue Service about it," however, is a regulation. In general, regulations are relatively more prevalent, and plans less prevalent, in market economies than in the U.S.S.R. This is because business policy can be stated fairly simply as "Do X if and only if it seems to be legal and profitable." If X is profitable, and if it does not get us into the toils of the law, there is no particular reason to discuss the desirability of doing X; and if X is both unprofitable and illegal, there is no particular reason why anyone should want to do it. It is a fact, in contrast, that Soviet institutions generate very large numbers both of plans and of regulations. It is perhaps an economic question why so many exist; it is certainly an economic fact that they do.

In the nature of things, plans are hardly ever fulfilled exactly. That is, the output of an enterprise is usually not exactly equal to the plan. Sometimes it is somewhat below, sometimes slightly above. If the enterprise produces many products, it may receive a plan for each; in some cases it may well fall short of, and in other cases exceed, plans. Since a plan is in principle an order, there is an important question of why the orders are not exactly executed. Soviet literature tends to talk in terms of virtue and vice, saying that good leadership leads to plan fulfillment, while bad leadership does not. But this statement is not very satisfactory, because it does not explain why management might arrive at any particular level of output and why this particular level is in some sense "best" for it. The problem of explaining output levels would be resolved by the existence of plans if we could say that deviations from plan were chance occurrences. When, however, it turns out that large groups of enterprises may all tend, for example, to have below-plan profits or above-plan wage payments then there is an economic phenomenon, worthy of direct scrutiny.

The instructions received by individual factories, farms and so on, include plans. The set of plans issued by each of the major centers of economic power are summarized in documents which we shall have occasion to discuss. These are also frequently referred to as plans, since they aggregate, in some sense, the orders issued by the particular agency in question. Thus, for example, the set of orders issued by the Ministry of Finance is summarized by the *State Budget of the U.S.S.R.*, which is one of the important economic plans. The set of orders regulating current production of the individual enterprises in industry and transportation is summarized in the annual *Production Plan*. The annual set of orders relating to construction of new plant and equipment is summarized in the *Plan for Capital Works*, which has a close connection with the state budget, since a large part of the funds used in construction come from the budget. The annual set of orders relating to the issue of credit by the banking system is called the *Credit Plan;* the annual set of orders relating the payment of wages to the value of retail trade is called the *Cash Plan.* Each of these five documents summarizes one aspect or another of the aggregate of instructions issued by the Soviet government to the enterprises which operate the plant and equipment which it owns; each also contains instructions to the collective farms, co-operatives, and so on which it regulates.

Readers familiar with British and American discussions of

economic planning may be surprised to note that I have used *plans* only in the plural, and that while I have mentioned familiar economic categories such as wages, construction of plant and equipment, wage payments and so on, I have not used the expression *national product*. It is true that Soviet economists use the word *plan* in the singular. When they do, in nine cases out of ten they are referring to the *Production Plan* only and not to the other four documents. It is therefore important that we inquire whether the five major economic documents I have mentioned are so interrelated that if one refers to one of them he finds only statements compatible with statements contained in the other four. In particular those who are interested in discussions of economic growth in other countries will wonder why the national product is not included in my listing. The answer which is compatible with the terminology so far developed is that there cannot be plans relating to the national product because orders relating to the level of the national product cannot be addressed to anyone. GNP is a synthetic number, which ideally could be compounded from other economic information, but it is not an instrumental variable, that is, it is affected by other things, but cannot be directly influenced.

I have referred to plans as documents, but I have given no particular clue about how these documents originate. To answer that question would require very much more information than anyone possesses on this side of the Iron Curtain. In 1945, I had occasion to be present at an interview between a group of American congressmen and the deputy chief of the State Planning Commission of the U.S.S.R. A plan for 1946–50 production was in the process of preparation; the press was full of it, and the congressmen wished to find out how the plan was prepared. The Soviet official described the process as follows: One day, he said, the commission received from "over there"—he pointed out of the window to the Kremlin, which was visible—a list of about twenty commodities, with levels of output to be reached in 1950. The commission then determined what production levels of other commodities would be needed in order to maintain output of the listed items. The commission then allocated a second, enlarged set of targets among the responsible ministries; these allocated their targets among their plants and sent these targets to the plants. After a while, a reverse flow of information began. The plants submitted estimates of the ways and means by which they could either achieve or come close to their targets; the ministries summarized these reports in discussions of ways and means by which they could carry out the instructions of the commission; and the commission prepared a volume (probably large and fat) for the government describing how it proposed to carry out the government's objectives.

This answer, of course, does not tell us why the government selected the particular commodities on the list, how it arrived at the desired levels of output, and what manner of adjustment was possible between the desires of one administrative agency and those of agencies at higher and lower levels. In fact, very little is known about these matters, except perhaps at the level of the individual plant. There have been enough plant officials who have defected from the U.S.S.R. in the postwar period for us to have some slight notion (however biased the sources on which it is based may be) about how this part of the process of issuing and obeying orders is carried on; but we have virtually no idea about how decisions are reached at higher levels of the administration.

The discussion of planning would be incomplete without some comment on Five Year Plans. These are the most dramatic economic pronouncements of the Soviet government and have been the subject of much debate, both on the emotional and intellectual planes. These plans serve two purposes. First, they force the Soviet administrative system to regard production problems as a whole, and this is a very useful exercise. Second, they are a concise statement of government objectives which can be used for public relations purposes.

It is easy, however, to show that Five Year Plans are of limited operational importance. Thus no Five Year Plan has ever begun on time and also survived for five years without major revision. The First Five Year Plan (1929–33) was rewritten by the 1930 Party Conference. The second (1933–37) was drastically altered after the Comintern Congress of 1935, which signalled a major change in Soviet foreign policy. The third (1938–42) was not completed until early 1939 and had to be discarded when war broke out in 1941. The fourth (1946–50) had to be drastically changed because of (*a*) inflationary pressure leading to the currency conversion of December, 1947, (*b*) the unexpected nature of world politics, and (*c*) the adoption in 1949–50 of major unscheduled construction projects.

The fifth (1951–55) was not approved until late 1952 and was drastically revised in early 1954 by the short-lived Malenkov program for consumer goods production. The sixth (1956–60) was shortly afterwards replaced by a Seven Year Plan (1958–65), but this plan was obviously revised in major respects in 1961.

To make these points is simply to warn against journalistic excess. Too often, Five Year Plans are considered as immutable, as if the Soviet government could only make decisions at five-year intervals. In part, the mythology of the Five Year Plans is perpetuated because the Soviet government pretends it never changes its mind, and issues reports on the fulfillment of plans which have, in the interim, been altered beyond recognition. In periods when statistics have been suppressed, such reports are indeed important statistical sources, but they should be viewed only as statistical sources. The Soviet government relies on annual and monthly plans to direct its enterprises, and these are the plans which are relevant for most analytical purposes. We may, of course, learn about Soviet economic policies as of the date of issue of a Five Year Plan; but we must not assume uncritically that these policies will remain fixed for very long. Some do and some do not.

The reader may have noted that I have so far not made any use of the word *price,* nor of the corresponding term *wage rates.* Of course, the Soviet Union uses money. Prices certainly exist, and we shall have occasion to discuss their roles. It is natural to inquire at this point whether there is any "price plan," to correspond to the "production plan" or to other plans which have been mentioned. The answer to this question, in a word, is "no." Prices are fixed by law in the U.S.S.R. Orders therefore exist which say "Pay X rubles for item Y." These orders are, however, in our terminology, regulations and not plans. They remain fixed over long periods of time. Soviet officials treat them in very much the same way as they treat accounting regulations in general. That is, they admit that any set of prices may have long-run consequences. These consequences are not considered to be of very great practical importance and do not, in fact, interest Soviet economists very much. Plans, on the other hand, interest them a great deal; and they consider that plans do have effects which are well worth studying.

We shall have reason to consider whether the Soviet government is right in considering prices as being of no importance, except as matters of accounting procedure. This problem is really the central one which we shall face. Economists, of course, have placed the analysis of price at the very center of economics, asserting that under competitive conditions, price measures scarcity and cost in a meaningful way. Economists would base their professional evaluation of a set of prices upon the way in which these prices either measure or influence economic activity. If Soviet prices are indeed of no importance, then we are shorn of one of our most important analytical devices. One might say that the essence of economic reasoning is in statements based on interpretations of prices. If prices have no meaning, then it would seem that conventional economic analysis is impossible. It is not clear whether anything can take its place.

Chapter 3   ENTERPRISES

The armies of most countries are divided into units: platoons, companies, regiments, brigades, divisions, corps. Each unit has a chain of command, and regulations exist which specify the relations among the members of the unit and between that unit and other units; however, any unit's life may be transient. It may be created for the sole purpose of training its members; it may be dissolved at the end of a time and its members scattered to the corners of the earth. In wartime, a unit may be sent to its death, just as its members may. Only prudence, money, and military doctrine limit the ability of the army command to create and destroy units of command.

In contrast, some government units have almost acquired immortality. In the United States, for instance, it would be impossible to imagine dissolving a state. States have been created; some have even been divided in two; but none has ever been abolished, nor does any mechanism exist for abolishing it. It would require special legal invention to achieve this end.

Somewhere in between any army company and an American state one finds the ordinary government-owned corporation. Consider, for example, Purdue University, my employer. It has a charter from the state of Indiana; about half its income comes from the state legislature; its trustees are appointed by the governor with the consent of the legislature. It is unlikely but not impossible that the governor or the legislature might wish to close down this organization. The university has financial resources, since half its income does not come from the state. It is a corporation, and its trustees and administration could perhaps operate a skeleton staff without state funds until they were replaced by more pliable personnel; but in this case, the university would not hesitate to appeal to public opinion and to use a wide variety of devices for support. Were Purdue someone else's employer, I should find the spectacle an instructive one; but I should not care to predict the outcome of the struggle.

When we say that Soviet industry is state-owned, we have not said very much. An individual plant might be owned in much the same way that an army company, with its equipment, is army-owned. It might belong to the Soviet government in the sense that the state of Mississippi belongs to the United States. To answer the question: "In what sense does the Soviet government own an enterprise?" we must turn to the regulations pertaining to business management in the U.S.S.R.

There have been 38,000 industrial enterprises completed or rebuilt since 1918; currently 800 to 1,200 industrial plants are put into operation each year. Individual plants tend to be large. In 1960, 62 percent of all plants employed over 500 persons, and 94 percent of all workers worked in such plants. Over half of all industrial workers were employed in plants of 5,000 or more workers. Almost two-thirds of the fixed assets of industry were in plants employing 5,000 or more workers. In the case of industry, at least, enterprises are large organizations.

Soviet administrative law recognizes two types of unit: the enterprise (*predpriiatie*) and the institution (*uchrezhdenie*). The institution is characterized by accountants as subject to *budget financing*. That is, institutions do not as a rule have any income. They receive an appropriation from some higher organization. The arrangements for institutions are very much like those of other countries with respect to state-owned schools, hospitals, fire departments, police departments, and the like. Even if they do charge fees to customers, these fees are not really at the disposal of the agency receiving them. From an economic point of view, it is safe to say that in the Soviet Union they are not very interesting, because most of them do not carry on what we should consider to be economic activity (that is, they do not provide goods or services which are marketable in most countries); and, as far as I can tell, they do not present control problems which differ in important and interesting economic respects from those of corresponding institutions in other countries.

Soviet enterprises, however, represent one of the unique

Soviet contributions to institutional arrangements. Accountants characterize enterprises as being "on a business basis" financially. The word *business* carries with it some flavor of "private enterprise," which is certainly irrelevant under Soviet conditions. It is therefore convenient to think of enterprises as having financial arrangements described by the Soviet portmanteau word *khozraschet,* a contraction of *khozyaistvenny raschet,* or "business accounting."

Soviet industry, transportation, construction, state-owned trade, and state-owned agriculture, then, are made up of a collection of enterprises, which (with some qualifications for agriculture) are run by rules in the *khozraschet* system. These enterprises are regulated (the word *planned* will turn out to be a better description) by a set of institutions which are governmental agencies and perform administrative functions. These regulatory agencies over most of Soviet history have been functional; that is, they have been organized by industry and branches of industry. In recent years, however (and to some extent in earlier periods as well), there have been regional industrial organizations with jurisdiction over many kinds of economic activity. Where the higher administration has been functional, the higher institutions have been called ministries (before the second world war they were called people's commissariats); the regional administrations are now called economic councils. In general, the regulatory agencies do not have any income of their own but are financed from taxation. Their personnel is comparable to that in a civil service. They have important economic functions, but these do not basically require special comment at this point in the discussion.

On the other hand, enterprises are quite a distinctive form of economic organization. From what has been said, we know that an enterprise administers a portion of the general fund of state property. The enterprise comes into being when this particular bit of property is turned over to it for operation. Its function is to carry out the plans of some administrative organ (an economic council or a ministry), using the principles laid down by the system of *khozraschet.* In other words, an enterprise's activities are bounded by a set of plans prepared by an institution, the accounting system (laid down by the Ministry of Finance), the basic physical facts which make up the plant itself, and the capacities and inclinations of the members of the enterprise itself.

Soviet law contains a number of interesting problems in connection with enterprises. Since the enterprise is a collection of people administering a body of fixed assets (from one point of view), it is tempting to view it as some sort of corporate body of which the members are those employed at the site in question. On the other hand, the purpose of the enterprise is to carry out the plans of some higher administrative agency. Consequently, from this point of view, the enterprise is a collection of people working for (in some sense) the institution; however, the terms on which they are employed are very special. The individual worker is not hired by a ministry or an economic council but rather by the enterprise itself. On the other hand, the ministry or economic council may replace the management of the enterprise, even if it does not hire the ordinary workers. The enterprise may enter into contracts with other enterprises, and it buys and sells. In so doing, it commits only itself and not the ministry or economic council. On the other hand, the ministry or economic council may specify what contracts the enterprise should agree to, even if it is not itself bound by these contracts. There is a rather interesting collection of legal problems, then, associated with the precise position of the enterprise in law. Fortunately these problems are of marginal practical importance to the economist.

The enterprise is headed by a director appointed by the ministry or economic council. His most important deputy is the chief engineer, who is concerned with the physical operation of the plant. The next most important person is the secretary of the Communist party organization in the plant. In the early period of Soviet history, when the other officials might reasonably be suspected of lack of sympathy with the political aims of the government, the secretary was perhaps more important than the director; and in occasional situations he still emerges as decisive.

The chief accountant is another extremely important figure in the plant organization, since he is obviously the expert on the financial position of the enterprise. It is particularly interesting, then, to notice that he is not, strictly speaking, responsible to the plant director nor to the ministry or economic council regulating the plant. Instead, he is appointed by and responsible to the Ministry of Finance, so that his position is in part to safeguard the financial interests which the state has in the successful operation of the plant.

The management of the plant includes the secretary of the

trade union having jurisdiction over the plant. Indeed, this official, like the chief accountant, is not responsible to the director or his superiors but to the trade unions. His activities are mainly concerned with the administration of certain social welfare functions. If the plant operates housing facilities, restaurants, recreational facilities, and the like, these are in trade union accounts. The trade unions are financed by the state and administer state spending on programs such as paid vacations, old-age pensions, and the like. These activities are considerable but mainly routine and non-controversial, so that from this point of view the trade union secretary is the representative of the social services program of the government. In addition, however, he has within the plant a variety of programs aimed at raising labor productivity. This is the main "political" objective of the Soviet trade unions. At various times, the government has particular problems which it wishes to resolve throughout the economy. The government may, for instance, wish to simplify production lines, to cut down hoarding of scarce materials, to economize on the use of fuel, to encourage inventive activity, and so on. In these cases, by activating the trade union organizations in the individual plants the government can obtain a body of personnel experienced in applying the general policy of the government to fit the conditions of the individual plant, without interfering with the daily operations of the director and chief engineer. The trade union representative has funds at his disposal (which we shall hear more about) which enable him to provide worthwhile supplementary cash rewards to individual workers within the plant, and thus a supplementary incentive system for particular purposes.

In addition to these officials, there are at times others attached to the plant administration for special purposes. If the plant is working on armaments orders, there may be a representative of the Ministry of Defense attached to the plant. The security aspects of the plant work will be in the Special Section, headed by a representative of the Ministry of State Security (or whatever the central police organ may be called at the time), and so on.

Students of government and administration will find some rather curious aspects to the arrangements which I have described. Here is a form of corporate organization which in practice has been used to build the second largest industrial power in world history; but a corporate organization whose legal status presents complications which are still imperfectly resolved. Its administration consists of a group of officials responsible to several different higher administrative institutions—yet who are supposed to divide up among themselves the various recognized functions of business administration. In theory, the director of the plant is responsible for the work of the plant; yet in theory also his authority in matters pertaining to plant "political issues," to plant accounts, to plant welfare programs, to plant security, and so on may be challenged by officials with a recognized status within the enterprise but not responsible to the same officials to whom the director is responsible. One is tempted to say that the organization is expressly designed to divide authority and to provide information about plant operations to a variety of potential administrative rivals.

We might also be tempted to say that no organization can serve so many masters. Indeed, in a situation in which the national political leadership was divided, paralysis of the activities of many individual enterprises might well occur. The seeds of such a situation existed briefly in 1953–54, when the government was headed by Malenkov (later Bulganin) and the party by Khrushchev. When Khrushchev was removed from office in 1964, the government was headed by Kosygin and the Party by Brezhnev. In diplomacy, this meant that foreign officials did not know to whom to talk. In business administration, it might have meant that plant directors and party secretaries might pull in opposite directions. For this reason, it is very difficult to imagine a secular state in the Soviet Union without major changes throughout the entire structure of economic administration.

The purpose of the enterprise is to carry out the plans given to it by higher administrative organs. These plans, as has been noted, are instructions, all of which in theory are binding but which actually have widely different practical weight in the eyes of the management. For the moment, we shall suppose the plans are data which fall from the blue without prior warning or notification. If indeed plans were prepared in this fashion, the Soviet economy could not operate effectively; for it is not possible to issue instructions intelligently if one does not know the capabilities of the agent who is to carry them out. Soviet literature on planning stresses over and over the importance of knowing what are the capabilities of the agent. If these are not known, then either the plans cannot be carried out (because they are impossible of achievement), or they do not utilize effectively the agent's resources. In this latter case, the planners (that is to say, the Soviet government) will not obtain as much from its resources as it could. But to find out the agent's capability the state must consult with him in preparing its plans. This is a question to which we shall return when we consider the central control apparatus.

The most important plan received by the enterprise is the production plan, which tells the enterprise how much it is to produce. In principle, at the beginning of each year the enterprise receives a schedule of its planned monthly output, so that an annual total is obtainable from the monthly totals. Actually, in some cases, the annual plans may not be available at the beginning of the year, so that the enterprise may have to work on the basis of monthly or quarterly instructions, during the early months of the year, without necessarily knowing what it is to do later on in the year. When work is not of a serial nature—in constructing very large pieces of machinery made to individual order, for example —the concept of monthly output will have to be interpreted in a special sense, since no work is completed, and the work in progress need not fall into neat monthly patterns. Nonetheless, the monthly production target is the most important single target for the individual enterprises.

The production plan is a *minimum*. In effect the enterprise is told, "In January, produce at least X units." The more is produced, the more pleased is higher authority. This fact is of interest, for it suggests that the Soviet economy can always absorb more, at existing prices, than is actually available. If this were the case, there would be what we should call excess demand. Conversely, if there were no excess demand in general, production plans would read, "Produce more than X units in January only if you have a customer."

If the plant produces more than one commodity, the production plan may list all the types separately, or it may list a total output by pricing the various items listed to obtain a value figure. Most large plants are in this position, so it is worthwhile to look briefly at this situation. Imagine a plant which makes tables and chairs. In general, the procedure used in the U.S.S.R. says, "Produce X chairs and Y tables at least. If you produce fewer than X chairs, you will be forgiven, provided you produce more than Y tables." This instruction is quite sensible, provided, of course, that a shortage of chairs may indeed be compensated for by an excess of tables. The fact that a plan exists does not mean that it will be carried out. Indeed a major administrative effort is needed within enterprises, and in the ministries and economic councils supervising them, to ensure its completion. Output is seldom at the planned level. It is not possible to obtain data on how far from plan the output of individual enterprises tends to be. However, for the period 1952-56 it is possible to give the plan fulfillment by union industrial ministries,[1] and by industrial ministries of the RSFSR (Table 3–1). Not all ministries are reported (the armaments industries, in particular, are probably mainly excluded). In this period, most ministries in any year produced between 95 and 105 percent of their plans. It is not a wild guess to suppose that the same was true of enterprises.[2]

TABLE 3–1
INDUSTRIAL OUTPUT, AS PERCENTAGE OF PLAN IN
REPORTING MINISTRIES, 1952–56
(Number of Ministries Reporting Given Percentages of Plan)

Output, in Percent of Plan*	Reporting Union Ministries					Reporting Ministries of the RSFSR†			
	1952	1953	1954	1955	1956	1952	1953	1954	1955
111 and over						1			
109–110							1	1	1
107–108	1		1	1		2		1	1
105–106			6	7	3		3	3	4
103–104	6	6	11	11	8	4	3	3	6
101–102	5	3	5	5	10	3	1	1	
99–100	13	5		2	3	3	2	1	1
97–98		1	1	2	1	2		1	2
95–96	2		1					1	
Under 95	2	1	1			1	1		
Total	29	16	26	28	25	15	11	13	15
Percentage reporting 99–100	45	30	0	8	12	20	20	8	6

* Decimal points are disregarded in a number of cases.
† No report for 1956 has been found.

Economists will wonder why a change in plans will cause enterprises to change their output; if they can explain why output changes in response to changes in plans, they may wonder whether

---

[1] That is, ministries responsible to the government of the U.S.S.R., rather than to the governments of the 16 republics making up the U.S.S.R.

[2] It is not possible to carry the table beyond 1956, because of the reorganization of the administrative structure in 1957–58, and because of changes in the format of the annual reports of the State Planning Commission.

the two changes should be equal, and if not, why not. Soviet explanations are not explanations: good directors and virtuous workers fulfill plans; incompetents and sinners do not. Moreover, the Soviet view is that overfulfillment of plan is always good. Actually, it could simply reflect administrative underestimation of the potential of enterprises, and overfulfillment by an industry could in principle lead to scarcity of the resources used by that industry.

It might be, of course, that enterprises produce more or less than planned because of random events in individual plants. But this does not seem to be the case. There are of course "accidents": the food industry may produce more or less than planned because of harvest fluctuations; plants do burn down and suffer other damage, and so on. But, as Table 3–2 shows, there is some connection between the percentages of plan fulfillment in individual industries in successive years. "Long-term accidents" are hard to explain.

TABLE 3–2
THE PERCENTAGE OF PLAN FULFILLMENT IN
UNION INDUSTRIAL MINISTRIES, 1955–56*
(Number of Ministries Reporting Given Results)

| | | Plan Fulfillment, 1956 (in percent) | | | | | |
		97–98	99–100	101–102	103–104	105–106	Mean
Plan Fulfillment	107–108					1	105
1955	105–106			1	4		103
(in Percent)	103–104		1	3	3	2	103
	101–102	1	1	2	1		101
	99–100		1				99
	Mean	98	101	104	104	105	

* Only twenty-one union ministries were common to both years. No attempt has been made to account for the output of ministries formed or disappearing during the two year period.

An explanation of planning is needed, so as to give a reason why enterprises' output changes in response to changed plans, but not necessarily by the amount of the latter. That problem will be the main burden of Chapters 4–6. It is true that such an explanation could be made in administrative, sociological, or psychological terms. But economists have a preference for an explanation which runs in terms of hypotheses which are familiar to them. It would seem odd if they could explain market systems (as they think they can) and be unable to explain other systems within their familiar framework of "scarce means and given ends." The attempt to find an economic explanation of the Soviet enterprise and planning system is thus a natural one.

The same sort of economic problem exists in connection with other "physical plans" relating to enterprises. These are supposed to give maximum amounts of labor and materials which the enterprise is supposed to use. Enterprises must pay attention to these restrictions, even though their primary concern is with the production plan.

Let us now consider the enterprise as a financial unit. Obviously the officials and the workers of the plant receive incomes. Moreover, the plant does not simply give away its output, but sells it. In fact, the management of the plant must "meet a payroll," as well as pay for the materials and supplies it uses, and also make certain payments, partly describable as taxes, to its owner, the state. If it is inefficiently managed, it will be unable to make its payments; its suppliers will not supply it (since they, too, must meet their own operating costs), and the production plan will therefore not be completed. In this sense, the plant management must be as conscious of costs as the management of a private enterprise, even though the Soviet manager is rewarded mainly for his output achievement, and only to a lesser extent for the profit his enterprise shows.

Effectively, the balance sheet of a Soviet enterprise may be considered as consisting only of short-term assets and liabilities. The fixed assets—the plant and equipment—are assigned by the state, and the corresponding liabilities item is entirely made up of the equity of the owner. Transactions involving plant and equipment, moreover, are handled in quite a different type of procedure from those involving current operations. The reasons for this separation cannot be understood in terms of the individual enterprise, but they will become clearer when investment financing is discussed.[3]

At the time the enterprise is organized, it is given a certain amount of working capital, and from time to time it may obtain a grant of additional working capital. In addition, it may borrow short-term funds from the State Bank. Experiments have been made with long-term credit in state industry, but little has been done to use it on a large scale. Finally, it may owe money to its suppliers. This last item, as we shall see, is not of great importance.

[3] Professor J. R. T. Hughes tells me that the business and banking principles and practice described in the remainder of this chapter are extraordinarily close to those of Britain in the mid-19th century. He refers the reader to books such as J. W. Gilbart, *The Principles and Practices of Banking*, London, 1871 edition. I join in Professor Hughes' surprise and delight.

With its "own" working capital and its borrowings, the enterprise may then buy materials and finance its current production. Assets include cash and accounts receivable, and inventories, which are divided into raw materials, goods in process and finished goods.

The cash which an enterprise has is entirely kept in a current account. Enterprises are not allowed to make payments in currency to other enterprises, and effectively they withdraw currency from the bank only to pay their workers. This fact has interesting consequences on the monetary system, and we shall consider these later on. Moreover, enterprises are not allowed to sell on credit, since the State Bank is the only source of commercial credit.

THE CURRENT ASSETS AND LIABILITIES
OF SOVIET ENTERPRISES, END OF 1960
(Percent of Total)

Assets		Liabilities	
Inventory	77.2	Own funds	38.8
Goods shipped	9.2	Bank credit	44.3
Cash	6.2	Accounts Payable	14.0
Receivables	7.0	Other	2.9
Other	.4		
Total	100.0	Total	100.0

The structure of current assets and liabilities of Soviet enterprises throughout the entire economy is given in the accompanying table. In comparison to data from private enterprise economies, these show very low accounts receivable and payable. Most of these accounts, moreover, are probably associated with tax payments. In recent years accounts receivable and payable have declined in importance. Total current assets have been rising rapidly, from 42.3 billion rubles in 1950 to 92.0 billion in 1960; inventory (including goods in process) rose from 29.5 billion to 71 billion rubles and thus rose more than total assets. Short-term credit increased from 17.3 billion to 42.7 billion rubles, or by 25.4 billion, accounting for about 60 percent of the increase in current assets. To give some meaning to these magnitudes, one might observe that total state taxation in 1960 came to 77 billion rubles, state enterprises had profits of 25 billion rubles, and retail trade was 78.5 billion rubles.

When an enterprise makes a sale, it draws a draft upon the buyer. This draft is accompanied by a bill of lading, showing that the goods have actually been shipped. The seller deposits this draft with his bank office, the bank office extends an advance on the draft and sends the papers to the buyer's branch of the bank. The buyer is then notified that a draft has been drawn on his account. He then has five days to file an objection; if he has made none, the draft will automatically be charged against his account; the seller's bank will be notified, and will then cancel the advance. The buyer, it should be noted, may only object to the payment on the grounds that the invoice does not correspond to the terms of his contract. If the invoice is correct, but the goods are not, the buyer must go through an arbitration procedure. A part of this procedure is made necessary by the fact that shipments of goods are frequently made by rail over distances of thousands of miles so that without some such procedure it would be difficult to dissociate the payments mechanism from short-term credit in general. The objective of this payments procedure is to ensure that cash is promptly paid to selling enterprises but in such a way that the bank does not become a party to the transaction or a claimant on the goods in shipment.

Let us look at the draft a little more closely, for it tells us something about Soviet business practices and their connection with planning. The draft may have two, three, or four names on it. If the buyer and seller are in regular contact, the draft may very well involve only these two enterprises; however, if the commodity in question is allocated centrally, or if the two enterprises have only occasional dealings, then each plant will have acted through what we would call a wholesale broker. Any ministry or economic council is apt to have two such brokerage agencies, one of which is a sales agency (*sbyt*), and the other of which is a purchasing agency (*snab*). The sales agencies prepare plans which specify how the output of the enterprises in their jurisdiction is to be sold; the buying agencies prepare plans which show the sources of the materials used by their enterprises. Materials balancing, which is the main Soviet technique for allocations, is concerned with this particular part of the Soviet planning mechanism. It will be discussed in more detail later on.

When transactions are carried out through this centralized distribution system, a single draft by the selling enterprise covers its sale to the sales agency of its ministry or economic council, the sale by that agency to the purchasing agency of the buyer's ministry or economic council, and the sale by the purchasing agency to the purchasing enterprise. This sounds complicated but in fact is relatively simple, since the wholesalers are paid a standard commission and do not ordinarily acquire title to the goods. It is for this reason that I have called them wholesale brokers, although they have no exact parallel in other economies.

The extent to which these intermediaries intervene in ordinary business operations depends a good deal upon economic conditions and upon government policy generally. In times when shortages are acute, the government has considerable difficulty in seeing that the scarce items are allocated to the users who have highest priority in the government's schemes. In such times, then, the activities of the "wholesale brokers" tend to expand. In times when shortages are less acute, such activities are less numerous and the brokers intervene less directly. While direct allocations might be said to be a principle which official Soviet thinking supports, it has turned out to be difficult to operate this system smoothly. The main source of difficulty—to anticipate a little—is that it is extremely hard to predict how much of any particular material any single user will really need to carry out a production plan, particularly if his rate of output is not constant but is changing over time.

We have now described the mechanism by which enterprises sell goods to one another. These transactions, of course, affect their cash position. So also, of course, do wage payments, since the enterprise must draw currency regularly from its account in order to keep its workers paid; but now we must consider the rest of the plant's operations and how they affect its financial position.

Suppose that the plant is producing at a constant rate, but its workers become less efficient. Then receipts from sales will remain constant, while wage payments will rise, causing the cash position to deteriorate. Likewise, if its labor productivity remains constant, but the plant starts wasting materials, its purchases of materials will rise, and its cash position will deteriorate. These are fairly obvious observations. There are some others which may be less obvious. Suppose we consider the typical steel mill, which aims at producing at a constant rate throughout the year. Most steel mills buy their coal from some distance away; and they can expect that in winter, coal deliveries are apt to be irregular due to the slowing down of transportation in the well-known Russian winters. On ordinary precautionary grounds, then, the steel mill will carry greater reserves of coal for its coking ovens in winter months than in summer months. If, however, the mill does so, it has more need for credit in winter than in summer.

If coal is in scarce supply, however, then regardless of the weather, the steel mill will wish to have a larger supply of coal on hand. If it does not, the mill may find itself unable to get coal because the mines are unable to satisfy all their customers. Thus a shortage of coal, whether it is induced by mismanagement in the coal industry or by the demands of third parties, will cause coal consumers to try to build up their stocks of materials. This circumstance, in terms of the allocations mechanism, will lead to difficulties in controlling the movement of coal. If coal users have ample funds of their own with which to buy coal, these funds will serve to impede the movement of coal in the directions wished by the government. Consequently, if coal users must borrow in order to carry their inventories, it is easier to restrict their purchases, since the banks can restrict their credit.

Suppose, now, a somewhat different case. We imagine a cotton mill, which spins the raw cotton, weaves it into cloth, and bleaches it. The plant management is able to spin and weave effectively but is having difficulty with its bleaching process. Purchases of cotton may remain constant and labor expenses be unaffected, while the output of finished cloth drops sharply. In this case, the cash position of the plant will worsen. If the enterprise has considerable funds of its own, it may be some time before this situation comes to the attention of the authorities. If, however, the plant relies on borrowed funds, then it will be forced to borrow, and the situation will shortly become apparent, increasing the eagerness of the plant to correct a deficiency in its own organization.

Finally, suppose that a plant produces goods of unacceptable quality. In this case, the goods are listed as "finished" in the production reports, but they are not sold because buyers will not take them. Once again, if the plant must rely upon the bank for funds, its situation will become apparent in relatively short order.

The banking system thus has, in principle, an important role in controlling the operations of enterprises. The actions of the plant management in accumulating inventories and in attempting to control costs affect the cash position of the plant and determine how much recourse it must have to bank financing. Local bank officials who are responsible for loans to the plant must be on the alert for such symptoms, being limited in the amount of loans they can make; and unusual demands for credit by any enterprise, or group of enterprises, are likely to cause difficulties for local bank officials with the management of the State Bank.

It is clear, however, that these credit controls are not equally effective in all sectors of the economy. Enterprises in heavy industry have traditionally been given more of their "own" working capital than those in consumer goods industries, so that they are less dependent upon the bank. Moreover, the enterprise, in dealing with the bank, has one important weapon. The production plan is the most important single order which the enterprise receives. If the enterprise can put up a strong argument that a loan is needed to enable it to complete the production plan, it is relatively hard for a bank officer to refuse the application. While bank management literature contains numerous examples of the use of credit control as a means of promoting industrial efficiency, it seems likely that this device is not as powerful as it might be and that it can be used much more effectively in industries in which production plans are of low national priority than in industries which have been given high priority in governmental policy generally.

Soviet banking practice is based upon what in English is called the real bills doctrine, which was popular in the early part of this century but (at least in the United States) has fallen into disfavor. That is, in general, bank loans are made only when they are secured by actual stocks of goods in the plant. The theory underlying this practice in a private enterprise economy is at least in part concerned with the risk taken by banks. In the Soviet Union, the view is taken that if loans are made only to finance stocks of goods, then they do not serve to increase the liquidity of enterprises. This view is a form of "neutral money" theory. It asserts that if loan transactions are made only in connection with specific goods transactions, then they do not have monetary repercussions.

If this view is correct, then the operations of the banking system may have an effect upon managerial efficiency but would not be expected to produce those problems which, in other economies, are considered to be peculiarly monetary. We shall later have occasion to discuss this problem in rather greater detail. For the present, it is sufficient that we have indicated the point of contact between enterprises and the banking system. It is important to understand that such a point exists, since otherwise a part of the mechanism of the Soviet economy would be obscured.

Now let us turn from our brief survey of the enterprise's balance sheet to a consideration of its earnings. One of the plans received by an enterprise is a plan which allocates the income which the enterprise will receive if its production is at the planned level. The price at which output is sold is fixed by the authorities, so that there is no difficulty in principle in calculating the revenue which will be obtained if the plan is fulfilled. (Of course, if the plant produces more than one kind of goods and fulfills some parts of the output plan but not others, the revenue attained will differ from this figure.)

If the plant produces consumer goods, we must distinguish between the amount that it receives from its customers and its own revenues. This is true because in the consumer goods industries there is a turnover tax, a generalized excise tax, which is levied on consumer goods. This tax is paid by the buyer but does not form a part of the revenue of the seller. Instead, the seller must pay every few days an amount equal to its planned turnover tax payments into the account of the Ministry of Finance. Its revenue, for accounting purposes, does not include the tax. Since this tax is the most important single source of Soviet budget revenue, we must mention it at this point.

If the plant operates as efficiently as it is supposed to, it will show a bookkeeping profit. This is the case even when the plant is actually receiving a subsidy. Very little is known in detail about Soviet subsidies, but the general outlines of the subsidization technique are clear. The wholesale brokers of an industry sell at an industry-wide price to all customers; however, the price which they pay to producing enterprises is based upon their planned costs. Thus some plants (or even all plants) in any industry may sell at a price which is higher than the national fixed price. Any subsidization which exists in the system thus occurs at the level of ministries or economic councils. In this way, plants are kept operating at close to a break-even point, which gives the administrative institutions some degree of effective supervision over their efficiency. Obviously, from the point of view of Soviet national economic policy, this practice raises a number of questions, which we shall wish to discuss later.

The profit which an enterprise makes is not considered as being simply "gravy" for the management. Indeed, since the enterprise is a part of the state mechanism, it would be inconsistent with Soviet policy toward these things for the management to dispose of the profits as it wished. Consequently, the planned profit is allocated to a number of possible objectives.

In 1960, profits of all economic organizations amounted to 25.2 billion rubles. Of these, 16.2 billion (64 percent) were paid into the budget; about 3 billion (12 percent) were used for capital investment by the enterprises themselves; about 3 billion (12 percent) were used to increase the current assets of enterprises and to cover certain planned losses. The balance of about 3 billion (12 percent) was available for a variety of other purposes, ranging from improvement in housing facilities of the enterprises to cash bonuses (of about 450 million rubles). It is clear that the various cash bonuses amount to a relatively small part of profits and of money available to the personnel of enterprises; however, this does not mean that bonuses are of negligible importance. Soviet managers talk as if these bonuses were indeed rather important, and it may be that indeed they are.

The important part of this profits plan is this: At regular intervals, at least monthly (and in some conditions more frequently), the plant management must make out-payments on the basis of planned profits. For example, if it is paying for expansion, management must make a deposit of funds to a construction account. If profit is not intended to be entirely used up by the several internal purposes enumerated, the balance is paid out to the Ministry of Finance as a "deduction from profits," and certain parts of the director's fund require regular payments. Consequently, even if a considerable profit is made ultimately, the enterprise will tend to be short of cash as long as its profit is not at the planned level, simply because the profits must be "supplied," whether or not they are earned in any particular month. At longer intervals, of course, an accounting is made with the Ministry of Finance, and at such times the discrepancy between actual and planned profits is taken care of.

One further aspect of plant finance arises because of the wearing out of plant. I hardly need expound on the fact that the wearing out of plant is a cost of production. In private enterprise, the firm will ultimately find itself with no productive assets if it does not include depreciation as a cost of production. The Soviet state, as owner of the plant, would be in a similar situation. Consequently, depreciation must be treated as a cost of production.

On the other hand, the revenue corresponding to this depreciation is a flow of cash. Private firms often find cash flow (income after taxes plus depreciation) as a useful measure of performance, particularly if they are expanding. So in the U.S.S.R., cash flow accounting is a useful measure of the amount of funds available to someone for expansion. Enterprises, therefore, would have funds to finance their own expansion if they retained the depreciation funds, and it is not necessarily the state's intent that particular enterprises expand. Consequently, enterprises must regularly pay sums into special depreciation accounts; these accounts may be released for construction purposes, but only at the discretion of the Ministry of Finance. If the ministry wishes, it may obviously allocate these funds for construction elsewhere, since the ministry is, legally, the owner of all state property and may therefore choose to allow some particular set of its facilities to deteriorate.

Depreciation in the U.S.S.R., as almost everywhere, is based upon initial cost, since it is difficult to revalue assets on the basis of replacement costs. From 1929, when industrialization began, until about 1950, there was a rapid rise in the price level, so that original cost was not a very good measure of replacement cost. As a result, depreciation accounting has been of relatively small practical importance over a good deal of Soviet history. On the other hand, the relative price stability of recent years, together with the continuing high level of investment, suggests that depreciation funds should become increasingly important as a source of funds for financing construction of new plants. Obviously, properly constructed national accounts would make some allowance for the change in price levels, if the difference between gross and net investment is properly to be measured. I shall not emphasize this particular problem because I am only secondarily interested in national income accounting. For students of these problems, I should point out that we should expect major difficulties in evaluating the true rate of net capital formation, because it is so hard to arrive at reasonable bases for estimating depreciation, on a national scale, in relevant prices.

At any rate, the value of fixed plant is estimated to have doubled from 1950 to 1960. Depreciation payments tripled, however. In part this is the result of revaluation, in part of increased rates. In 1960, 9.1 billion rubles were paid into such accounts. Of this, 5.4 billion was allocated to capital repairs. The balance, 3.7 billion rubles, is greater than the 3.2 billion in retained profits which were used for new construction; but only a small part of the former was spent on investment.

Chapter 4

THE ECONOMIC THEORY OF OUTPUT-MAXIMIZING ENTERPRISES

This chapter and the two which follow it present a microeconomic theory of the behavior of Soviet enterprises. This theory is different from the analysis of private firms, because it assumes the Soviet enterprise seeks to maximize output. Private firms are normally assumed to maximize profit. In this chapter, it is assumed that enterprises are confronted with fixed prices, but plans play no role in the analysis. Thus this chapter is only a first approximation to reality. To present an economic theory of planning, it is necessary to specify how plans affect the terms on which enterprises buy and sell. This specification is given in Chapter 5 and formalized in Chapter 6, which is thus a second approximation to reality, and includes both fixed prices and planning.

Any simple hypothesis about the behavior of an economic organization is suspect. Private firms certainly do not always seek to maximize profits on a day-by-day basis; and it is often said of very large private corporations that the sales department tries to maximize sales, the production department tries to minimize average cost, the personnel department to maximize average labor productivity, and the accounting department to minimize reported profits. Nevertheless, the profit-maximization hypothesis introduces an important ordering and simplification into economic analysis. It is justified if the simplifications it makes are consistent with experience, and if it suggests an approach to the analysis of real situations. In particular, it can only be rejected if a precisely stated hypothesis of a different nature turns out to be a significantly better explanation of an important body of economic data.

When it is assumed that Soviet enterprises seek to maximize output, the assumption plays the same simplifying role in the analysis of Soviet enterprises that the profit-maximization hypothesis plays for private firms. From this hypothesis there will be derived propositions about how Soviet enterprises may be expected to react, and it may be shown that these expected reactions are different from (although not altogether unrelated to) the reactions of private firms. The advantages which this particular hypothesis has at the present time are three. First, it has no theoretical competitors, for the only accounts of Soviet enterprise are institutional or sociological in nature, and do not provide the basis for an analysis comparable in any sense to that possible for private enterprise economies using a profit-maximization hypothesis. Second, it is intuitively plausible in the same sense that the profit-maximization hypothesis is acceptable. Private firms say that they are in business to make profits. Soviet enterprises and the Soviet press say that enterprises exist in order to produce at least as much (and if possible more) than state plans call for. Third, the hypothesis is a simple one. It is easy to make a theory complicated; but until a simple theory clearly breaks down, it is preferable to a complicated one.

There have been cases reported, of course, where Soviet-type enterprises did not try to maximize output. In some of the European satellites there are enterprises which produce solely for export. They do not maximize output, but only seek to meet foreign demand. These do not fit into the present analysis. It is also true that the Enterprise Fund, from which bonuses are paid to management and workers, is calculated on the basis of a scale which depends not only on whether output is at least as great as planned, but also on whether profits are at least as great as planned. A management which sought to maximize bonuses in the short run might well give up some output to achieve some profit. And so on.

The most important simplification introduced by this analysis is that conditions of certainty are assumed. All economic theory (including this) becomes unpleasantly difficult if uncertainty is present. In a first approach, it is prudent to pretend that there is no uncertainty. But it is well to illustrate how uncertainty may affect the output maximization hypothesis.

Suppose the monthly output plan is 100 units in January. The enterprise managers feel that they could produce 120 units in January. However, they may feel that if they do, they may receive real and psychological reward in early February, but the March plan may be increased to 130. If they make 105 units in January, they will receive some rewards, and be less likely to have a sudden increase in their plans. In this case, their problem is to keep output slightly above plan, even if it is below capabilities. Our theory will not take account of this possible behavior pattern, which is suggested by some circumstantial evidence. We cannot do everything at once.

Output and profits are not the only possible indices of plant performance. For example, average labor productivity is a gauge often used to measure the performance of enterprises. Generally speaking, the question in controlling managerial efficiency proceeds in this sequence: (1) is output at planned levels; (2) if not, is the enterprise holding its costs and profits at planned levels; (3) if not, is labor productivity at planned levels? Generally, investigation of management does not go beyond these points. Only in special circumstances are there clean-cut investigations of waste of materials, of pile-up of work in process, and so on. But management may be called to task for violations of dozens of instructions. There is no difficulty if we wish to complicate our hypothesis.

Let us introduce the ways in which Soviet enterprises may be expected to differ from private enterprises by imagining an economic organization to which both profits and output are important; in particular, suppose that the welfare of the managers is a "weighted average" of the two. That is, $U = \alpha x + (1 - \alpha)y$, where x is output, y profits, and U a reward.[1] This is a simple sort of utility function, but most administrative systems of bonuses must be simple. Suppose now that $C(x)$ is the total cost of producing x units of production; that the price of the finished goods is p; and hence, that $y = px - C(x)$. We now observe that:

$$U = \alpha x + (1 - \alpha)\, y$$
$$= \alpha x + (1 - \alpha)\,(px - C(x)) = \alpha x + (1 - \alpha)\,px - (1 - \alpha)C(x)$$

We select the optimum level of U

$$\frac{\partial U}{\partial x} = 0 = \alpha + (1 - \alpha)\,p - (1 - \alpha)\,\frac{\partial C}{\partial x}$$

$$\frac{\partial C}{\partial x} = \frac{\alpha + (1 - \alpha)\,p}{1 - \alpha} = \frac{\alpha}{1 - \alpha} + p$$

[1] Mathematicians will recognize that I am here using a special case: in a system satisfying

$$dU = U_x dx + U_y dy$$

the partial derivatives U_x and U_y are constants, and $U_y = 1 - U_x$. This special case illustrates sufficiently the point.

so that marginal cost equals price if and only if $\alpha = 0$. (This is the case where profit is maximized.)

Note that if $0 \leq \alpha \leq 1$, then $\frac{\partial C}{\partial x} - p = \frac{\alpha}{1 - \alpha} \geq 0$. (If $\alpha = 1$, marginal cost will be infinite. This is to be expected. Since no constraint on costs has been introduced, producers will produce an infinite amount!) Thus, if $\alpha \neq 0$ (output counts for something in the utility function), marginal cost will exceed price. This consideration suggests that the more output-oriented the firm, the greater will be its marginal cost at equilibrium. Let us see what happens to marginal cost as α increases. The last result, rewritten in the form $\frac{\alpha}{1 - \alpha} = \frac{\partial C}{\partial x} - p$ may be differentiated with respect to α : $\frac{\partial}{\partial \alpha}\left(\frac{\alpha}{1 - \alpha}\right) = \frac{\partial^2 C}{\partial x \partial \alpha}$. Since $(\alpha/1 - \alpha)$ necessarily increases as α increases, the left side of this expression is positive. The right side must therefore be positive also. An increase in the utility of output, relative to that of profits, means an increase in marginal costs.

This result suggests that if marginal costs are an increasing function of output, the less important profits are in the utility function, the greater output will be. This proposition can be demonstrated graphically. Let us assume provisionally the U-shaped average cost function used in ordinary theory. (See Figure 4–1, page 54.) As is familiar to us all, profit is maximized at output q_1; but the firm can expand output beyond q_1. In fact it *may* expand output as far as q_2; even if it wished, it could not expand output beyond q_2, because it would be unable to pay for the cost of producing.[2]

If the enterprise, then, maximizes output (profit being of no consequence) the average cost curve of the enterprise represents its supply curve. This is obviously true if we allow the average revenue function *(AR)* to rise and fall and if we observe that maximum output traces out the line *AC* for levels of output at least as great as q_0.

Moreover, if price falls below the lowest point on the average cost function (corresponding to output q_0), the enterprise will produce nothing, so that a "reservation price" is assumed, even under conditions of maximized output. If price should be at the reserva-

---

[2] We disregard, of course, the possibility of the enterprise's drawing large cash reserves, that of its receiving an unlimited subsidy, and other unenlightening possibilities.

tion level (and only then), the enterprise will behave as if it were purely competitive.

For the output-maximizing enterprise, the condition that average cost equals price is necessary but not sufficient. This condition is satisfied for two levels of output, q_4 and q_2, in Figure 4–1. The first, however, is a point of *minimum* output. In order that output

FIGURE 4–1

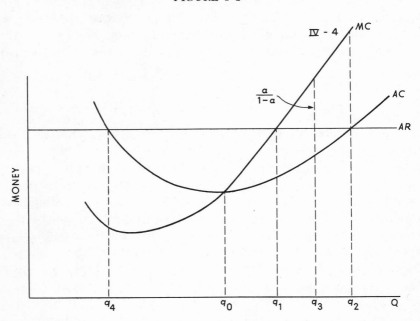

be maximized, it is thus necessary that average cost be increasing. It is more convenient, perhaps, to say that marginal cost exceeds average cost, which is implied by increasing average cost.[3]

The case in which the firm maximizes some weighted average of prices and output is obviously "between" the profit-maximizing and the output-maximizing cases. In this case, the supply function is given by the rule (which was derived above)

$$[3] \quad \frac{d}{dx}\left[\frac{C(x)}{x}\right] = \frac{1}{x}\frac{dC}{dx} - \frac{1}{x^2}C(x) > 0$$

$$\frac{dC}{dx} - \frac{1}{x}C(x) > 0$$

$$\frac{dC}{dx} > \frac{C(x)}{x}$$

$$\frac{\partial C}{\partial x} - p = \frac{\alpha}{1 - \alpha}$$

That is, in Figure 4–1, output is at q_3, where the (vertical) distance between marginal cost *(MC)* and price *(AR)* is equal to $\alpha/(1 - \infty)$. If price changes, the quantity supplied will trace out a curve which falls $\alpha/(1 - \alpha)$ units below the marginal cost curve, provided that this curve is above average cost. There is thus a reservation price in this case too, but it is higher than that in the case in which output is maximized. (This is true because average cost is rising at all levels of output greater than q_0.)

The graphical equivalent to the evaluation of $(\partial^2 C/\partial x \partial \alpha)$ given above is the following: if the importance of output to the welfare of the enterprise (α) increases, so does $\alpha/(1 - \alpha)$. Consequently, at any given price, output will rise to a point where the vertical distance between marginal cost and average revenue is equal to $\alpha'/(1 - \alpha')$. Supply depends both on price and on α; given α supply is a function of price.

The foregoing discussion now enables us to provide a rationale for having drawn a U-shaped average cost function. If prices are fixed, the average cost function must rise beyond some finite level of output. If it did not, enterprises, whether they maximized output or profits, would never have any bounds to the amounts they produced. On the other hand, we all think we know that there are economies of scale at some point in the production process, regardless of the objectives of managers. We are left with a U-shaped cost function.

Reasoning of this sort tells us something about the connection between wages and productivity, and from this we can make some statements about the demand for inputs in enterprises having welfare functions of this sort. Thus, if

$$U = \alpha x + (1 - \alpha) y$$

where x = output, y = profits, and $0 \leq \alpha \leq 1$, there is a production function relating output to inputs $v_1 \ldots v_n$:

$$x = x (v_1 \ldots v_n)$$

If the inputs sell at prices $w_1 \ldots w_n$, and the price of output is p,

$$y = px - \Sigma w_i v_i$$

If optimum amounts of the inputs are used, then for every $i = 1$, $\ldots n$,

$$\frac{\delta U}{\partial v_i} = 0 = \alpha \frac{\partial x}{\partial v_i} + (1 - \alpha)\left[p \frac{\partial x}{\partial v_i} - w_i\right];$$

so that

$$w_i = \frac{\alpha + p(1 - \alpha)}{(1 - \alpha)} \frac{\partial x}{\partial v_i} = \left[\frac{\alpha}{1 - \alpha} + p\right]\frac{\partial x}{\partial v_i}$$

If only profit is maximized, so that $\alpha = 0$, then the familiar result follows:

$$w_i = p\frac{\partial x}{\partial v_i} \quad \text{(Wages equal the value of the marginal product.)}$$

We may also, by a simple rearrangement of terms, find that

$$\frac{\alpha}{1 - \alpha} = \frac{w_i}{\partial x/\partial v_i} - p$$

This condition holds, however, for all inputs. For inputs i and j, then,

$$\frac{w_i}{\partial x/\partial v_i} = \frac{w_j}{\partial x/\partial v_j}$$

or

$$\frac{w_i}{w_j} = \frac{\partial x/\partial v_i}{\partial x/\partial v_j}$$

This statement, that the marginal productivities of different factors are proportional to their prices, is familiar to students of private enterprise. It is interesting that so far there is no difference between the two sets of results; however, the general condition

$$\frac{\alpha}{1 - \alpha} = \frac{w_i}{\partial x/\partial_i} - p$$

means that

$$-\frac{\alpha}{1 - \alpha} \frac{\partial x}{\partial v_i} = p \frac{\partial x}{\partial v_i} - w_i.$$

The right-hand side is a measure of the profit obtained from selling the output of the marginal unit of the $i'th$ input. If $\alpha = 0$, profit maximization occurs, with the familiar result that .wages equal the value of the marginal product. In other cases, however, this result would not be valid. If $\alpha > 0$, the marginal unit of output will be sold at a loss.

Proceeding as before, let **us** consider what happens if output becomes more important, and profits less important as a determinant of enterprise behavior. That is, we consider the effect of increasing α. First, we make some rearrangements of terms:

$$\frac{\alpha}{1-\alpha} = \frac{w_i}{\partial x/\partial v_i} - p$$

Then

$$\frac{\partial}{\partial \alpha} \frac{\alpha}{(1-\alpha)} = -\frac{w_i}{(\partial x/\partial v_i)^2} \frac{\partial^2 x}{\partial v_i \partial \alpha}$$

The left side is positive, and $w_i / \left(\dfrac{\partial x}{\partial v_i}\right)^2$ is positive. Therefore, $\dfrac{\partial^2 x}{\partial v_i \partial \alpha} < 0$. Hence, as output becomes more important (and profits less important) to the enterprise, the marginal productivity of inputs will fall.

This result suggests that firms which try to maximize output will use more inputs under given conditions, and use them less productively than firms which seek to maximize profits. This is an interesting conclusion, if true. Let us see if it is defensible. We start from a "Marshallian-Hicksian" sort of analysis. Then ordinary theory about productivity says that there will be average and marginal productivity curves of the general form shown in Figure 4–2.

FIGURE 4–2

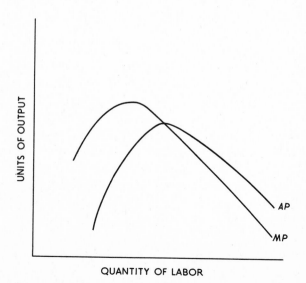

QUANTITY OF LABOR

We shall see later the rationale for this conformation. If the firm is selling at a fixed price, then average revenue product curves and marginal revenue product curves may be obtained by changing the vertical scale of measure: units are multiplied by product price to give values. On the other hand, if the wage rate is given, then the average (variable) cost is shown by a horizontal line. In this case, we assume (as in Soviet practice) that enterprises pay no in-

FIGURE 4–3

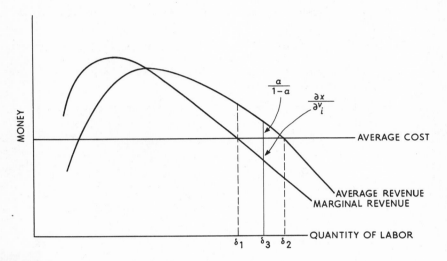

terest on their capital. If fixed costs are present, "average cost" becomes "average variable cost" and "average total cost" will be the "sum" of this line and a suitable rectangular hyperbola. The results are quite comparable, but make for messier diagrams.

It is well known, of course, that an enterprise maximizing profits will select employment level δ_1, at which marginal cost equals marginal revenue. The demand for labor is the marginal revenue curve in this diagram and thus (apart from a change in scale) the marginal productivity curve of the preceding diagram; but if the enterprise maximizes output, subject to the condition that average revenue equals average cost, then the enterprise will employ δ_2 units of labor. The average revenue product curve is thus the demand curve for the input. If δ_2 units are employed, total output will be greater, and average productivity and marginal productivity will be less.

When both output and profits are taken into account, we make use of the equation

$$p = \frac{\alpha}{1 - \alpha} + \frac{w_i}{\partial x / \partial v_i},$$

derived above, to obtain the relation

$$\frac{p(\partial x / \partial v_i) - w_i}{\partial x / \partial v_i} = \frac{\alpha}{1 - \alpha}$$

This asserts that the marginal profit from hiring additional labor is equal to the quantity $\alpha/(1 - \alpha)$. Consequently, a demand curve for the input is obtained by a vertical displacement of the marginal revenue curve. Average and marginal output, then, are in this case intermediate between the two extreme cases.

These results suggest that it should be worth making a formal statement of what the equilibrium conditions are for enterprises which maximize output, subject to the constraint that revenue must equal cost. Let output be x; x is a function of inputs $1 \ldots n$, so that $x \equiv x (v_1 \ldots v_n)$. Maximization is subject to the constraint that revenue equals costs. Let λ be a Lagrange multiplier, p the price of the commodity, and w_i the price of the $i'th$ input. Then the function to be maximized is

$$G \equiv x - \lambda (px - \Sigma w_i v_i)$$

This means that

$$\frac{\partial G}{\partial v_i} = 0 = \frac{\partial x}{\partial v_i} - \lambda \left(p \frac{\partial x}{\partial v_i} - w_i \right) = \frac{\partial x}{\partial v_i} - \lambda \frac{\partial y}{\partial v_i},$$

so that for every $i = 1, \ldots, n$,

$$\frac{1}{\lambda} = \frac{\partial y / \partial v_i}{\partial x / \partial v_i} = \frac{\partial y}{\partial x}$$

is the marginal profit from the sale of an additional unit of output. (In contrast, in the case of the profit-maximizing firm, the Lagrange multiplier turns out to equal marginal cost.) By a straightforward manipulation,

$$\frac{\lambda \, p - 1}{\lambda} = \frac{\left(\dfrac{\partial x}{\partial v_i} \Big/ \dfrac{\partial y}{\partial v_i} \right) p - 1}{\dfrac{\partial x}{\partial v_i} \Big/ \dfrac{\partial y}{\partial v_i}} = \frac{\dfrac{\partial x}{\partial v_i} p - \dfrac{\partial y}{\partial v_i}}{\dfrac{\partial x}{\partial v_i}} = p - \frac{\partial y}{\partial x},$$

which, of course is marginal cost; but

$$0 = \frac{\partial x}{\partial v_i} - \lambda \left(p \frac{\partial x}{\partial v_i} - w_i \right) = (1 - \lambda p) \frac{\partial x}{\partial v_i} - \lambda w_i ,$$

so that

$$\frac{\lambda p - 1}{\lambda} = \frac{w_i}{\partial x / \partial v_i}$$

The left side is independent of i. Consequently, for any pair of inputs, $i, j,$

$$\frac{w_i}{w_j} = \frac{\partial x / \partial v_i}{\partial x / \partial v_j}$$

That is, marginal products are proportional to wages in the output-maximizing enterprise, as they are in competitive firms.

The relation between price and marginal cost may now be derived:

$$\frac{\lambda p - 1}{\lambda} = \frac{w_i}{\partial x / \partial v_i} = \frac{w_i v_i}{x} \cdot \frac{1}{\dfrac{\partial x}{\partial v_i} \cdot \dfrac{v_i}{x}} = \frac{w_i v_i}{x} \cdot \frac{1}{\eta_i}$$

The quantity η_i is the partial elasticity of output with respect to changes in the $i'th$ input. The left side, as we have seen, is marginal cost. Denoting this as M, we have

$$M \eta_i = \frac{w_i v_i}{x}$$

Summing over all inputs, we obtain average cost A:

$$M \sum_1^n \eta_i = \frac{\sum_1^n w_i v_i}{x} = A$$

This result is purely formal; however, the condition that output is maximized means that price equals average cost. Making this substitution, then, we find that

$$\frac{A}{M} = \frac{p}{M} = \Sigma \, \eta_i$$

The importance of this proposition is that marginal cost represents the change in the value of resources resulting from a unit change in output. If an industry has several enterprises, each of which has its own production function, then each enterprise will have a different set of output elasticities (η_i). Consequently, for any given price, the different enterprises will have different marginal costs. The total amount of resources used by the industry can be made to change if a given total output is reallocated among the producing enterprises. Suppose that factor prices are fixed and that for each firm the η_i are given numbers (i.e., are independent of output levels and of the amounts of inputs used). Let there be n firms, such that for the $j'th$ firm $\Sigma\eta_i$ is a number K_j. Then there will be n different

ratios $\dfrac{p}{M_j} = K_j$, if the firms all sell at the same price.

On the other hand, if it be desired that each firm have the same marginal cost, M, it will be necessary to select n distinct prices, so as to equalize the n different ratios

$$\frac{p_j}{K_j} = M$$

It is for this reason that planning for output-maximizing enterprises requires a good deal of information. If prices are the same for all enterprises selling a given product, then, in general, it would be possible to reduce the social cost of a given level of output by reallocating output differently among the different enterprises. On the other hand, if the marginal costs of all enterprises are the same (as is necessary for minimizing the total cost of a given level of output), then the price charged by each enterprise must (in principle) be different. It is not possible, however, to set such prices without information concerning the production function of each enterprise, since without such information the quantities K_j cannot be determined.

In a purely competitive economy, prices are equal to marginal costs. The effect of a reallocation of resources among firms or industries can therefore be calculated if prices are known. But in an economy where enterprises maximize output, prices do not have this meaning. The central regulatory or planning authority must have information about each firm to judge the effects of resource changes. The next point is to show that output-maximizing enterprises will respond in a definite fashion to changes in product or input prices.

If an enterprise sells at a fixed price p, then it will maximize its output x, if, and only if, it maximizes its total revenue px. It is formally simpler, and of no practical importance, to present the problem in terms of revenue maximization. That is, the firm maximizes the function

$$G = px - \lambda(px - \Sigma w_i v_i)$$

subject to

$$0 = px - \Sigma w_i v_i$$

The equilibrium conditions are that

$$\frac{\partial G}{\partial x_i} = p\frac{\partial x}{\partial v_i} - \lambda\left(p\frac{\partial x}{\partial v_i} - w_i\right) = 0 \qquad (i = 1, \ldots, n)$$

This may be rewritten

$$0 = (1 - \lambda)\,p\frac{\partial x_i}{\partial v_i} + \lambda w_i$$

and if a new variable μ is defined such that

$$\mu = \frac{\lambda}{\lambda - 1}$$

the equilibrium conditions and constraint take the form

$$0 = p\frac{\partial x}{\partial v_i} - \mu w_i \qquad\qquad (i = 1, \ldots, n)$$

$$0 = px - \Sigma w_i v_i$$

If a single input price, say the *j'th,* changes, the effect on the equilibrium is given by the system

$$0 = p\sum_k \frac{\partial^2 x}{\partial v_i\,\partial v_k}\frac{dv_k}{dw_j} - w_i\frac{d\mu}{dw_j} - \mu\delta_{ij} \qquad (i = 1, \ldots, n)$$

$$0 = p\Sigma\frac{\partial x}{\partial v_k}\frac{dv_k}{dw_j} - \Sigma w_k\frac{dv_k}{dw_k} - v_j$$

$$0 = \Sigma\left(p\frac{\partial x}{\partial v_k} - w_k\right)\frac{dv_k}{dw_j} - v_j$$

$$= -(1 - \mu)\Sigma w_k\frac{dv_k}{dw_j} - v_j$$

$$= -\Sigma w_k\frac{dv_k}{dw_j} - \frac{v_j}{1 - \mu}$$

The solution, in the variables $\dfrac{dv_1}{dw_j}\ldots\dfrac{dv_n}{dw_j},\ \dfrac{d\mu}{dw_j}$ thus is the solution of the augmented matrix system, written in block form

$$
\left[
\begin{array}{c|c|c}
p \dfrac{\partial^2 x}{p\partial v_i \partial v_j} & -w_i & \mu \delta_{ij} \\
\hline
-w_j & 0 & \dfrac{v_j}{1-\mu}
\end{array}
\right]
$$

If the price of the product changes, the effect on the equilibrium is given by the system

$$
0 = \frac{\partial x}{\partial v_i} + p\Sigma \frac{\partial^2 x}{\partial v_i\, \partial v_k} \frac{dv_k}{dp} - w_i \frac{d\mu}{dp} \qquad (i = 1, \dots, n)
$$

$$
0 = x + p\frac{\partial x}{\partial v_k} \frac{dv_k}{dp} - \Sigma w_k \frac{dv_k}{dp}
$$

$$
= x + \Sigma \left(p\frac{\partial x}{\partial v_k} - w_k \right) \frac{dv_k}{dp}
$$

$$
= x - (1 - \mu) \Sigma w_k \frac{dv_k}{dp}
$$

$$
= \frac{x}{1 - \mu} - \Sigma w_k \frac{dv_k}{dp}
$$

The solution, in the variables $\dfrac{dv_1}{dp} \dots \dfrac{dv_n}{dp} \dfrac{d\mu}{dp}$ thus is the solution of

the augmented matrix sytsem, written in block form

$$
\left[
\begin{array}{c|c|c}
p \dfrac{\partial^2 x}{\partial v_i\, \partial v_j} & -w_i & -\dfrac{\partial x}{\partial v_i} \\
\hline
-w_j & 0 & -\dfrac{x}{1-\mu}
\end{array}
\right]
$$

The matrices of these systems (omitting the last column) are bordered symmetric patrices of second-order partial derivatives of the production function. They thus have points of resemblance to the matrices discussed in the literature on firms in purely competitive industries. We do not have occasion to make much use of these systems. It is sufficient to point to the fact that the behavior of Soviet enterprises confronted by changes in input and output prices is determinate in the same sense that the behavior of such firms is determinate.

Having established that the inputs $v_1 \dots v_n$ depend upon the prices of inputs and of output, we may outline the derivation of the supply function of the output of the enterprise. Since G is output plus a Lagrangian term,

$$G = x - \lambda \left(px - \Sigma\, w_i v_i \right) = x\,(1 - \lambda p) + \lambda \Sigma\, w_i v_i = x$$

So that

$$x\,\lambda\,p = \lambda \Sigma\, w_i v_i$$

Therefore also

$$x = \frac{\Sigma w_i v_i}{p}$$

If this last expression is differentiated with respect to p

$$\frac{dx}{dp} = \frac{\Sigma\, w_i \dfrac{\partial v_i}{\partial x}\dfrac{dx}{dp}}{p} - \frac{\Sigma\, w_i v_i}{p^2}$$

$$0 = \left(\frac{\Sigma\, w_i \dfrac{\partial v_i}{\partial x}}{p} - 1 \right)\frac{dx}{dp} = \frac{\Sigma\, w_i v_i}{p^2}$$

$$= \left(\Sigma\, w_i \frac{\partial v_i}{\partial x} - p \right)\frac{dx}{dp} - \frac{\Sigma\, w_i v_i}{p}$$

$$= -\frac{\partial y}{\partial x}\frac{dx}{dp} - \frac{\Sigma\, w_i v_i}{p}$$

$$dx = \left[-\frac{\Sigma\, w_i v_i}{p} \bigg/ \frac{\partial y}{\partial x} \right] dp$$

Since v_i and $\dfrac{\partial y}{\partial x}$ are functions of p, x may be expressed as a function of price by integration:

$$x(p) = \int_0^p C(z)\, dz$$

where C is the contents of the square brackets, p having been replaced by the variable of integration z. The contents of the brackets are certainly positive, since $\Sigma w_i v_i$ is positive, and $\dfrac{\partial y}{\partial x}$ is negative. Hence $x(p)$ is positive for all positive p.

It might be objected that if rewards to management are not strictly proportional to output, then management should wish to maximize a function of output rather than output itself. If, however, this function is non-decreasing, then the results here should hold. It might also be objected that Soviet enterprises have a profits plan, which in general is positive. This situation, however, is equivalent to treating planned profits as a cost, so that only above-plan profits are "true" profits, just as only "above normal" returns are profits in the theory of pure competition.

There is a more important objection to be raised, however. It has been assumed that enterprises were rewarded solely on the basis of output. This is only a simplification of the true situation, in which profits are of some importance in determining the reward of management. To grant the practical qualification does not diminish the theoretical interest of these results; but a more important objection is that in the analysis so far, it has been shown only that if enterprises seek to maximize output, a determinate outcome obtains (under conditions of certainty) whenever input and output prices are fixed; if these prices change in continuous fashion, output and input levels will also vary continuously, and no importance is assigned to any plans (in the sense in which the word has been used). That is, the enterprise will do what prices and the production function enable it to do, and price regulation alone determines how the system will operate.

There is one sense in which plans can enter this analysis. We assume the production function to be given, in such a way that given prices p, w_1, . . . , w_n, the enterprise will produce quantity x' and use input quantities v_i', . . . , v_n' . Imagine, however, that the enterprise is given also some other "plan" quantities $x'' > x'$, $v_i'' < v_i'$, . . . $v_n'' < v_n'$, and these other quantities are called plans. Then, in effect the plan constitutes an order to develop a different production function. Such a theory would state that the incentive scheme depends upon a special "profit" function of the form

$$y \left(x' - x'' \right) - \Sigma\, \Omega_i \left(v_i' - v_i'' \right)$$

where y and the Ω_i are rewards which vary with the extent to which production is above plan and inputs below plan. This function (rather than output) is to be maximized subject to the budget constraint. To the extent, however, that output was the main consideration, y would have large absolute value and the Ω_i small absolute values, and the problem would tend to return to that already described.

There is, however, an important sense in which "plans" can enter into the analysis of Soviet-type enterprises. In order to see how plans in fact work, it will be convenient to break off the theoretical discussion for the moment to return to a description of Soviet practice. When the institutional environment has been specified more precisely, it will be possible to give formal economic content to the concept of "plan" at the enterprise level. That is, it will be suggested that plans have a very definite economic role, which is more than an alteration of the incentive scheme. Plans alter the range of choice open to management and do not merely serve to make management utility functions different from what they seem to be in the suggestion made in the preceding paragraph. Thus, they will be shown to be constraints, not part of the function to be maximized. This formal difference will separate managers from planners, as seems only reasonable in the light of our direct observations.

Chapter 5 : SURPLUSES, SHORTAGES, AND DIRECT CONTROLS

  The discussion of enterprises has so far assumed simply that all prices are fixed. This statement has been interpreted to mean that the enterprise sells whatever it produces at a price which does not change, no matter how much is sold. This interpretation means that the demand for the output of enterprises is perfectly elastic. Likewise, the assumption that input prices are fixed has been interpreted to mean that enterprises can buy as much as they wish at a fixed price, so that the supply curves for inputs used by individual enterprises are perfectly elastic. These assumptions amount to saying that the conditions facing Soviet enterprises are like those of purely competitive firms. This point was, as far as I know, first made by Reddaway in a book that is now little known, despite its considerable interest.[1] Under the analysis so far, if Soviet enterprises behave differently from purely competitive firms, it is because they seek to maximize output rather than profits. The analysis of this problem is straightforward enough and may be conducted along lines familiar to us thanks to the work of Hicks and Samuelson.

  I should like to modify the assumptions about the price system in one more important respect, by introducing the concept of multiple pricing. This concept, as I shall present it, is a rather general one and can apply to private enterprise economics as well as to Soviet-type economics. It is not a concept in common use, at least in English-language and Soviet bloc economics. In English literature it is not used because economists writing on price control have mainly dealt with wartime situations, in which those subject to regulations were relatively patriotic and law-abiding. In the

---

[1] W. B. Reddaway, *The Russian Financial System* (London: 1935).

Soviet literature, prices are generally considered of little interest; therefore, the very interesting practices of the Soviet bloc governments in this respect have not been discussed from a theoretical point of view.

It is convenient to begin with some institutional background, so that it will be clear what the real problems are. I shall therefore discuss three distinct cases drawn from Soviet bloc experience: retail trade, transactions among enterprises, and agriculture. After the discussion of the facts, I shall present a theoretical model which will indicate how these problems can be more generally formulated.

Soviet retail stores sell their goods at prices which are fixed by higher administration. They are permitted, under specified conditions, to hold sales, at which they may mark goods down by specified percentages. Stores' sales correspond roughly to the sales conducted periodically by private enterprises to eliminate stocks cf slow-moving goods and are mainly of interest to technicians. The maximum discount permitted is regulated, as are the frequency and duration of the sales. Since all the stores are government-owned, it would clearly not make sense for any one store to have a price policy of its own which would enable it to attract sales from other stores. In this case, low markups would be basically achieved at government expense, because the income of the store itself is determined by the difference between its buying prices and its selling prices. This difference is set at a level which corresponds to the operating costs which the store is supposed to have, in its plan, plus a small profit margin. The store, operating at planned costs, could then reduce its selling prices only by cutting the prices at which it bought and thus by cutting either the profit margins of producers and distributors of the goods or the income of the government, which collects profits and turnover taxes in the distribution process.

If the retail trade system worked perfectly, then the amount of each good sold by the stores would be exactly equal to the amount which consumers wanted. The stores would be able to supply every buyer, because they would have on their shelves the goods buyers wanted. If, by chance, one store lacked a particular item, then either another store in the community would have it, or the store would be able to guarantee delivering in a reasonable time. The delivery of goods to the stores, being regulated by the plans of wholesalers, would guarantee this result.

Suppose, however, that consumers want more or less of some particular item than the production plans call for. This situation will have an observable effect. If the production rate is too great, the factories will supply the wholesalers, and the wholesalers will supply retailers with more goods than can be sold. The goods will accumulate in inventories. Conversely, if the production rate is too small, then existing stocks will vanish as they are bought by consumers.

The retailers have some recourse against surplus output. They can resist buying goods they don't want. In this effort, they can derive some help from the banking system, which does have credit plans limiting its loans to individual stores. Producing enterprises, however, work on longer-term contracts, which are co-ordinated with production plans; unless production plans can be changed, they will continue to deliver goods to the wholesale branches of the Ministry of Trade or the co-operatives.

Against shortages, however, the retailers do not have effective recourse, since they cannot in general buy directly from producers. The wholesalers have somewhat greater recourse, since they may try to find other sources of supply. Some kinds of consumer goods are produced by enterprises in many different administrative jurisdictions; and sometimes, by asking a different ministry, or by looking in a different part of the country, it is possible to find available plant capacity. In particular, local industry (industry regulated by cities) or producer co-operatives are rather more able to change their production schedules than the larger plants controlled more directly by the central authorities. Their output, it is true, tends to be of lower quality.

In an economy with a price mechanism, the surpluses would tend to cause prices to fall, and shortages would tend to cause prices to rise; this possibility is ruled out, for practical purposes, in the U.S.S.R. Consequently, the only adjustment possible is through changes in output. These may be difficult to achieve, for a variety of reasons.

One reason it may be difficult to increase production is that existing plant is inadequate; in this case, the government may be unwilling to expand capacity at once, and even if it were willing, construction takes time. A second reason, however, is that the government has fixed the prices at which producers may sell and has specified production plans in a way which does not make enterprises willing to alter their operations.

Suppose, for instance, that the production plan of an enterprise calls for the production of a stated number of yards of cotton cloth. The enterprise produces two kinds of cloth, one of which contains 20 percent more thread than the other because it is more tightly woven. A yard of fine cloth uses 20 percent more raw material than a yard of coarse cloth and will be correspondingly more expensive to produce. The manufacturer, then, can produce coarse cloth more cheaply than fine cloth and will do so unless there is a corresponding price differential in his selling price. Moreover, even if such a differential exists, he may produce only coarse cloth, if he has trouble getting thread, since a given amount of cotton thread will enable him to produce 20 percent more yardage of coarse cloth than of fine cloth. If his rewards depend mainly on his output, measured in yards, he will be disinclined to pay any attention to the Ministry of Trade, which wants more fine cloth. The Ministry of Trade will be unable in any short period to change prices or the system of measuring output for the production plan, for these are not under its jurisdiction but under that of the producing industries.

The effect of this situation is that consumers will be forced to buy things they would rather not buy, given the structure of prices. Under these conditions, the employees of retail stores will be tempted into a peculiar form of economic crime. If they purchase (without stealing) the goods in greatest demand, they can resell them at a profit. The store will suffer no financial loss, but in fact price controls will be violated; therefore, store managers must guard both against pilfering and against purchases by employees. Such transactions would not be detected by bookkeeping audit; but they would lead to private retail trade, which is against state policy.

In recent years, it has often been observed by unsympathetic foreigners that some items, such as automobiles, cameras, record-players, tape-recorders, and so on, were extremely difficult to obtain. Foreign tourists are approached by Soviet "spivs," and are asked to sell such items. Foreigners are inclined to ascribe the phenomenon to Russian mechanical inefficiency. The Soviet press ascribes it to bourgeois mentality on the part of foreigners and spivs alike. Economists, however, may readily see in this phenomenon the consequences of price fixing in circumstances wherein the assortment of goods produced does not in fact change rapidly in response to changes in consumer demand. The Soviet term *bureaucracy*, which is applied to cases of unintelligent administrative inflexibility, does not cover the phenomenon. It is not the case that enterprises produce the wrong kinds of goods because they are stupidly inflexible. Rather, the enterprises know how to maximize their rewards, which are for fulfilling production plans, and do so in the way which is most advantageous to them. Thus, we may say that enterprises are intelligently inflexible, though their behavior has untoward social consequences.

Let us now generalize on this phenomenon. We suppose that there is an increase in investment, carried out in such a way that personal incomes and prices are unchanged, output of investment goods is increased, and output of consumer goods is decreased. In this case, it may well be that output of all goods becomes less than the amounts demanded. (The same sort of thing would happen if income and capital goods output increased by the same amounts and consumer goods output remained constant.) In this situation in a market economy, consumer goods prices would rise to levels equating supply and demand. This cannot occur under actual Soviet practices. The practical difficulty that occurs is that stores will sell goods as rapidly as they can be brought into the stores; despite this fact there will be unsatisfied customers. In particular, people may be inclined to buy as much as they can, since they can always resell (presumably at a profit) to those who were at the other end of the queue. The trading system thus has a choice of rationing goods systematically or of using a first-come-first-served policy which tends to favor what the Soviet press calls speculation.

The retail trade policies, then, amount to saying to consumers, "You may buy all you want at a fixed price, providing that you do not buy more than the planned output. No matter how much you are willing to pay, you may not have more than this amount." The retailer, simultaneously, is told he may buy at a stated price, for resale at a stated price, up to the limits of what is available. In extreme cases, where rationing exists, consumers must register with a particular store, and the store receives supplies on the basis of the number of customers registered with it.

Thus far, the only fact claimed is that the supply of goods to retail stores is perfectly elastic up to a limit imposed by production plans and existing inventories; however, in the case of retail trade, there is a marginal source of supply of foodstuffs. This exists because collective farms and their members produce some goods which they are allowed to sell on a market where prices are not controlled. Prices on this market therefore rise if prices in the state and co-operative stores are such that excess demand exists. Normally, the free market prices are perhaps 20 percent above the fixed prices. This normal discrepancy reflects the fact that variety is apt to be slightly greater, quality slightly better, and service faster in the free markets, especially on fresh vegetables, fruit, and dairy products; but under conditions of extreme inflation, the discrepancy can rise enormously. At such times, moreover, manufactured goods tend to become illegally available at high prices.

Soviet writers state correctly that this free market has provided only a small (and generally decreasing) share of the retail goods available for consumers; but its share of food sales is larger, especially in the categories listed. Moreover, the interesting feature of the market, for present analytical purposes, is that it alters the supply function. The consumers are told, "Up to the limits of planned retail sales, you may buy at the fixed price level. If you buy more, you may do so at the higher prices prevailing in the free market."

Let us consider transactions among enterprises. These, as we know, take place on the basis of contracts which are concluded between an enterprise and either a sales (sbyt) organization or another enterprise. These sales are supervised by the sales and supply (snab) organizations of the ministry or economic council. The process of organizing inter-enterprise transactions is referred to in Russian as *material and technical supply,* or more simply as *supply (snabzhenie).* As we may by now anticipate, there are plans drawn up for supply. In principle, there are two kinds of supply plans. Decentralized plans leave the enterprise free to select its customers, or at least to select them from among certain classes. For instance, a clothing plant may be free to sell to any wholesale trading system, a sawmill may be free to sell to any construction organization in its region, and so on. In other cases, supply is said to be centralized, and particular purchases, together with quantities to be sold, are specified in detail. The documents which summarize the centralized supply plans for a commodity are referred to as *materials balances.* The materials balance for a commodity is thus a two-dimensional table. Along one dimension—say, the rows—the sources of the commodity are listed. These include individual plants (if these are not very numerous) or ministries or economic councils (if plants are very numerous) plus reduction in government stockpiles and imports (if these are involved). The other dimension—say, the columns—lists the users of the commodity, the individual plants (or if these are very numerous, the ministry or economic council), additions to government stockpiles, and exports (if these are involved). An entry in this table thus is a number giving the physical quantity of the commodity which source X is to sell to user Y.

The plan represents a double set of orders. It orders sellers to provide not less than a given amount to a given user, and it orders buyers to buy not more than a given amount from a given source. The administration of these plans has given rise to a considerable body of literature and has presented a number of practical problems. The materials balances exist in order to ensure that goods are used to further the purposes of the state. The number of such plans fluctuates greatly. The higher the pressure upon the economy, the more such balances are prepared, because the greater is the likelihood that otherwise enterprises would not allocate materials in the interests of the state. On the other hand, the administration of such balances is extremely difficult. If an enterprise produces more than the plan calls for, this is cause for rejoicing by the production authorities; but it calls for adjustment, in process, of a number of materials balances. Obviously, there is an increase in the quantity of its output which is available for distribution; but, also obviously, it may require above-plan quantities of inputs. In some cases, the allocation authorities must have to prevent plants from producing above plan, by holding back materials which they would require. In a situation in which a materials balance is even of the order of 20×20—twenty sources and twenty users—adjustments for above-plan and below-plan output are both numerous and difficult.

Materials balances must be based upon experience. If a supplying industry, for example, contains some modern, efficient enterprises and some old, inefficient enterprises, the allocations system must recognize this fact. On the other hand, if the plan relies solely on past experience, the plan will not be an order for an enterprise to use its materials more economically; therefore, in practice, plans must compromise between recognition of past abilities and the desire to improve efficiency. Consequently, some leeway must exist in planning, and those administering a materials balance must be prepared to revise their instructions as events develop. Such a revision means that the *snab* and *sbyt* distributors must have some freedom to adjust their operations in the course of any planning period.

A particular difficulty exists because the materials balances relate current purchases to current output. If the output of an enterprise is increasing, however, a part of its purchases will be devoted to current output, but some will be devoted to inventory. If materials balances are based on past purchases, such balances will tend to overestimate the requirements of enterprises with constant output. Where material balances are based on actual past consumption, they underestimate the requirements of enterprises with rising output. In fact, the calculation of requirements has caused continuing problems; and there is a large literature on how important, and also how difficult, it is to obtain a workable means of establishing the requirements of individual enterprises. A great part of current practice is based on complicated bureaucratic guesswork.

The effect of introducing a materials balance system into the enterprise's world is primarily to alter the terms on which it trades. Instead of the rule being "You may buy materials of this sort at price P," the rule becomes "You may buy materials of this sort at price P, but you may buy only Q units." A somewhat more complicated rule is this: "You may buy materials of this sort at price P; for every unit of your output this month, you may buy Q^1 units of this input next month." In either case, the rule amounts to this: "However much you pay, you cannot buy more than so many units of inputs in a given month." This statement formally is very similar to the rule existing for trade.

Of course, we must not exaggerate the power of the materials balance system. Experience shows that the very complexity of the Soviet economy means that plant managers have some freedom to maneuver. It is certainly the case, for instance, that materials balancing has been unable to control the use of fuels. For many years, it was the attempt of the planners to restrict the use of high-quality coal to certain industries and regions. In fact, there was always a tendency for the producers of relatively high-grade coal to sell to consumers who preferred it to the alternative, "preferred" sources of low-grade coal. Enterprises in the Moscow area, for example, were in practice able to use more Donets coal and less local coal than the authorities wanted. Enterprises in the Volga were in practice able to use more Kuznetsk coal and less Urals coal than they were supposed to. It is apparent that buyer-seller relations are often strong enough in industries producing and using bulk commodities to evade some part of the materials balance controls. It is clear that prices had something to do with this desire: in the examples cited, the cost per unit of heating power of the lower grades of coal was relatively high. It is also clear that the producers of high-quality coal had better equipment and could more easily fit an old customer into their schedule than the producers of the low-quality coal. The elaborate control mechanism we have described did not fully determine what actually took place. Students of particular Soviet industries, then, cannot but be impressed by the pressure which enterprises can and do exert upon the central authorities, as well as by the power of the latter.

Suppose that an enterprise is unable to buy as much of a given input as it would like, because the supply is centrally allocated by a materials balance. Then its supply appears to be perfectly elastic up to the limit imposed by the balance, but completely bounded. Is it true, however, that the enterprise is stopped from further purchases? Experience suggests that in a great many cases, enterprises have some further recourse. Consider the metal-working or machinery plant which buys parts. If it is able to secure only a limited number of parts, it may undertake to manufacture some parts on its own. Such parts will probably cost more than the output of specialized parts plants.

It is also true that the enterprise may find sources of supply not subject to the same materials balance. The materials balance often applies to a set of enterprises under some single administrative jurisdiction. For instance, the allocation of tractor parts probably governs the output of a particular collection of enterprises. If a user can find an enterprise in some other jurisdiction which will accept the order, it can in fact obtain additional parts. Thus small enterprises under the jurisdiction of cities in fact seem to do odd jobs for larger plants. They are usually relatively inefficient and sell at higher prices than regular producers.

The attitude of the regulatory authorities towards such practices varies. Generally speaking, they encourage initiative which leads to increased output. On the other hand, cases of this sort generally involve higher cost. Consequently, the press makes frequent mention of initiative to use local resources (which is good) and of wasteful purchase of high-cost material (which is bad). We need only observe the fact that many enterprises do use "byproducts," the output of "local industry," and the like, to supplement, at higher prices, the supplies available through materials balance systems.

In agriculture, the collective farm has traditionally confronted' a situation which I shall now describe. I should emphasize that since the death of Stalin there have been rather drastic changes in farm price policy, so I am not trying to describe in detail 1964 reality. I am interested in Stalinist farm pricing because it differs most widely from what we are accustomed to in the West, and is therefore of greater academic interest. It will also be a most dramatic example of the general principle of the pricing system which I am suggesting we should consider as being relevant to a discussion of Soviet-type economics. Recent changes have made Soviet agriculture conform more closely to the enterprise system I have already described. The process of adjustment, however, requires an understanding of the older system as well as the newer. When we come to write Soviet agricultural history for the past decade, we shall, I think, find it helpful to think of it in the terms I am proposing. At the moment, however, I am interested in theory, not in history.

The grain-producing collective farm has traditionally disposed of its output according to the following procedure. The acreage it devoted to various uses was determined by a plan from the Ministry of Agriculture. The machinery it used was hired (until 1958) from machine-tractor stations, which were sometimes part of the ministry and sometimes a special, separate ministry. The rental was paid in kind. The disposition of output was as follows. An allowance was first made for seed grain. Then "compulsory deliveries" were made. These normally bore some relation to the yield but in some years were based solely on acreage. Compulsory deliveries were sales to the Ministry of Procurements at a low price, which remained fixed from 1931 until the 1950's, despite considerable increases in all other prices. The machine-tractor station was then paid in grain, the grain being priced at this same level. Then, apart from the compulsory deliveries, the Ministry of Procurements bought additional grain at a price several times higher than the compulsory delivery price. The amount sold in this way was not fixed rigidly. The balance of the output was mainly distributed to members of the farm, in proportion to the amount and kind of work they had done. (The relative, but not necessarily the absolute, pay-scales were fixed.) This formed the basis of their diet over the coming year. Some part of the grain, however, might be sold on the open market for what it would bring. Thus, a large part of the farm output was sold as compulsory deliveries, but a large part of the farm cash income came from sales at the two possible levels of higher prices. Of course, farms producing "technical crops" (sugar beets, cotton, oil-bearing seeds, etc.) sold all their output for cash, and farmers were paid in cash rather than in kind; but here, too, there was more than one price paid.

Finally, the incomes of the farmers (as distinct from the farm) were made up of (1) payments in kind, just mentioned; (2) cash payments from the farm, allocated on the same principle as payments in kind; (3) income from the sale of the produce received from the farm (when they did not consume it); and (4) income from selling the output of small private plots of land which they were allowed to use for their own purposes. The farmer derived most of his cash income from this source, and of course most of his food was produced on the farm.

It is therefore true for a considerable part of the Soviet economy that the statement "Prices are fixed" is only a partial description of the supply conditions faced by individual buyers, whether these are individuals or enterprises. It is more correct to say that prices are fixed on purchases which do not exceed particular limits. These limits are included in plans of various sorts, the materials balances and retail trade plans being the most important. It may be true that quantities greater than these limits may not be purchased at any price. It is true, however, that in a great many cases additional amounts may be acquired from sources not covered by the limit, but at higher prices. Consequently, it is reasonable to approximate the supply function facing individual buying enterprises as a series of "steps": up to the limit of a plan, they buy at lower prices; larger amounts may in fact be bought at higher prices. (If not, the "higher price" may be assumed to be infinite.)

One feature of Soviet distribution systems has not, probably, been sufficiently stressed. That is the limitation of particular buyer groups to particular sources of supply. For example, for a twenty-year period, electric power-generating plants serving household consumers in a broad belt running east from Leningrad and Minsk to the Urals were supposed to be designed to burn peat rather than coal; other power plants were designed to burn sub-bituminous coals and lignite rather than bituminous coal. This prescription of fuel did not necessarily correspond to the costs of fuels in these areas but was intended to reduce the transport of coal by the railroads. Many plants would prefer to use long-haul coal, on grounds of price, rather than the high-cost, low-quality fuel found in their neighborhood. Again, agricultural organizations have been encouraged to set up subsidiary enterprises to produce building materials, although these are probably more costly than similar materials available for urban and industrial construction. This situation undoubtedly reflects pressure on materials balances supplying the building industry.

It must therefore be assumed that the "fixed prices" of Soviet economics are very numerous and vary, for any commodity, according to the administrative structure of the economy. One important tendency, since 1957, has been the breakup of a number of industrial ministries and the transfer of enterprises in their jurisdiction to regional economic councils. One purpose of this change was to simplify distribution and pricing. It had frequently been the case that goods were shipped very great distances, because buyers were in fact unable to buy readily from nearby enterprises which happened to belong to a different ministry. There is reason to suppose that in fact several prices still exist in any region, for individual commodities, where the commodities are produced by enterprises in several administrative jurisdictions. Even if each jurisdiction has fixed prices of its own, there may still be a variety of prices quoted. Enterprises may prefer the lower prices but be unable to secure more than small amounts of supplies at such prices.

This aspect of Soviet pricing has tended to be obscured by our image of modern industry as a mass production phenomenon. Those articles of heavy industry which are produced in considerable number do tend to be concentrated in single plants. Thus, there are several Soviet automobile factories, but any particular model is produced in only one plant; thus, the price of that plant is a nation-wide price. There are, however, many types of goods which are produced in a great many plants. Indeed, in some cases, production may be said to occur all over the country. Building materials are of this sort. Indeed, there is no reason why any large user of many building materials, hardware, and so on should not find it convenient to make them itself. Thus, collective farms, construction ministries, city governments, and so on have all made certain kinds of supplies for their own construction programs. Even though cement plants have tended to be grouped into special organizations, bricks, roofing, and nails have been made in many places. The mass production metal-using industries do tend to make their parts rather than to buy them, as do the corresponding American firms; but such a policy is a tendency, not an absolute fact. Whenever parts come from several sources, or whenever several agencies produce a single item, we may suspect that prices will be different.

There has been some interest in the United States over the so-called Liberman proposals. In 1964 an experiment was made in the Kiev region to eliminate certain defects in the distribution system. This new technique is to be expanded in 1965. As I understand the system, retail stores are able to contract directly with factories of their own choice. The factories are able to complete their production plans only if they can produce goods acceptable to retail stores. The effect of this change is that quality competition of a sort is introduced into consumer goods industries even though prices are still fixed. Also, wholesalers are less apt to accumulate stocks of unsalable goods. The theory of quality selection under conditions of monopolistic competition has been discussed by Chamberlin and Brems, and is doubtless transformable to the case where enterprises maximize output rather than price. I have not discussed it in detail because the regulations surrounding Soviet practice are not yet clear, and because the system itself is only partly approved by the Soviet government. But the experiment should be mentioned, because it has sometimes created the impression that a "market mechanism" is being encouraged. This impression does not yet seem justified.

In order to present a theory in which (*a*) individual goods may have more than one price and (*b*) the quantity which may be bought or sold at any price is fixed by a plan, it is necessary to revise the theoretical structure presented in Chapter 4. This will be done in the following chapter, which is, I hope, made more intelligible by the fact that the phenomena about to be analyzed have been described in a more intuitive way.

Chapter 6

PLANS AND THE OUTPUT-
MAXIMIZING ENTERPRISE[1]

This chapter will reconstruct the theory of output-maximizing enterprises given in Chapter 4 in the light of what has been said about multiple price systems in Chapter 5. The formal problem involves recasting the statement "Prices are fixed" to take into account the qualification "but the amounts which may be bought at a fixed price are limited by plans." This recasting operation will be mainly formulated in terms of Soviet economics; but it would apply, with fairly obvious modifications, to any system in which prices are fixed administratively at levels which do not equate supply and demand.

In the specific Soviet examples that have been discussed, we may distinguish two cases, which may be represented in diagram-

FIGURE 6–1

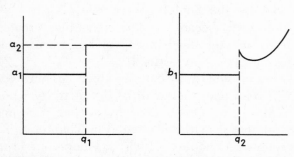

matic form. The first case is that of Soviet retail trade and is shown in the left-hand diagram. The buyer is told, "You may buy up to

---

[1] Professor Morton Kamien has suggested that it might be simpler to use Kuhn-Tucker or programming methods involving inequalities, in place of these Samuelsonian maximization methods. Through ignorance, I am unable to do more than convey his suggestion to readers at this time.

amount q of food at state retail price a_1. If you wish more, you may buy on the free market at price a_2." The step function illustrated in the left-hand diagram is a marginal cost function, relating the cost of the $q'th$ unit to the quantity already bought. In private enterprise economies a function of this sort exists in the labor market, where the rule is phrased, "If you employ a worker for more than H hours a week, you must pay him overtime."

In the diagram, an upward step is shown, because most explicit steps in Soviet price systems are upward. An example of a Soviet price system with a downward step will be given below. In private enterprise economies, a price system with a downward step is common in the case of public utilities. Here the rate per kilowatt hour of electricity used may be fixed at price p_1 for the first q kilowatt-hours used per month and drop to p_2 for additional electricity used. The second example is from one variant of the numerous U.S. farm price support programs: "If you plant no more than x acres you are eligible to price support at price p_1; if you plant additional acres you are not, but must sell at a lower market price p_2."

The right-hand diagram corresponds to the rule: "You may purchase parts up to quantity q_2. If these are not enough, you must make the rest yourself." Here the solid line to the right of q_2 is a marginal cost function. The diagram shows that the buyer will buy parts rather than make them. Of course, one could devise situations in which the buyer would prefer to make parts. In this case, the marginal cost function would look like that in Figure 6–2.

FIGURE 6–2

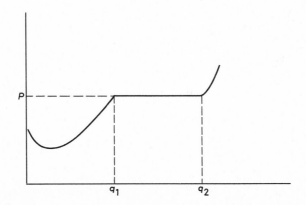

Here, if fewer than q_1 parts are needed, it is cheaper to manufacture them. If the enterprise is allowed to buy q parts at price p, it will do so; and $q_2 = q_1 + q$. If more than q_2 parts are needed, however, marginal cost will once again be the relevant criterion.

Formally we observe that "price" in this system is a marginal cost (or revenue), and that marginal cost depends upon the quantity bought. This situation is not unlike the situation in the theory of monopoly; but in that theory it is usually convenient to formulate the analysis in terms of average cost (or revenue), since most theory assumes that in any market there is only one price.[2]

Total revenue or total cost functions and the corresponding marginal functions are then derived from the average functions. In this case, it is easier to start with marginal functions and to derive total and average functions from them. Thus if $p(x)$ is the marginal cost of the $x'th$ item purchased,

$$\int_0^x p(z)\,dz$$

is the total cost; and

$$\frac{1}{x}\int_0^x p(z)\,dz$$

is the average cost of x units.

Particular interest in applications to the Soviet economy is attached to the case in which the marginal cost function is a step function, of the sort on the left of the first diagram. In this case, the integral representing total cost given above is replaced by the Stieltjes integral:

$$\int_{z \leq x} dp(z)$$

If there is only a single step, this integral may be written out in the form

$$\int_{z \leq x} dp(z) = \begin{cases} p_1 x, \text{ if } x \leq x_1 \\ p_1 x_1 + p_2(x - x_1) \text{ if } x > x_1 \end{cases} \tag{6-1}$$

Here x_1 is the plan—that is, the upper bound of the amount which may be bought at price p_1. Consequently, the average cost function

---

[2] An exception, of course, is the theory of discriminating monopoly; but this theory is not in a very solid formal state.

is perfectly elastic only on part of its range:

$$\frac{1}{x} \int\limits_{z \leq x} dp\,(z) = \begin{cases} p_1, \text{ if } x \leq x_1 \\ p_1 + p_2\,\dfrac{x - x_1}{x} \text{ if } x > x_1 \end{cases} \tag{6-2}$$

In the case of the collective farm selling at compulsory delivery prices, procurement prices, and free market prices, there are two steps. Thus the total revenue function is

$$\int\limits_{z \leq x} dp\,(z) = \begin{cases} p_1\,x, \text{ if } x \leq x_1 \\ p_1\,x_1 + p_2\,(x - x_1), \text{ if } x_1 < x \leq x_2 \\ p_1\,x_1 + p_2\,(x_2 - x_1) + p_3\,(x - x_2) \text{ if } x > x_2 \end{cases} \tag{6-3}$$

In this case, x_1 represents the quantity of compulsory deliveries and $(x_2 - x_1)$ the quantity of procurements; therefore, average revenue is

$$\frac{1}{x} \int\limits_{z \leq x} = (z)\,dp \begin{cases} p_1, \text{ if } x \leq x_1 \\ p_1\dfrac{x_1}{x} + p_2\,\dfrac{x - x_1}{x}, \text{ if } x_1 < x \leq x_2 \\ p_1\dfrac{x_1}{x} + p_2\,\dfrac{x_2 - x_1}{x} + p_3\,\dfrac{x - x_2}{x}, \text{ if } x > x_2 \end{cases} \tag{6-4}$$

These functions depend upon the prices which are set. The derivatives with respect to any of the prices may readily be computed. They will not be discussed, because we assume that in the U.S.S.R. prices change only infrequently. Changes in plans also affect the total and average expenditures. In this last example,

$$\frac{d}{dx_1}\left[\int\limits_{z \leq x} dp\,(z)\right] = \begin{cases} 0 \text{ if } x \leq x \\ p_1 - p_2 \text{ if } x > x_1 \end{cases}$$

$$\frac{d}{dx_2}\left[\int\limits_{z \leq x} dp\,(z)\right] = \begin{cases} 0 \text{ if } x \leq x_2 \\ p_2 - p_3 \text{ if } x > x_2 \end{cases}$$

$$\frac{d}{dx_1}\left[\frac{1}{x}\int\limits_{z \leq x} dp\,(z)\right] = \begin{cases} 0 \text{ if } x \leq x_1 \\ \dfrac{p_1 - p_2}{x} \text{ if } x > x_1 \end{cases} \tag{6-5}$$

$$\frac{d}{dx_2}\left[\frac{1}{x}\int\limits_{z \leq x} dp\,(z)\right] = \begin{cases} 0 \text{ if } x \leq x_2 \\ \dfrac{p_2 - p_3}{x} \text{ if } x > x_2 \end{cases}$$

In principle, the marginal cost function might be continuous or have many steps; in practice it is possible to assume that it has one step. This mathematical convenience reflects the fact that multiple pricing presents administrative inconveniences; and in the present state of the art, it is very difficult to administer systems which are mathematically more general. On the other hand, as we shall see, it is often simpler to retain the generalized form, since otherwise it is necessary to specify all the separate plans and to determine which plans are overfulfilled and which are underfulfilled.

It is convenient to have a precise terminology for dealing with these matters. The terms *total expenditure function* and *average expenditure function* will be used to denote, respectively, the functions

$$\int_{z \leq x} dp\,(z) \quad \text{and} \quad \frac{1}{x} \int_{z \leq x} dp\,(z)$$

The marginal expenditure function is $p\,(z)$; the value of this function for some $z = z_0$ will be called a *price*. If the marginal expenditure function is a step function, then the price is defined for some interval of z, rather than merely for particular values of z. The values of z for which $p\,(z)$ is discontinuous will be called *plans*. (In private enterprise economies, *direct controls* would be the more customary terminology.) Our discussion of Soviet practices has asserted that prices are regulations, which tend to be fixed for prolonged periods of time. Plans, however, change regularly. From a theoretical point of view, it is of interest to consider both types of change.

Formally, we assume that the enterprise maximizes output, subject to the condition that total revenue equals total cost.[3] If output x is a function of the inputs, so that $x = x\,(v_1 \ldots v_n)$, then the maximum must be sought for the function

$$G \equiv x\,(v_1 \ldots v_n) - \lambda \left[\int_{z \leq x} dp\,(z) - \sum_1^n \int_{z_i \leq v_i} dw_i\,(z_i) \right] \quad (6\text{--}6)$$

That is, values of $v_1 \ldots v_n$ (and hence of x) must be sought for which this function is maximized. The necessary conditions for this (disregarding corner solutions) are that for each $i = 1, \ldots, n$,

---

[3] In Chapter 4, it turned out to be simpler if it was assumed that enterprises maximize total revenue rather than output. If the marginal revenue function were a step function with decreasing steps, maximization of total revenue is not necessarily the same as maximization of total output. In this chapter, then, the latter will be explicitly considered.

$$0 = \frac{\partial x}{\partial v_i} - \lambda \left\{ \frac{\partial}{\lambda x_i} \left[\int\limits_{z \le x} dp\,(z) \right] - \frac{\partial}{\partial v_i} \left[\int\limits_{z_i \le v_i} dw_i\,(z_i) \right] \right\}, \quad (6\text{--}7)$$

so that

$$\frac{1}{\lambda} = \frac{\dfrac{\partial}{\partial v_i} \left[\int\limits_{z \le x} dp\,(z) \right] - \dfrac{\partial}{\partial v_i} \left[\int\limits_{z_i \le v_i} dw_i\,(z_i) \right]}{\dfrac{\partial x}{\partial v_i}} \quad (6\text{--}8)$$

This condition means that enterprises employ factors of production in such a way as to equalize the losses incurred from hiring marginal units of the various inputs. Suppose, now, that each of the marginal expenditure functions associated with revenue and with the cost of the *i'th* input consists of two prices and one plan (that is, they are step functions with one discontinuity point). Then the *i'th* equilibrium condition may be expressed in one of the following ways, depending upon which pair of "steps" is relevant.

	If $x \le x_o$ and	If $x > x_o$ and
$v_i \le v_o$	$\dfrac{1}{\lambda} = \dfrac{p_1 \dfrac{\partial x}{\partial v_i} - w_{i1}}{\dfrac{\partial x}{\partial v_i}}$	$\dfrac{1}{\lambda} = \dfrac{p_2 \dfrac{\partial x}{\partial v_i} - w_{i1}}{\dfrac{\partial x}{\partial v_i}}$
$v_i > v_o$	$\dfrac{1}{\lambda} = \dfrac{p_1 \dfrac{\partial x}{\partial v_i} - w_{i2}}{\dfrac{\partial x}{\partial v_i}}$	$\dfrac{1}{\lambda} = \dfrac{p_2 \dfrac{\partial x}{\partial v_i} - w_{i2}}{\dfrac{\partial x}{\partial v_i}}$

(6–9)

From Formula (6–9) the relation between average and marginal costs may be obtained, as in Chapter 4. If the enterprise is producing and hiring inputs above plan,

$$w_{i2} = \left(p_2 - \frac{1}{\lambda} \right) \frac{\partial x}{\partial v_i}$$

$$\frac{w_{i2} v_i}{x} = \left(p_2 - \frac{1}{\lambda} \right) \frac{\partial x}{\partial v_i} \cdot \frac{v_i}{x} = \left(p_2 - \frac{1}{\lambda} \right) \eta_i$$

$$\frac{\Sigma w_{i2} v_i}{x} = \left(p_2 - \frac{1}{\lambda} \right) \Sigma\, \eta_i = \frac{w_{j2}}{\partial x / \partial v_j} \Sigma\, \eta_i$$

The quantity on the left represents the average cost of producing

x units, assuming all inputs are priced at the above-plan prices. The quantity $(p_2 - 1/\lambda)$ equals marginal cost. The fraction $w_{j2}(\partial x/\partial v_j)$ is the cost of producing a marginal unit of x by increasing the use of an arbitrary input j; $\Sigma\ \eta_i$ is the sum of the partial output elasticities. The algebra is unaffected, however, if it should be the case that some of the quantities in question are below-plan quantities.[4] Thus, in general, whatever the state of affairs with respect to plan fulfillment, $MC = K.AC$ when $K = 1/\Sigma\ \eta_i$. This result means, as before, that unless the production functions are also known, so that K may be calculated, the social cost of reallocating output among enterprises cannot be ascertained from price data.

Diagrammatically, a marginal expenditure function which is in steps is associated with an average expenditure function with cusps.

FIGURE 6–3

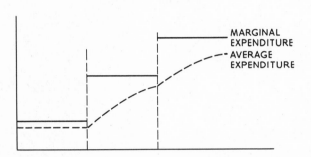

The average expenditure function will always come closer to the marginal expenditure function, within the limits of any step of the marginal revenue function. If the last step has no finite bound, then as quantity goes to infinity, average expenditures will move to equality with marginal expenditure.

The effect of a change in plan is to change the points of discontinuity in marginal expenditure, and hence to move the average expenditure function. Thus in Figure 6–4, the plan has changed from q_1 to q_2.

This diagram shows that if enterprises had marginal revenue functions which were increasing step-functions, an increase in plan

---

[4] The condition that output is to be maximized means that if the equilibrium conditions are satisfied for both below-plan and above-plan quantities, the latter are to be preferred. Since there is a finite set of inputs, no difficulty exists on this score.

would represent a decrease in average revenue for enterprises which were producing above plan. Such an increase would thus induce them to reduce output, other things remaining equal.

In contrast, an increase in input plans lowers the average cost of inputs in enterprises using above-plan amounts. It would therefore lead to an increase in output.

FIGURE 6–4

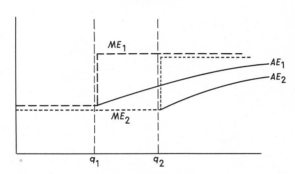

If the authorities wished to make enterprises respond to increases in plan by increases in output, they would make marginal revenue curves decreasing step functions. Then an enterprise producing above plan would find its average revenue increased when the plan increased, and it would increase its output.

Prices charged by enterprises to buyers do not in fact change with the seller's output, and it may be suggested that an analysis based on step-functions is inapplicable when applied to enterprises' revenue functions. But Soviet tax laws may be interpreted in such a way that they introduce step-functions into marginal revenues. The following example is only slightly modified from the tax laws of the early 1950's.

An enterprise sells at price p, and has an output plan q. If the actual output is less than or equal to q, the enterprise pays "deductions from profits" of $(p - r)$ per unit to the budget, leaving it an "effective average revenue" of r. Its planned cost is c, and its planned retained profit is $(r - c)$ per unit on output less than or equal to q. These planned retained profits are allocated to inventory expansion, construction, etc., and are considered as a fixed cost. (The enterprise must make the expenditures, whether or not the profits are earned, as was explained in Chapter 3.) Suppose that output is above plan. Then deductions from above-plan profits are at a figure higher than the deductions on below-plan output. "Planned cost" on above-plan output is the same as on below-plan output, so that as output rises above plan, "effective marginal revenue" drops from r to r', at the rate of output q. In this case, an increase in the production plan increases effective marginal revenue (and hence effective average revenue) at levels of output greater than q.

FIGURE 6-5

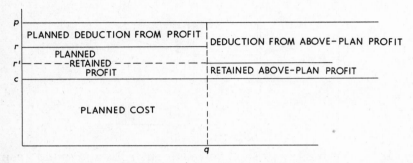

An apparent paradox in the foregoing discussion may puzzle readers familiar with Soviet incentive schemes. These schemes provide more funds to enterprises which fulfill output plans than to those which do not, and one might expect marginal revenue functions to have an upward step rather than a downward step at the planned level of output. But these schemes are allocations of sums to purposes other than current production (i.e., for social services, bonuses, etc.) and hence decrease the ability of the firm to expand output, given its cost function. The main purpose of the schemes, however, is to alter cost functions, rather than to displace the equilibrium point on a given cost function. Thus an increase in incentive payments has the short-run effect (in Marshallian terms) of reducing, but the long-run effect of raising, the equilibrium level of output. The persistence of such schemes suggests that shifts of cost curves may be more important to industrial management than movements along given cost curves.

Suppose an enterprise sells at fixed prices (no step-function for marginal revenue or for inputs) in the short run, where there may be changes in labor, capital being held constant. Then the output of the enterprise will be at q_1. If a plan is introduced, so that when the enterprise wishes to produce more than q_2, it must pay labor at

FIGURE 6–6

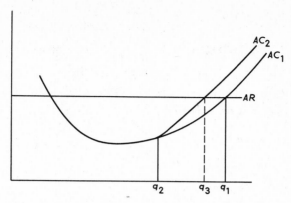

a higher wage rate, there will be a new average cost curve AC_2 for $q > q_2$, which increases relative to AC_1 as q becomes large. As a result there will be a change in equilibrium output from q_1 to q_3. The amount of the decline depends upon how much steeper AC_2 is than AC_1. That is, it depends upon how much more above-plan labor costs than below-plan labor. If the prohibition on above-plan labor is absolute, then the cost of above-plan labor is infinite. Then AC_2 is discontinuous (or vertical) at q_2, so that output is reduced to such a level that no labor would be used above plan.

Let us now consider a change in planned employment, say an increase. This means that the enterprise can employ more labor at a low price before it must employ high-priced labor. Hence the average cost curve AC_1 will be relevant to some level of output ($q_{.1}$) higher than formerly (q_2). Instead of the curve AC_2 there will be a new average cost curve AC_3. Output, instead of being q_3, will be q_5.

FIGURE 6–7

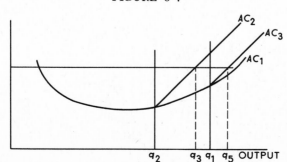

It may be shown that only if the prohibition on above-plan labor is absolute (AC_2 and AC_3 become vertical, at q_2 and $q_{.1}$ respectively) will the change in *output* exactly equal $(q_{.1} - q_2)$. In general, AC_2 is steeper than AC_3, so that output will rise by more than $(q_{.1} - q_2)$.

The effect of changes in individual plans is shown by differentiating the equilibrium conditions [Formula 6–7] and the zero profit condition in Formula (6–6). If Θ is a plan parameter, then it is necessary to solve the system

$$0 = \frac{\partial^2}{\partial v_i \, \partial \Theta} \left[\int_{z \le x} dp(z) - \int_{z_i \le v_i} dw_i(z_i) \right] -$$
$$\frac{\partial}{\partial \Theta} \left[\frac{1}{\lambda} \frac{\partial x}{\partial v_i} \right] (i = 1, \ldots, n) \tag{6–10}$$

$$0 = \frac{\partial}{\partial \Theta} \left[\int_{z \le x} dp(z) - \sum_{1}^{n} \int_{z_i \le v_i} dw_i(z_i) \right]$$

This formulation is much too general for practical purposes, and it will be sufficient to work it out in detail for the case in which each marginal expenditure function has a single step, as in Formulas (6–1) and (6–2). This means that

$$\int_{z \le x} dp(z) = p_1 x_1 + p_2 (x - x_1)$$

$$\int_{z_i \le v_i} dw_i(z_i) = w_{i1} v_{i1} + w_{i2} (v_i - v_{i1})$$

where x_1 and v_{i1} are plans for outputs and inputs.

The first case to be considered involves a change in the single input plan, v_{j1}. For the first n equations,

$$0 = \frac{\partial^2}{\partial v_i \, \partial v_{j1}} [p_1 x_1 + p_2 (x - x_1) - w_{i1} v_{i1} +$$
$$w_{i2} (v_i - v_{i1})] - \frac{\partial}{\partial v_{j1}} \left[\frac{1}{\lambda} \frac{\partial x}{\partial v_i} \right]$$
$$= \frac{\partial}{\partial v_{j1}} \left[\left(p_2 - \frac{1}{\lambda} \right) \frac{\partial x}{\partial v_i} + w_{i2} \right] \tag{6–11}$$
$$= \left(p_2 - \frac{1}{\lambda} \right) \sum \frac{\partial^2 x}{\partial v_i \, \partial v_k} \frac{\partial v_k}{\partial v_{j1}} + \frac{1}{\lambda^2} \frac{\partial x}{\partial v_i} \cdot \frac{\partial \lambda}{\partial v_{k1}}$$
$$= (p_2 \lambda + 1) \sum \frac{\partial^2 x}{\partial v_i \, \partial v_k} \frac{\partial v_k}{\partial v_{j1}} - \frac{1}{\lambda} \frac{\partial x}{\partial v_i} \frac{\partial \lambda}{\partial v_{k1}}$$

For the last equation,

$$0 = \frac{\partial}{\partial v_{j_1}} \{p_1 x_1 + p_2 (x - x_1) - \Sigma [w_{k_1} v_{k_1} - w_{k_2} (v_k - v_{k_1}]\}$$

$$= \sum_1^n \left(+ p_2 \frac{\partial x}{\partial v_k} - w_{k_2} \right) \frac{\partial v_k}{\partial v_{j_1}} - w_{j_2} \qquad (6\text{--}12)$$

$$= \frac{1}{\lambda} \sum \frac{\partial x}{\partial v_k} \frac{\partial v_k}{\partial v_{j_1}} - w_{j_2}$$

Thus this is a system with the augmented matrix

$$\begin{bmatrix} 0 & \vdots & (1 + p_2\lambda)\dfrac{\partial^2 x}{\partial v_i \, \partial v_k} & \vdots & -\dfrac{1}{\lambda} \dfrac{\partial x}{\partial v_j} \\ \cdots & \cdots & \cdots & \cdots & \cdots \\ w_{j_2} & \vdots & -\dfrac{1}{\lambda} \dfrac{\partial x}{\partial v_i} & \vdots & 0 \end{bmatrix} \qquad (6\text{--}13)$$

The matrix of this system is symmetrical, and is a bordering of the matrix of second-order partial derivatives of the production function. It will be familiar to economists. It has been assumed, to simplify exposition, that outputs and inputs are above plan, so that p_2 and w_{j_2} appear in the matrix. Actually, solutions may involve either p_1 or p_2 and w_{j_1} or w_{j_2}. As in (9), any of four situations may turn out to be relevant.

If a change in the revenue function is involved, Θ in (10) must be set equal to x_l; and (11) and (12) may then be revised accordingly.

There does not seem to be very much advantage in pursuing the mathematical formalities beyond this point. It has been shown that if plans are interpreted formally as points of discontinuity in marginal expenditure functions, then quite definite theoretical consequences follow. The combination of price regulations and plans then gives a clear set of constraints to enterprises, and changes in the constraints yield changes in output and inputs which are precisely defined once production functions are known. This is precisely the situation as regards the theory of competitive enterprises. If it be argued that this situation is not very useful as long as production functions are not known, the theorist can but give a reproachful glance to his colleagues in empirical economies.

The discussion given here is certainly artificial in one respect. It has been assumed that the plans for individual inputs and output are all independent. This assumption reflects our general unwillingness at this point to say anything of plans, except that they are given to enterprises "from outside." As a matter of fact, a major task of the administrative authorities is to coordinate plans, so that a combination of them is selected which is in some sense optimal. This fact means that it is unlikely that the plans of an enterprise will be changed one at a time. Instead, changes in output plans will be accompanied by "suitable" changes in input plans. That is, there is some sort of functional relationship among the various plans. The task of the planners is to select a "wise" functional relationship. In later chapters, the problem of defining "wise" will be discussed. Although this problem is central to the normative economics of the Soviet system, it is not very important in this book, for we are more interested in the workings of the system than in the wisdom or folly of its leadership.

The system just described has some further consequences from the point of view of welfare economics. It was observed in Chapter 4 that output-maximizing enterprises would not produce at that level of output which minimized average cost unless prices happened to be fixed at a particular level which led to such a result. The question may be asked whether a system of planning can yield this result, if prices are set by regulation. The answer might be given that if controls are enforced with sufficient vigor, the average cost curve may be made perfectly inelastic at a level of output where average cost is minimized.

It appears dangerous to assume such perfection in any administrative system; but, provided only that enforcement exists to a sufficient extent to create a step in marginal cost, it may be theoretically possible to achieve this particular result by planning. Thus (see Figure 6–7) if, without a plan, output would be at q_1 and it is desired to hold it to the more efficient level q_2, it may be possible to do so by setting a sufficiently low plan q_3. The enterprise will exceed this level of output but will produce only q_2, which is the desired level.

Since the cost to the enterprise of producing q_2 will be such as to leave it no profit, it might be objected that there is no advantage in having this level of output and a plan, as compared to having output of q_1 and no plan. That would indeed be a valid criticism if the economy as a whole generated zero profits in both circumstances. If, however, the state imposed a tax which fully accounted for the difference between the cost of below-plan and the cost of above-plan labor, then the shift from q_1 to q_2 would be accompanied by an increase in tax revenue. Or, if consumer welfare were a part of the social welfare function, something equivalent

FIGURE 6–8

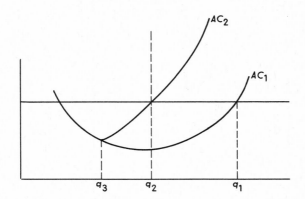

to income from overtime pay could accrue to the household sector as a result of this change.

Calculations of this sort, however, depend upon some information about the average cost function which would prevail if in fact supply functions for inputs were perfectly elastic and unbounded, at the level of prices prevailing for below-plan quantities. Any change in input prices is bound to affect the average cost of producing a given output. If the prices on below-plan quantities of inputs are administratively fixed, there is no particular reason to associate them with prices which in some sense *should* be used to calculate the average cost function relevant for this sort of calculation.

A system with multiple pricing may be capable of producing economic behavior which will not occur if the marginal expenditure function does not have steps and hence coincides with the average expenditure function. The most familiar demonstration of this sort pertains to the supply of overtime labor in the private enterprise market. In conventional indifference curve analysis, we assume that the individual's welfare depends on his leisure time and goods consumption. A familiar diagram appears in Figure 6–9.

In the case of a straight pay schedule, the worker will supply $24 - L_2$ hours of work per day in order to obtain G_2 units of goods; but an overtime system offers him one (lower) rate for work up to

H hours and a higher rate for additional work. In this case he will work $24 - L_1$ hours and obtain G_1 units of goods. There is no straight time scale (given a twenty-four-hour day) which will induce him to accept this combination of goods and leisure.[5] Specifically, he

FIGURE 6–9

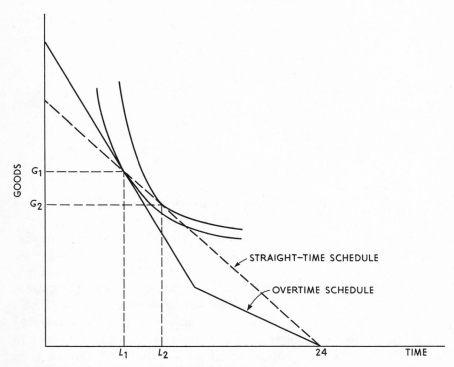

will work longer hours and acquire more goods under an overtime system than under a straight time pay system.

A somewhat less familiar case is that of rationing. Thus in Figure 6–10, the individual may buy up to a stated amount in state stores at relatively low prices and additional amounts on the free market at higher prices. In this case, assume that his welfare depends upon the amount of goods he buys and on his cash savings. (Dynamic aspects of the problem are ignored.) In this case, given rationing and two sets of prices, he will buy G_1 units of goods and save S_1 units of money. If, however, he had the same money income

[5] There is, however, a reduced straight-time wage that will put him on the same indifference curve that he is left on with overtime. But straight time pay would lead him to work less and have fewer goods.

and paid a price equal to the average of rationed and free market goods prices which he actually pays, he would buy G_2 units of goods and save S_2 units of money. In this case, multiple pricing causes him to save more than he would save under a unified system.

FIGURE 6–10

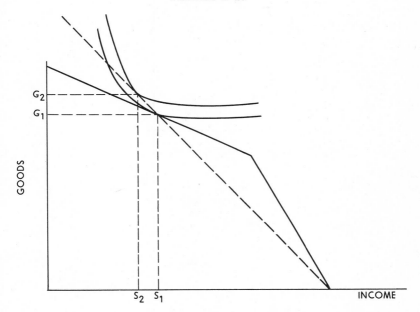

In discussing enterprises' purchases of inputs, making use of the familiar isoquant analysis, we must distinguish four cases when we are dealing with two inputs, i and j:

1. The enterprise buys below-plan amounts of i and of j.
2. It buys above-plan amounts of i and below-plan amounts of j.
3. It buys above-plan amounts of j and below-plan amounts of i.
4. It buys above-plan amounts of i and of j.

An isocost line in this case may have zero, one, or two breaks in it, depending on where it lies with reference to the plans. Each isocost curve changes direction as it crosses a line marked "plan." Enterprises' average and marginal costs for individual inputs will differ, and the marginal rates of substitution between inputs will be affected by plan changes. This is because even if there are only four slopes represented in all the isocost lines, the slopes of isocost lines in any segment of the quadrant may be affected by changes in plans. Also, the meaning of average cost and marginal cost of an input is obscured.

It may be particularly noted that if the difference between price levels is sufficiently marked, an equilibrium point may exist along an isoproduct curve which is convex upward. This corresponds to the case of increasing returns for an input. Output-maximizing

FIGURE 6–11

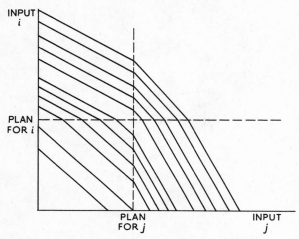

firms would never tolerate increasing returns in the absence of plans restricting inputs; however, if the "kinks" in the isocost functions are sufficiently sharp, they may lead to equilibrium under conditions of increasing returns.

Economists are apt to think in terms of isoproduct curves which are convex to the origin, because under conditions of pure competition (that is, for the only case studied in much detail in the literature) it is generally accepted that only such curves yield an equilibrium point in which more than one input is used. It is worthwhile to look briefly at an example. Suppose an electric generating plant, the equipment of which can be adjusted to burn either fuel oil or natural gas. Given the heating capacity (*Btu* per pound, calories per kilogram, etc.), it is possible to include both fuels as inputs in the plant's production function; moreover, one fuel may be substituted for the other in a manner which is independent of the amounts of either used in a given period of time (disregarding the time needed to adjust the burning equipment). (That is, the isoproduct curve is a straight line.) Then, a comprehensive analysis shows that if the relative price of oil rises above the relative heating capacity of oil, the plant will convert to gas; if it drops below, the plant will convert to oil. In other words, the plant will burn either oil or gas, but not both, under given market conditions.

The analysis given here says that if there is planning of the sort which exists in the Soviet Union, the plant may be allowed to buy only a limited quantity of one of the fuels. In this case, over a period of time, it will shift from one kind of fuel to the other, thus using both, even though the prices of the two fuels remain constant. This result would not take place in a market system, because it is ordinarily assumed that if a price exists, the user may buy any quantity he desires at that price. If he could not the price would be at some other level.

Suppose now an economy consisting of n firms each seeking to maximize output, given a set of expenditure functions and production functions. It is natural to inquire about the existence of general equilibrium in a system of this sort. In discussing this problem, it will be convenient to replace the Stieltjes integral by another notation, so that we shall write

$$w(x) = \int_{z \leq x} dp(z)$$

Moreover, we shall assume that there is a different expenditure function governing purchases between each pair of enterprises. Thus $w_{ij}(x_{ij})$ will denote the total cost of x_{ij} units of output by the i'th enterprise purchased by the j'th enterprise; however, we shall also assume that the total cost of the i'th enterprise depends on its total output, so that there exists a function, $w_i\left(\sum_k x_{ik}\right)$, representing the total cost of the i'th enterprise. Thus

$$0 = W_1\left(\Sigma_k x_{k1}\right) - w_{12}(x_{12}) - \ldots - w_{1n}(x_{1n})$$
$$0 = -w_{21}(x_{21}) + W_{\cdot 2}\left(\Sigma_k x_{k2}\right) - \ldots - w_{1n}(x_{2n}) \qquad (6\text{–}14)$$
$$0 = w_{n1}(x_{n1}) - w_{n2}(x_{n2}) - \ldots + W_n\left(\Sigma_k x_{kn}\right)$$

is a system representing the fact that the cost of production of each enterprise is equal to its revenue from its sales to all other enterprises; however, since the cost of each enterprise is equal to the sum of its payments to all other enterprises, the sum of $(n-1)$ of these equations is equal to the remaining equation. (That is to say, there are only $n-1$ independent equations here, since Walras' law holds.) If, however, one of the commodities (say the n'th) is a numeraire, or unit of account, we may introduce the monetary definition

$$w_{ni}(x_{ni}) = \int\limits_{z \leq x_{ni}} dp_{ni}(z) = \int\limits_{0}^{x_{ni}} dz = x_{ni}$$

$$W_n(\Sigma\, x_{in}) = x_n$$

There are thus n independent conditions. A solution to this system exists if there exists a set of non-negative numbers x_{ij} which satisfy it. There are of course $(n^2 - n)$ of these numbers, which should mean that there are many solutions, if these conditions were the only information known; however, for each enterprise we have established equilibrium conditions [Formula (6–8)] relative to its $(n - 1)$ inputs. These depend in part upon the prices in the marginal expenditure functions (which are part of the data) and in part upon marginal physical productivities, which the enterprise controls by adjusting its inputs.

Given an income function and a production function, as in Formula (6–6), the enterprise maximizes output. That is, the enterprise determines the level of each input which will satisfy Formula (6–8). Strictly speaking, the enterprise considers the effect of successive increments of each input until it finds that level which yields Formula (6–8) as an equality. In ordinary problems $\partial x/\partial v_i$ is considered to decline in a known way as v_i increases, so that knowing the equilibrium value of $\partial x/\partial v_i$ means knowing the equilibrium value of v_i. Consequently, given a set of expenditure functions, the corresponding values of the arguments x_{ij} in Formula (6–14) are known, and the conditions imposed by Formula (6–14) on the expenditure functions will be sufficient to ensure that there is a single solution to the system.

The short discussion given here does not constitute a proof of the existence or uniqueness of equilibrium. It is at best the sort of proof which satisfied nineteenth century economists. To examine in detail the conditions for existence and uniqueness of equilibrium would require a much more complicated discussion than can now be undertaken; however, the basic work in this area by writers such as von Neumann, Arrow, and Debreu should be referred to as the point of departure for such a treatment.

One more problem remains: the discussion of general equilibrium assumed the existence of n enterprises. In most economic discussions, it is convenient to group enterprises into industries. Lange has shown that in the case of purely competitive private enterprise systems, two commodities may be considered a single commodity if their prices move proportionately. This demonstration is possible because of the connection between prices and marginal costs in such an economy. On the other hand, Chamberlin and Triffin have shown that if "numbers are small," so that each seller in a market must take into account the effect of his actions upon the actions of others, it is analytically more convenient to consider each firm as if it were a separate industry.

Our discussion has shown that if two enterprises sell at the same price but have production functions with different elasticities of output, they will have different marginal costs. Conversely, if they are to have equal marginal costs, they must sell at different prices. This result suggests that it may be analytically impossible to combine Soviet enterprises into industries, just as it may be impossible to combine oligopolistic firms; but the problem has not been explicitly discussed, and it will be useful to consider it briefly.

The problem to be discussed may be formulated as follows: suppose that it is desired to predict the behavior of a group of enterprises in response to some change in their environment. This prediction may be possible only if information about each individual firm is available. If so, any prediction about the group is the sum of predictions about its members; but it may be that all enterprises will react in the same way to the change. If so, it will be unnecessary to know anything in detail about individual enterprises, for the group will behave as if it were a single unit. To the extent that this second possibility is the true one, it is certainly possible to speak of an industry as a meaningful economic category.

The analysis has so far assumed that each enterprise has a production function and that the output and the inputs are sold on the basis of some set of expenditure functions. The general equilibrium analysis assumed that a different expenditure function prevailed for transactions between every pair of enterprises. Suppose we consider now enterprises i and j, both of which have transactions with a third enterprise, k. Suppose the expenditure functions of i and j are $w_i(x_i)$ and $w_j(x_j)$. (We may suppress the subscript k to simplify notation.) Then it would seem that i and j form an industry with respect to k, provided that there is a function, $w(x)$, such that

$$w(x_i + x_j) = w_i(x_i) + w_j(x_j)$$

Observe that if $w_i(x_i) = px_i$, $w_j(x_j) = px_j$, for some number p, then the function $w(x) = px$ has the property in question. This case is the case of unified prices; if enterprises i and j always buy or sell at the same price p, their expenditure functions may be combined.

Suppose, however, that i and j have marginal expenditure functions which are step functions with a single step, as in Formula (6–1). Then

$$w_i(x_i) = \begin{cases} p_{i1}\, x_i \text{ if } x_i \leq x_{i1} \\ p_{i1}\, x_{i1} + p_{i2}\,(x_i - x_{i1}) \text{ if } x_i > x_{i1} \end{cases}$$

$$w_j(x_j) = \begin{cases} p_{j1}\, x_j \text{ if } x_j \leq x_{j1} \\ p_{j1}\, x_{j1} + p_{j2}\,(x_j - x_{j2}) \text{ if } x_j > x_{j1} \end{cases}$$

If there exists a function $w(x)$ satisfying Formula (6–15), then it is also true that

$$\frac{\partial w}{\partial x_i} = \frac{\partial w}{\partial x_j} \qquad\qquad (6\text{–}16)$$

The functions w_i and w_j above have, however, partial derivatives according to the following rules.

	if $x_i \leq x_{i1}$	if $x_i > x_{i1}$
if $x_j \leq x_{j1}$	$\dfrac{\partial w_i}{\partial x_i} = p_{i1}$	$\dfrac{\partial w_i}{\partial x_i} = p_{i2}$
	$\dfrac{\partial w_j}{\partial x_j} = p_{j1}$	$\dfrac{\partial w_j}{\partial x_j} = p_{j1}$
if $x_j > x_{j1}$	$\dfrac{\partial w_i}{\partial x_i} = p_{i1}$	$\dfrac{\partial w_i}{\partial x_i} = p_{i1}$
	$\dfrac{\partial w_j}{\partial x_j} = p_{j2}$	$\dfrac{\partial w_j}{\partial x_j} = p_{j2}$

$$(6\text{–}17)$$

(If the marginal expenditure functions have more than one discontinuity, then it would be necessary to construct a more complicated table along the same lines. The entry in the $m'th$ row and $r'th$ column of this table would then be the following.)

$$\frac{\partial w_i}{\partial x_i} = p_{ir} \quad \frac{\partial w_j}{\partial x_j} = p_{jm}$$

The conditions under which Formula (6–16) will hold may then be formulated as follows: For every price in the marginal expenditure function of i there is an equal price in the marginal expenditure function of j, and vice versa. Moreover, enterprise i sells to k (buys from k) above plan if and only if enterprise j also sells to k (buys from k) above plan. This condition is a fairly strict once. If Lange's proposition about purely competitive enterprises were transferable to Soviet-type enterprises, it would be possible to omit the second part of the condition, beginning with "moreover."

One qualification should be noted, however. Suppose that planning is perfect in the following sense: enterprises may purchase above-plan quantities only if they pay an infinite price. Then they will be unable to pay any price other than the lowest one in the step function. In this case, the only relevant portion of Formula (6–17) is the upper left box; consequently the second part of the condition will be true but vacuous. In this case, there is a modified condition: Formula (6–16) will be true, under conditions of perfect planning, if and only if enterprises i and j buy (sell) at the same price.

A somewhat more flexible concept of *industry* may be obtained if probabilistic notions are introduced. Suppose a (large) group of N enterprises, all buying (selling to) some enterprise k in amounts near the planned levels; suppose that the actual quantity of purchases is a random variable, so that the probability of a given member of the group exceeding its plan is q and the probability of its falling below plan is $(1 - q.)$ Then, if p_1 is the price for below-plan purchases and p_2 the price of above-plan purchases, the expected value of

$$\sum_{i=1}^{N} \frac{\partial w_i}{\partial x_i}$$

is equal to $N\left[p_1\left(1 - q\right) + p_2\,q\right]$. In this case, the expected value may be used as a substitute for an industry expenditure function.

It does not seem unreasonable to apply the concept of stochastic industry expenditure function to sectors of the Soviet economy in which there are large numbers of enterprises—for example, agriculture, retail trade, construction by enterprises subordinate to the republics, and consumer goods production of various types.

Indeed, a survey of Soviet literature on management problems suggests that in fact Soviet planning authorities make an important practical distinction between cases in which it is possible to consider each individual enterprise and cases in which only classes of enterprises may be analyzed. Even in some branches of heavy industry, the "class" is more important as a control unit than the enterprise. Individual coal mines are seldom discussed except on a "for example" basis; but the problems of a coal-producing *region*, such as the Kizel basin, form a recognizable topic. Naturally, Soviet managers are no more probability theorists than, say, economists at the National Bureau of Economic Research; however, both groups use, in practice, what may best be termed an intuitive probability concept.

To summarize the results of this chapter we may state that:

1. It is possible to introduce planning and multiple pricing into the theory of output-maximizing enterprises. When this has been done, it turns out that prices may be assumed to be fixed, and output and inputs of enterprises become functions of plans. They are not, however, necessarily *equal* to plans, unless the plans are perfect so that deviations from plan are impossible. This result is important, for it provides a theoretical explanation of why enterprises produce and buy amounts which differ from planned amounts.

2. Given the equilibrium conditions for enterprises of this sort, it is possible to construct a general equilibrium system at the order of mathematical technique used by Walras, Pareto, or Barone. It is not yet clear whether this model will stand up to the rigors of the more recent theoretical advances.

3. The general equilibrium system does not guarantee optimality in at least one sense. Given the same selling price for two enterprises, equilibrium does not ensure that social costs of production are minimized. That is, the marginal costs of the two enterprises will ordinarily differ, so that in principle the same output could be achieved at lower cost if it could be reallocated between the two.

4. The introduction of multiple pricing may lead to patterns of resource use which would not be achieved in any single-pricing system. It would be possible to use multiple pricing in a way that would ensure that enterprises produce at a level of output which minimizes costs under some assumed system of prices. There is, however, no unique answer to the question of how this system of prices should be constructed.

5. The aggregation of enterprises into industries, for theoretical purposes, is possible under restrictive conditions. Enterprises must certainly have marginal expenditure functions with the same prices. Given this condition, they may be aggregated if planning is perfect (i.e., controls admit of no above-plan purchases at finite prices), or if all enterprises in the group simultaneously operate at above or below the plan, or if the concept of "industry" corresponds to an expected value of a sum rather than to a true sum. The situation of Soviet industries thus seems to bear some similarity to that of industries in private enterprise economies; when the number of enterprises is small, the concept of *industry* becomes unsatisfactory.

PART II

Macroeconomics

Chapter	INTRODUCTION TO
7	SOVIET MACROECONOMICS

Given a theory about how individual enterprises react to their surroundings, it is possible to consider the behavior of aggregations of enterprises. For most economists, this activity is the most interesting, because it is more "real." Instead of dealing with arbitrary inputs $x_1 \ldots x_n$ and arbitrary outputs $y_1 \ldots y_m$, we can give our groups the names of real occupations and industries. By dividing the economy into a few main parts, we hope to reduce real problems to some manageable degree of simplicity. In private enterprise economies, we set up macroeconomic hypotheses by dividing firms into a few main groups with different kinds of behavior (that is, different maximization problems to solve). We now have some basis for doing the same for the Soviet economy, because we have shown how enterprises may react to changes in their environment, including, in particular, changes in plans.

The hypotheses we shall discuss assert that it is useful to divide enterprises into three groups (at least): industry, agriculture, and construction; that it is useful to distinguish between the farm and the non-farm population; and that the Soviet state may (for our purposes) be represented by a fiscal system (the State Budget) and a monetary system (the State Bank), which are conceptually and institutionally distinct. For some purposes, we shall make groupings or subdivisions of these main categories.

In the previous discussion, a sharp distinction has been made between the state and the enterprises it owns. Attention has been focussed on explaining enterprise operations, given a set of arbitrary plans externally imposed. For all practical purposes, the state has had no function but to prepare plans; and its plans might have been prepared by rolling dice. This presentation had its justification, but it was certainly not complete.

The Soviet state plays several roles in the economy. First, it purchases almost all "final output" not purchased by households. That is, it purchases the social services which are provided free to households, it purchases most new capital goods, and it purchases military equipment. To pay for this final output, it must either raise taxes or borrow. As a very large buyer, the state has an influence on the outcome of economic processes. As a taxer, it affects the ability of other economic units to do what they might wish. These functions of the state could not be inferred from the previous discussion of enterprises.

The Soviet state also prepares plans. Our discussion of plans has so far concentrated on showing how plans affect enterprises. Usually, however, discussion of planning concentrates on quite a different matter: Suppose the economy worked according to plan. What plan would produce the best result? (Clearly some definition of *best* is needed.)

A plan, as we have seen, is an order of the form "Do at least (or at most) X." Manifestly, what the recipient of the order does depends, in some degree, upon his resources and desires as well as on the order itself. Imagine, for example, that the plan says, "Build an oil refinery at town N," but that the recipients of the plan want to build a steel mill at town M and have the funds to do so. In this case it will be relatively hard for the state to get its order executed. If the recipients of the plan have no money, then the state may issue its plan in the form "Take this money (but no more) and build an oil refinery at town N." Then it will be relatively easy to get its order executed.

The fulfillment of plans, then, depends partly upon the existence of regulations which make it hard for enterprises and individuals to do other than carry them out. A part of the discussion of Soviet macroeconomics consists in an explanation of how the entire control process fits together. In this discussion, for instance, it may be very important to show that a particular sector receives funds from some sources but not from others. One aspect of Soviet macroeconomics, then, is a specification of the flow of funds.

If the flow of funds could uniquely determine the output and allocation of goods within the economy, the state would need only fiscal and monetary controls. Conversely, if output and allocation of goods could be determined without reference to the flow of funds, the state could limit itself to planning these directly. The most interesting—and least studied—problem in Soviet macroeconomics is the problem of specifying the connection between plans, on the one hand, and the regulatory fiscal and monetary powers of the State, on the other hand.[1] Despite a generation of experience, the Soviet state has not dispensed with either kind of control; and one should surmise that both kinds are necessary (neither, by itself, is sufficient) to ensure that the economy does what the state wants. There is now, however, no way of proving the validity of this statement, so it must remain a surmise.

The most unusual feature of Soviet macroeconomics, of course, is that prices may be taken as fixed numbers, with one group of exceptions.[2] This statement does not necessarily mean that all prices do remain fixed, but it does mean that decisions to change them are not automatic, and do not necessarily take into account what we might call *excess demand*.

For any set of prices, a flow of money receipts is determined by the levels of output of the various goods and services. These in turn vary in response to the plans. It may happen that the receipts of some sector are larger or smaller than what is needed to carry out the intentions of the state.[3] In these circumstances, the state may carry out something which amounts to a price change. But this change may be quite independent of what we should call *market conditions*.

For example, suppose that perfect controls exist in some industry, so that the enterprises of that industry cannot increase their output beyond some quantity q. At quantity q, they make a profit, even though for any arbitrarily small increase in output to $(q + dq)$ they would suffer a loss (because marginal costs all become infinite at output q. It may be that the state does not wish investment in this industry and will wish to use the profits elsewhere. The state

[1] It is only fair to add that the relation between "real" and "monetary" phenomena continues to be bothersome in the economics of private enterprise economies.

[2] The prices at which individual collective farm members sell to individual city dwellers vary according to market forces. Certain other prices may vary "sympathetically" with these open market prices.

[3] A sum is "needed" if it induces the recipient to do what the state wants. It is "not needed" if it can be reduced without causing the recipient to do less preferred things.

may do so by reducing the price which the enterprise receives for its product, leaving the industry price (paid by buyers) unchanged. The difference will then accrue to the state as a turnover tax. Alternatively, the state may allow the enterprise to earn the profit but may then require the enterprise to pay its profits to the Ministry of Finance.

In these two cases, we can see how tax changes may be equivalent to certain kinds of price changes. It might also be, however, that the industry's sales price and the price received by the enterprise would both be cut. This arrangement would, of course, increase what we might call *excess demand* for the ouput of this industry. That is, shortages would increase, and the pressure for greater materials balances by users of the good would rise. This change would also decrease the purchasing power of the industry, by reducing its profit; and this might very well be the objective of the state. Thus it is not really possible to discuss prices in the Soviet context, without giving consideration to matters which are considered either part of investment finance or public finance in other economic systems.

From this very brief introduction, it will be clear that macroeconomic analysis of the Soviet economy is very intimately associated with the analysis of government policy. It is of course true that in private enterprise economics today, the government frequently buys as much as one-quarter of the total national output (as in the U.S.) and carries out up to half of total investment (as in France or Italy). No macroeconomics of a twentieth century economy can ignore government. But the Soviet state, as we shall see, is overwhelmingly important in Soviet macroeconomics. One way of formulating the central issue of Soviet macroeconomics is: what are the limits of the ability of the state to determine the course of events? These limits certainly exist. If they did not, the Soviet economy would produce more than it actually does—at a minimum the U.S.S.R. would outproduce the rest of the world both in consumer goods per capita and in military equipment. To explain why the U.S.S.R. produces no more than it does, it is not enough to mutter about capacity or diminishing returns or limited resources. It is necessary to show some sort of economic process which at any moment limits the amount of output which can take place.

Since macroeconomics, in the case of the U.S.S.R., is very closely associated with the analysis of government policies and since macroeconomics deals, in part, with limits which the economy places upon the government's ability to achieve certain kinds of objectives, it might be expected that macroeconomic analysis should be very highly developed in the U.S.S.R. To date, however, it has not been.[4] Many parts of the analysis given here are set forth in Soviet literature, particularly that dealing with financial institutions; but there is no explicit Soviet model of macroeconomic equilibrium, either static or dynamic. The reasons for this situation are in part political and in part professional. Some digression on this point is in order.

In the late 1920's, industry and urban trade was mainly socialized (although the *khozraschet* system was only in an early stage); rural trade and distribution were still dominated by a market mechanism. An increase in industrial investment had the immediate effect of raising urban income and the demand for food in urban areas. It thus indirectly raised rural income and the demand for manufactured goods in rural areas. The exact relation between increases in urban and rural income depended on *(a)* urban propensity to buy food, *(b)* rural propensity to buy manufactured goods, and consequently *(c)* the rural propensity to sell food (in order to make such purchases); and *(d)* the relative prices of food and manufactured goods.

So long as increased industrial investment could be accompanied by sufficient increases in the flow of manufactured goods to the rural areas, no problems arose. If, however, urban demand for manufactured goods were sufficiently high, or if sufficient resources were absorbed by industrial investment itself, the flow of goods to rural areas would decline, and (in direct response) the flow of food to the cities would decline. In the absence of foreign exchange reserves to pay for food imports, this decrease in the urban food supply would operate as an effective limitation on the level of industrial investment. A number of Soviet economists established the formal connection between these various factors, and

---

[4] It is less surprising that microeconomics should be little developed. Marxists deny that economics is a set of constrained maximum models, and they would maintain that it is nonsense to distinguish between the state and the enterprises it owns. The economic theory we have presented they would presumably replace by a sociological or administrative theory to explain why enterprises do not do exactly what they are supposed to do. Economists, however, might find it hard to superimpose macroeconomics upon a microsociological or microadministrative model. Suffice it to say that there has been no basis for this approach as yet.

concluded that (a) an investment program could not exceed some particular magnitude at any time; (b) consequently, growth rates in industry could not exceed certain limits which depended on the propensities given above; (c) there was a necessary connection be-tween rural and urban output which could change only gradually over time.

Some of the economists who held this view may have held it with regret, wishing that industrial development could be more rapid. Others, however, may have favored agricultural development in principle and used the model to buttress their support of measures favoring agriculture. In any event, the model has the curious property of being quite right and quite wrong. As a description of the situation of the 1920's, the economists' models were quite right. But when the Soviet government decided to proceed with rapid industrialization, it simply destroyed the market mechanism on which they relied. By doing so (to cut a painful story short) the U.S.S.R. achieved growth rates in industry which nobody had believed would be possible, and the Soviet government underlined the superiority of its economic theorizing by executing quite a few of the economists who had maintained that the government could not do what in fact it was doing.[5]

Stalin's dictum "There are no fortresses which Bolsheviks cannot storm" had an unfortunate effect on Soviet macroeconomics. One must imagine that Soviet economists, in contemplating the graves of their colleagues, may have hesitated to say publicly that there was a limit to the amount of investment which the country could carry on; but quite apart from this factor, they must have been impressed by the growth rates actually achieved. It is not surprising, really, that many of them apparently came to believe that the only obstacles to increased growth rates were particular survivals of market mechanisms and that these could more or less readily be removed. On both grounds, then, macroeconomic analysis would tend to stop being an object of serious study in the U.S.S.R.

Some Soviet macroeconomic theory might have survived this collapse, except for a line of argument which reached its culmination with Stalin's 1952 work, *The Economic Problems of Socialism in the U.S.S.R.* This line of argument ran as follows: Economics is

---

[5] Nicholas Spulber, *Soviet Strategy for Economic Growth* (Bloomington: Indiana University Press, 1964), is a discussion of these and related issues.

a science and therefore seeks to find out economic laws. In particular, the maximal growth of output is the basic economic law of the Soviet economy. This means that the Soviet government, through its planning and other powers, has chosen those policies which in fact have led to more rapid growth than any other policies could have achieved. The function of economics is to demonstrate that these last two assertions are true.

Manifestly it is convenient for the head of a one-party government to be able to show that his actions are not the result of individual caprice, but rather of historical necessity. In the particular case in point, it was an extremely touchy matter to argue that the Soviet Union could have expanded output more rapidly than it actually had and an equally touchy matter to argue that it could not have expanded output more rapidly than it actually had. The first argument is an implicit criticism of government policy, the latter of Soviet institutions.[6] Manifestly no economic analysis can survive this pair of alternatives.

The Soviet government has always been secretive on economic matters. Even in countries whose governments are not secretive, academic economists are badly informed on the real economic issues of the day, for they do not have the time or the incentive to keep up with what is happening. Their contribution to economics is to provide ideas (most of them bad, but a few outstandingly good) for the rest. With Soviet academic economists unable to suggest that growth might have been faster or slower than it actually was, and with Soviet government economists prevented by security regulations from describing what was happening, it is no wonder that Soviet economics seemed unsatisfactory to foreigners in 1952.

In the past decade, of course, there have been changes in this situation. Some of these changes may be associated with "de-Stalinization." More important, of course, are the changes which modern technology may force upon Soviet economics. The advantages of using digital computers in accounting are clear; it is natural to imagine an extension of computing techniques to planning. But the advantages cannot be attained unless the computers are told what to do; ultimately an economic model will be necessary as part of a computer program. Faced with a choice between paper-

---

[6] In the next chapter, it will be pointed out that Stalin made the second point. Nobody else in the U.S.S.R. could have done so in 1952.

and-pencil methods and sloppy theory on the one hand or computer methods and adequate theory on the other, it is possible that even Marxists may prefer to permit the development of explicit and consistent economic theory.

It is idle to speculate whether the development of Soviet economic theory would lead to changes in Soviet attitudes toward prices. Meanwhile, however, it is possible to theorize about fixed price macroeconomic systems, as will be demonstrated. This theorizing is done at a great distance from Moscow, and it is academic theorizing—that is, it is based on ignorance of most of the real problems that have affected the Soviet economy. Some problems, however, cannot be concealed, and some have even been cautiously discussed in the Soviet press. These can be treated theoretically.

First, however, it is necessary to discuss macroeconomic variables. In the foregoing chapters, the economy was treated as an aggregation of enterprises. It was considered possible, in some cases, to aggregate enterprises into industries. Suppose, however, that an aggregation such as "consumer goods industry" or "agriculture" is considered. Here, enterprises producing many commodities are involved. The theorist is inclined to assume that consumers buy a single, homogeneous commodity; but such an assumption is artifice, and it is desirable to show what connection there may be between a homogeneous imaginary commodity of theory and a collection of diversified commodities such as make up the real world.

The macroeconomist, assuming that there is a homogeneous "consumer good" or "labor force" may also explain himself by saying that one aspect of his model deals with flows of money expenditures and that money expenditures are products, in some sense, of prices and quantities; so macroeconomics may be considered as a theory of how price and quantity indices will behave, as compared to data on spending. As we know, however, indices depend ultimately on enterprise performance. Thus something must be said about the connection between output in enterprises, separately recorded, and the behavior of macroeconomic variables.

In this discussion, we shall provisionally retain our agnosticism about plans. In discussing enterprises, plans (from a formal point of view) were externally imposed data, and no assumptions at all were made about the purpose of plans, or indeed about their consistency, attainability, or connection with government objectives. It is desirable to assert as little as possible about the policy contents of plans, when formal analysis is in progress. This is because plans may be good or bad morally, sensible or foolish politically, consistent or inconsistent with the government's own objectives, and conducive either to the happiness or misery of the population. From the present standpoint, an important problem is simply to show how plans affect the course of events. Later, when the formalities have been taken into account, it is possible to consider these other aspects of planning. We shall therefore end our analysis at the point where discussions of planning usually start—with these moral, political, policy, and welfare aspects of planning.

Suppose that prices are fixed and that there exists a macroeconomic variable Y defined on some set of n enterprises, such that

$$Y = \sum_{i=1}^{n} p_i\, x_i$$

We consider the effects of a change in plan π, which is assumed to be of such a nature that outputs are differentiable functions of the plan, as in Chapter 6.

$$\frac{dY}{d\pi} = \Sigma\, p_i\, \frac{dx_i}{d\pi}$$

For every enterprise, price is related to marginal costs by the relationship

$$p_i = K_i\, \frac{\partial C_i}{\partial x_i}$$

where K_i is equal to the sum of output elasticities. (If $K_i > 1$ there are increasing returns to scale, and if $K_i < 1$ there are decreasing returns.)[7] Thus

$$\frac{dY}{d\pi} = \Sigma\, K_i\, \frac{\partial C_i}{\partial K_i}\, \frac{dK_i}{d\pi}$$

[7] If $x = x\,(v_1, \ldots, v_n)$

$$dx = \Sigma\, \frac{\partial x}{\partial v_i}\, dv_i$$

$$\frac{dx}{x} = \Sigma \left(\frac{v_i}{x}\, \frac{\partial x}{\partial v_i} \right)\left(\frac{dv_i}{v_i} \right) = \Sigma\, \eta_i\, \frac{dv_i}{v_i}$$

Assume a proportional increase in all inputs, so that $\dfrac{dv_j}{v_j} = r,\ (j = 1, \ldots, n)$

$d \log x = r\, \Sigma \eta_i = rK.$

Enterprises seek, however, to maximize output. Since

$$p_i \frac{dx_i}{d\pi}$$

is the change in their revenue which occurs as a result of the change in plan,

$$p_i \frac{dx_i}{d\pi}$$

will also equal the change in total costs resulting from the change in plan:

$$\frac{\partial C_i}{\partial x_i} \frac{dx_i}{d\pi}$$

Hence

$$\Sigma K_i \frac{\partial C_i}{\partial x_i} \frac{dx_i}{d\pi} = \sum \frac{\partial C_i}{\partial x_i} \frac{dx_i}{d\pi} \, ,$$

so that

$$0 = \Sigma \, (K_i - 1) \, \frac{\partial C_i}{\partial x_i} \frac{dx_i}{d\pi}$$

It is now convenient to present this result in terms of a statistical identity. For any pair of variables, V, W, taking on observed values $V_i, W_i \, (i = 1, \dots, n)$,

$$\frac{1}{n} \Sigma \, V_i \, W_i = M \, (V) \, M \, (W) + \sigma \, (V) \, \sigma \, (W) \, r \, (V,W) \, ,$$

where M denotes mean, σ standard deviation, and r the correlation coefficient. For the preceding formula, therefore,

$$0 = M \, (K_i - 1) \, M \left(\frac{\partial C_i}{\partial x_i} \frac{dx_i}{d\pi} \right) + \sigma \, (K_i) \, \sigma \left(\frac{\partial C_i}{\partial x_i} \frac{dx_i}{d\pi} \right) r \left(K_i, \frac{\partial C_i}{\partial x_i} \frac{dx_i}{d\pi} \right)$$

$$M \left(\frac{\partial C_i}{\partial x_i} \frac{dx_i}{d\pi} \right) = - \frac{\sigma \, (K_i) \, \sigma \left(\frac{\partial C_i}{\partial x_i} \frac{dx_i}{d\pi} \right) r \left(K_i, \frac{\partial C_i}{\partial x_i} \frac{dx_i}{d\pi} \right)}{M \, (K_i) - 1}$$

The left side of this expression is

$$M \left(\frac{\partial C_i}{\partial x_i} \frac{dx_i}{d\pi} \right) = \frac{1}{n} \sum \frac{\partial C_i}{\partial x_i} \frac{dx_i}{d\pi} = \frac{1}{n} \frac{dY}{d\pi}$$

(n, of course, is the number of enterprises).

We have shown that enterprises operate under conditions of increasing average cost. That means they produce at levels of output where there are decreasing returns to scale, so that $K_i < 1$. This means that the denominator on the right is negative. The sign of the right side is therefore equal to the sign of the numerator, but the numerator is the product of two non-negative numbers (the standard deviations) and a number between -1 and $+1$ (the correlation coefficient). We have then the result: Under (the usual) conditions of decreasing returns to scale,

$$\text{sign} \left[M \left(\frac{\partial C_i}{\partial x_i} \frac{dx_i}{d\pi} \right) \right] = \text{sign} \left[r \left(K_i, \frac{\partial C_i}{\partial x_i} \frac{dx_i}{d\pi} \right) \right] = \text{sign} \frac{dY}{d\pi}$$

That is, a change in plan increases Y if and only if marginal outlays are increased more in industries with larger returns to scale than in industries with smaller returns to scale.

The analysis of enterprises assumed that enterprises were rewarded on the basis of their output, so that they wished to maximize output. This does not imply, of course, that over the range of enterprises constituting Y, the planners wish to maximize Y. Suppose, however, that they did wish to maximize Y. It would then be necessary that $dY/d\pi = 0$. In this case it would be necessary that the numerator on the right be zero. This will be the case if any of the three terms constituting it is zero. In particular, Y reaches an extremum if $\sigma(K_i) = 0$. That means that K_i is the same in all enterprises. Two interpretations are possible: (1) For all enterprises, the ratio of marginal cost to average cost must be the same. (2) For every enterprise, returns to scale must be the same.[8] Y will also reach an extremum, however, if

$$r \left(K_i, \frac{\partial C_i}{\partial x_i} \frac{dx_i}{d\pi} \right) = 0$$

that is, if the changes in outlay induced by the changes in plan are independent of the rates of return in the various enterprises.

These results are expressed in terms of outlays

$$\left(\frac{\partial C_i}{\partial x_i} \frac{dx_i}{d\pi} \right)$$

There is a question also of the connection between maximizing Y and maximizing outputs. We assume here that the p_i are different,

---

[8] In the limiting case in which returns to scale are 1 in all enterprises, we have Barone's case. Here there is only one plan producing positive output, that which would have occurred if prices had been set so as to force enterprises to produce at the level of output-minimizing average cost.

and that the outputs x_i in question may refer to different goods. Applying the statistical expansion to

$$M\left(\frac{\partial C_i}{\partial x_i}\frac{dx_i}{d\pi}\right)$$

we find that

$$\frac{1}{n}\frac{dY}{d\pi} = M\left(\frac{\partial C_i}{\partial x_i}\frac{dx_i}{d\pi}\right) = M\left(\frac{\partial C_i}{\partial x_i}\right)M\left(\frac{dx_i}{d\pi}\right) + \sigma\left(\frac{\partial C_i}{\partial x_i}\right)\sigma\left(\frac{dx_i}{d\pi}\right)r\left(\frac{\partial C_i}{\partial x_i},\frac{dx_i}{d\pi}\right)$$

If Y is maximized, this expression is equal to zero, so that

$$M\left(\frac{dx_i}{d\pi}\right) = -\frac{\sigma\left(\frac{\partial C_i}{\partial x_i}\right)\sigma\left(\frac{dx_i}{d\pi}\right)r\left(\frac{\partial C_i}{\partial x_i},\frac{dx_i}{d\pi}\right)}{M\left(\frac{\partial C_i}{\partial x_i}\right)}$$

Economists have come to think of changes in aggregate output in terms of production indices. These indices, however, have inconvenient statistical properties. Historically, they came into use because data were inadequate to make a complete enumeration of commodities and because the available data were obviously not random samples of the population of outputs and prices. The index is a stratified sample, which is taken as an approximation of a true value such as $M(dx_i/d\pi)$, which cannot actually be computed. This formula gives us the result.

A plan which maximizes Y also satisfies the condition:

$$\text{Sign}\left[M\left(\frac{dx_i}{d\pi}\right)\right] \neq \text{sign}\left[r\left(\frac{\partial C_i}{\partial x_i},\frac{dx_i}{d\pi}\right)\right]$$

Thus this plan is associated with increasing outputs if and only if the plan increases output more in enterprises with low marginal costs than in enterprises with high marginal costs. Moreover, if changes in plan do not affect output by the same amounts in all industries [so that $\sigma(dx_i/d\pi) \neq 0$], then a plan which maximizes Y will not also maximize output [$M(dx_i/d\pi) = 0$] unless either $\sigma(\partial C_i/\partial x_i) = 0$, or

$$r\left(\frac{\partial C_i}{\partial x_i}\frac{dx_i}{d\pi}\right) = 0$$

The first condition means that all enterprises have the same marginal cost. The second means that changes in output are independent of marginal cost.

Thus a plan which maximizes Y provides that the ratio of

average cost to marginal cost shall be the same for all enterprises. If it also maximizes output marginal cost is the same for all enterprises, then—since price is equal to average cost for each enterprise —we may say that a plan simultaneously maximizes Y and output if prices are the same for all enterprises. In general, this condition obviously is not met when Y refers to several kinds of goods.

Suppose, now, that the plan maximizes aggregate output but does not necessarily maximize Y. In this case $M\left(dx_i/d\pi\right) = 0$, and we have

$$\frac{1}{n}\frac{dY}{d\pi} = M\left(\frac{\partial C_i}{\partial x_i}\frac{dx_i}{d\pi}\right) = \sigma\left(\frac{\partial C_i}{\partial x_i}\right)\sigma\left(\frac{dx_i}{d\pi}\right)r\left(\frac{\partial C_i}{\partial x_i},\frac{dx_i}{d\pi}\right)$$

$$= \frac{\sigma\left(K_i\right)\sigma\left(\frac{\partial C_i}{\partial x_i}\frac{dx_i}{d\pi}\right)r\left(K_i,\frac{\partial C_i}{\partial x_i}\frac{dx_i}{d\pi}\right)}{1 - M\left(K_i\right)}$$

In this case, if the standard deviations are all different from zero and if enterprises produce under conditions of decreasing return to scale,

$$\text{Sign}\left(\frac{dY}{d\pi}\right) = \text{Sign}\left[r\left(\frac{\partial C_i}{\partial x_i},\frac{dx_i}{d\pi}\right)\right] = \text{Sign}\left[r\left(K_i,\frac{\partial C_i}{\partial x_i}\frac{dx_i}{d\pi}\right)\right]$$

For plans which maximize aggregate output, then, the following conditions are equivalent.

1. The plan increases Y.

2. Output increases more in response to changes in plan in enterprises with high marginal cost than in enterprises with low marginal cost.

3. Outlays increase more in response to changes in plan in enterprises in which returns to scale are high than in enterprises in which returns to scale are low.

The concept "a plan which maximizes a variable V" applies, of course, only to a given set of conditions. The plan, in macroeconomics, is "dynamic," in the sense that the production function of each enterprise at time t_o is a function of outputs at times $t < t_o$. This is because the plant, equipment and inventories have been built up from the output of previous periods, and the output at any period is a function of the plan at that period. Consequently, if we could characterize the plan as a number or vector π, it would be a number or vector which was a function of time, $\pi\left(t\right)$, since it exists at any date. An output vector X, then, is a function not only of $\pi\left(t_o\right)$ but also of $\pi\left(t - \Theta\right)$, for every $\Theta < t_o$. Strictly speaking, then, a "plan which maximizes" is one for which $\dfrac{\partial V}{\partial \pi}\bigg|_{t\,=\,t_0} = 0$;

however, the fact that this equation holds does not mean that $\left(\dfrac{\partial Y}{\partial \pi}\dfrac{d\pi}{dt}\right)\bigg|_{t\,=\,t_0\,+\,dt} = 0$. In other words, a "plan which maximizes V"

does so at an instant of time, under conditions which are given at that instant but which change in amounts influenced by the plan.

There arises in this connection the "index number problem," which has caused such difficulties to statisticians. This is the problem which arises in connection with measuring rates of growth in the U.S.S.R. with a view to determining whether Soviet growth is or is not slowing down and whether Soviet growth is or is not more rapid than that of (say) the U.S. Let us compare the relation between percentage changes in a macroeconomic variable Y and percentage changes in physical output of individual enterprises.

$$\frac{1}{n}\frac{dY}{d\pi} = \frac{1}{n}\,\Sigma p_i\,\frac{dx_i}{d\pi} = \frac{1}{n}\,\Sigma\,p_i\,x_i\left(\frac{1}{x_i}\frac{dx_i}{d\pi}\right) = \frac{1}{n}\,\Sigma\,p_i\,x_i\,\frac{d\log x_i}{d\pi}$$

Using the expansion given above

$$\frac{1}{n}\frac{dY}{d\pi} = M\,(p_i\,x_i)\,M\left(\frac{d\log x_i}{d\pi}\right) + \sigma\,(p_i\,x_i)\,\sigma\left(\frac{d\log x_i}{d\pi}\right)r\left(p_i\,x_i,\,\frac{d\log x_i}{d\pi}\right),$$

but

$$\frac{1}{n}\,Y = M\,(p_i\,x_i),$$

so that

$$\frac{1}{Y}\frac{dY}{d\pi} = \frac{d\log Y}{d\pi} = M\left(\frac{d\log x_i}{d\pi}\right) + \frac{\sigma\,(p_i\,x_i)\,\sigma\left(\dfrac{d\log x_i}{d\pi}\right)r\left(p_i\,x_i,\,\dfrac{d\log x_i}{d\pi}\right)}{M\,(p_i\,x_i)}$$

The rate of growth of Y will not equal the rate of growth of output unless the second right term vanishes. If this is to be the case, one of the following must be true:

1. All enterprises have the same total revenue $[\sigma\,(p_i x_i) = 0]$.
2. All outputs change in the same proportion.

$$\sigma\left(\frac{d\log x_i}{d\pi}\right) = 0$$

3. There is no tendency for output of enterprises with large revenues to change either more or less rapidly than output of enterprises with small revenues.

$$r\left(p_i\,x_i,\,\frac{d\log x_i}{d\pi}\right) = 0$$

The first two possibilities may be dismissed in a general way. The third deserves the following comment. Suppose that the output of new enterprises is small, that it grows rapidly at first, and that as it approaches its "rated capacity" it grows only slowly. Then, in fact, enterprises with small revenue will be growing rapidly compared to those with large revenue. Or, suppose the effect of technical change is to create economics of scale which formerly did not exist. Then investment will be concentrated in the smaller plants, and their output will rise more rapidly than in the older plants. Neither of these possibilities need be discussed in detail. The point is that there are various reasons to suppose the third term will not, in general, vanish.

So far, it has been assumed that prices are invariant. Suppose a general change in prices. What happens to the bias, that is to the difference

$$\frac{d\log Y}{d\pi} - M\left(\frac{d\log x_i}{d\pi}\right)?$$

Price changes are decided independently of output changes. Then, denote by dr a change in price structure.

$$\frac{d}{dr}\left(\frac{d\log Y}{d\pi} - M\,\frac{d\log x_i}{d\pi}\right) =$$

$$= -\,\frac{\sigma\,(p_i\,x_i)\,\sigma\left(\dfrac{d\log x_i}{d\pi}\right)r\left(p_i\,x_i,\dfrac{d\log x_i}{d\pi}\right)}{[M\,(p_i\,x_i)]^2}\,\frac{dM\,(p_i\,x_i)}{dr}$$

Using reasoning similar to that already shown, we find that

$$\frac{dM\,(p_i\,x_i)}{dr} = \frac{1}{n}\sum\frac{dp_i}{dr}\,x_i = \frac{1}{n}\sum p_i\,x_i\,\frac{d\log p_i}{dr}$$

$$= M\,(p_i\,x_i)\,M\left(\frac{d\log p_i}{dr}\right) + \sigma\,(p_i\,x_i)\,\sigma\left(\frac{d\log p_i}{dr}\right)r\left(p_i\,x_i,\frac{d\log p_i}{dr}\right)$$

Substituting, therefore,

$$\frac{d}{dr}\left[\frac{d\log Y}{d\pi} - M\left(\frac{d\log x_i}{d\pi}\right)\right] = -\left[\frac{d\log Y}{d\pi} - M\left(\frac{d\log x_i}{d\pi}\right)M\left(\frac{d\log p_i}{dr}\right)\right]$$

$$\times\,\frac{-\,\sigma^2\,(p_i\,x_i)\,\sigma\left(\dfrac{d\log p_i}{dr}\right)\sigma\left(\dfrac{d\log x_i}{d\pi}\right)r\left(p_i\,x_i,\dfrac{d\log x_i}{d\pi}\right)r\left(p_i\,x_i\dfrac{d\log p_i}{dr}\right)}{[M\,(p_i\,x_i)]^2}$$

If there is no change in the average level of prices,

$$M\ [(d \log p_i)/dr] = 0$$

and the first term vanishes. The second term will vanish if any one of the following is true:

1. All enterprises have the same total revenues.
2. All outputs change proportionately.
3. All prices change proportionately.
4. There is no tendency for output of enterprises with large revenues to change more or less rapidly than output of enterprises with small revenues.
5. There is no tendency for prices charged by enterprises with large revenues to change either more or less than prices charged by enterprises with small revenues.

Three of these conditions, (1, 2, and 4) have already been met. Of the others, No. 3 is not very interesting; but it seems that No. 5 should not, in general, be assumed true. Here is an obvious possibility: Suppose that prices charged include taxes, that some goods are bought by the state, and that the state expands more the enterprises from which it buys than the enterprises from which it does not buy. In this case, since the state has no reason to tax itself, it will have relatively low prices (or it will lower prices relatively more) in the large plants (from which it buys) than in the small plants (from which other consumers buy). Thus (1) in general there is a difference between percentage changes in value and percentage changes in volume, even if prices are fixed, and (2) in general this difference responds to changes both in the level and in the structure of prices. Hence production indexes, which are of the form of the variable Y in our problem, may in general be expected to differ from the average change in output $M\ [d \log x_i/d\pi]$ of the same set of commodities; moreover, the difference depends in general upon the set of prices used as weights. Analogous propositions may be derived about price index problems.

This is the problem which has preoccupied möst Sovietologists concerned with economic measurement and with macroeconomic variables. I have not dealt with it in this book because I feel that it is not of great theoretical interest, and its practical implications have been explored elsewhere.[9] In the following discussion, then, these problems will in the main be disregarded. It will be assumed merely that if prices are given, values and outputs move in the same direction and that if output is given, values and prices move in the same direction.

Since macroeconomic analysis is less formal, and more immediately translatable into visible categories of human endeavor, than microeconomics, it seems useful to summarize, with heroic brevity, a few salient facts about the U.S.S.R. These serve to clarify the frame of reference within which the analysis takes place. In particular, it is desirable to give orders of magnitude of phenomena; and for this purpose value data[10] will often be used.

[9] The practical implications are considerable. Gerschenkron has shown that if 1899 prices are used as weights, one would conclude that U.S. machinery output in 1939 was 5.5 times as great as in 1899; if 1939 prices are used as weights, one would conclude that U.S. machinery output declined 45 percent in the same period. Alexander Gerschenkron, *A Dollar Index of Soviet Machinery Output, 1927–28 to 1937*, Report R–197 (Santa Monica, Calif.: The RAND Corporation, April 6, 1951).

[10] Unless otherwise specified, all statistical information is taken from the statistical yearly, *Narodnoe Khozyaistvo SSSR*. An effort has been made to use only "hard numbers," so as to avoid the numerous controversies about index numbers and the like. International comparisons have also been avoided, where values are involved. The main reason for including statistical material in this discussion is that it justifies assertions that "*A* is large (or small) compared to *B*." Since the discussion, in any event, is a simplified view of reality, it is desirable to simplify by eliminating the unimportant rather than the important factors from this discussion. It may be added that in 1960 the U.S.S.R. altered its price system by dividing all money values and prices by ten (and issuing new bank notes in exchange for old at this ratio). Soviet statistical sources have now revised earlier data in the same way. All values in this book are likewise in the "new rubles." Readers comparing these value data with Soviet publications issued before 1961 will therefore find these figures are one-tenth as great as those originally published.

Chapter 8 AGRICULTURE

Winston Churchill tells of an evening he spent in reminiscence with Stalin. Each agreed that the second world war had had its tense moments. To Churchill, however, nothing compared in difficulty and strain to the Gallipoli campaign of the first world war. To Stalin, nothing compared with the collectivization of agriculture in 1931–32. The Soviet government has held that this extraordinary step, and the convulsions it caused, were necessary and desirable; but it has laid its main claim to achievement upon the construction of industry. What is the connection, if any, between these two sets of policies?

In 1927, as in 1910, 90 percent of the Soviet population was engaged in agriculture. Today, less than 50 percent is rural (we do not have figures for agricultural employment). If the Soviet population had remained constant, 40 percent of it, or perhaps 80 million people, might be said to have been moved physically from village to town in a period of thirty-five years. Births, deaths, and population growth, of course, make a statement impossible; but, generally speaking, this is the order of magnitude of the migration into the cities. Quite apart from the change in land tenure and farming methods, such a change would of necessity be a revolutionary one.

It would be extremely hard to give in a short space any adequate discussion of the collective farm system. One may only refer to Jasny's monumental work and to the considerable body of polemic literature on the subject. I should like, however, to discuss the problem of Soviet agricultural policy as a part of its industrialization program. It is quite clear that Soviet economic policy has been formulated in terms of cities and industry. The very earliest Marxist document, the *Communist Manifesto* of 1848, speaks of "the idiocy of village life." In striking contrast to political thinkers elsewhere, Soviet leaders have extolled the city and industrial life. The rural community is to be remade into the image of the city, and the concept of a farm as a "factory in the fields" has remained before their eyes.

There are two ways of looking at Soviet farm policy. The first is to see it as mainly concerned with operating farms and with the relations among rural people. This approach is a natural one in many respects. All Western countries with long histories (that is, every one but the United States, Canada and Australia) have had complicated problems of land tenure, and continuing land reform movements. They have frequently overshadowed production and distribution problems. In any case, these countries have usually had governments which had no reason to have a unified economic policy in which farm policies were adopted because of urban problems. Consequently, to look at Soviet agriculture as one would look at the agriculture of any other country is a natural first step. Indeed, such a study is, within limits, both interesting and valid.

Some of the basic problems of Soviet agriculture, however, have nothing to do with agriculture as such, but have to do with industry. If we understand this fact, we learn something of use to the analysis of Eastern Europe (and probably Communist China); and we can see some of the obstacles which some underdeveloped countries face.

The Soviet Union in the late 1920's was a poor credit risk. Even if it had wished to, it could not have financed industrialization by borrowing abroad. In order to import capital goods on a large scale, it had to export more agricultural goods, and to import fewer manufactured consumer goods. Thus, foreign trade policy, as well as the increases in domestic investment, necessitated decreases in domestic consumption and increases in savings. Besides increasing savings, the Soviet Government had also to ensure that savings were channeled into industrial rather than agricultural investments. The Soviet government had also to divert labor resources out of agriculture into industry. This movement of labor would be facilitated, if the urban standard of living rose more (or fell less) than the rural. These features of Soviet development policies would be relevant for any industrializing country.

The Russian Revolution was ultimately led and won by the Communists (then called Bolsheviks). They were a city party, and could obtain rural support only by supporting a program of land tenure which eliminated large land holdings. These large estates had produced most of the farm surplus, for peasant agriculture tended to be virtually subsistence farming. During the 1920's, therefore, there was a persistent problem of getting food for the cities and for export. Insofar as peasants had larger incomes, they were interested in improving their farms and were neither able nor willing to provide funds for industrial development. (In this respect, they were not very different from the former landlords, who were inclined either to spend their incomes or to invest in agriculture.) An increase in industrial investment, in these circumstances, meant mainly an increase in farm prices. City food supplies would tend to become short, and farmers would actually cut back on their deliveries unless manufactured goods were sent to the villages. Thus it was hard to raise urban living standards relative to rural ones.

The Soviet government had to make sure of a city food supply if it was to proceed with industrialization. Moreover, it had to raise funds for investment. In practice, it is almost impossible to collect food directly from individual peasant households. It would have been equally hard to collect money income taxes from the peasants. The practical way of procedure was to centralize the harvesting of grain in such a way that it would be collected physically in a relatively small number of places and sold at a profit which could be used to finance investment. The size of the investment program was such as to require reduction in urban consumption as well as rural—this is why the turnover tax was introduced. But to establish a differential between urban and rural standards of living, it was necessary to put especially low prices on payments to the farm sector. It is in this sense that the costs of industrialization were borne by the peasants. They were in any case the bulk of the population. They also had to be the least favored, since a major purpose of the program was to move many of them into the cities.

Of course, this economic logic formed only a part of the discussion at the time. The Soviet government, as Marxists, felt that the problem of the farm surplus should be analyzed in terms of property relations. It would have maintained that the problem arose because the wealthy peasants were holding back supplies, for the sake of self-enrichment. This was certainly true in the sense that the less wealthy were certainly on a subsistence basis and probably had very little surplus at all. But the "wealthy" peasants of the 1920's were not very wealthy by any reasonable standards and in any event were reacting to the "scissors" or "parity ratio" (the ratio of farm prices to manufactured goods prices) more or less as economic theory would have predicted. The Soviet government maintained that only the abolition of private farming would help the situation, so it replaced private farming with collectivized agriculture. If the Soviet government were correct in its assessment, its problem should have been resolved.

The elimination of private agriculture took place in 1930–33 and was peculiarly ferocious. Some millions of persons were arrested and either deported to the east to set up new farming areas, or put into forced labor camps to carry on construction work for industry and transportation. In revenge, peasants who were put into collective farms against their will slaughtered livestock and even, according to some reports, Soviet officials who came to operate the new system. The official statistics show a decline of one-third to one-half in the livestock population of the country over this period. In 1932, in the middle of the process, there was a severe crop failure; and there have been repeated accounts of famines in some farm areas. In general, there is no reason to doubt Stalin's characterization of the period as the most difficult of Soviet history. No discussion as brief as this one can do it justice.

Soviet farm policy originally expected that collective farms would be a transitionary institution and that state farms would be the ultimate form of farm organization. The state farm is literally a state enterprise which happens to be employed in agriculture. Its employees are in law and practice like factory workers. They receive money wages, the head of the farm is appointed by a higher body, and the accounts of the farm are kept virtually like those of any enterprise. These farms have proved to be a continuous source of disappointment, however, for the typical farm operation. They do function relatively well in specialized cases—for example, the production of vegetables outside the large cities is often carried out by state farms—but the grain farm has, until recently, generally been a collective farm.

Initially, the collective farm was conceived of as the economic unit corresponding to the village. In most of the U.S.S.R., peasants lived in villages rather than on the land, and the collective farm membership could thus be geographically defined. Very large collective farms were at first attempted, but these turned out not to function well. Only in 1950 was it decided to proceed to the formation of larger farm units, and in that year the number of separate farms was reduced by about 80 percent.

One of the important features of collective farming was the introduction of farm machinery for the main field operations. Indeed, collectivization and mechanization were very closely associated in all discussion of the subject. The agrarian legislation of the revolutionary period, in general, had tended to distribute land in relatively small units, which were too small to permit the individual peasant to use power machinery. Combining the land into larger units made it easier to use power machinery. The slaughter of horses, the movement of many peasants into the cities, and the deportation of others made it highly desirable to introduce power machinery. The Soviet government then made a virtue of necessity and mechanized ploughing and harvesting, particularly of grain; however, it was confronted by an acute shortage of machinery and of personnel trained to use it and, in addition, by peasant hostility to the new system. Hence it did not make the machinery directly available to the new farms but established a system of machine-tractor stations. These were state-owned; each served a number of farms; and their services were paid for in kind, at prices which added to the profit the state received from farming.

It would be very interesting to know how much of the opposition to collective farming was due to the farm institutions themselves and how much was due to the combination of taxes and compulsory deliveries which went along with them. Viewed historically, it is not possible to separate the two. The Soviet government did not collectivize agriculture until it had a need for more grain and more tax revenue, so it is a matter of conjecture what might have happened if it had attempted the measures separately.

The collective farm system, of course, survived the initial difficulties. During the war, it tended to break down in the areas under German occupation, because German policy, though partly aware of its usefulness in securing grain deliveries, was not particularly concerned in making any Soviet economic institution work. Without support of government, and particularly in the absence of adequate machine-tractor station service, the collective farms tended to fall apart. They were re-established without much visible trouble when the Soviet army regained possession of its former territories.

In the rest of the country the system survived, despite severe shortages of parts for machinery and of petroleum products. Soviet trucks and tractors were to a very considerable extent equipped with gas-generator units and burned wood fuel in areas where wood was plentiful. The shortage of fuel might have been expected to produce great difficulties, especially in the winter of 1942–43, when Baku, then the main source of Soviet crude oil, was isolated from the rest of the country by the German advance to the Volga. Moreover, the draft of men into the armed forces affected the collective farms far more acutely than the factories, since the less skilled farm labor was much less likely to be exempted from service. Using predominantly the labor of women, and forced to get along with far less mechanical aid than before, the system survived the war.

The collective farm system at that time showed, however, an important economic trait, which had apparently not been anticipated and which lent a distinctive feature to wartime and postwar Soviet monetary problems. Over the 1930's retail prices rose steadily, as also did urban money wages. The prices paid for compulsory deliveries and for crediting payments to the machine-tractor stations were fixed for twenty years at 1930–31 levels. By 1940, it was generally the case that collective farmers received their food from the farms, but very little cash. On the other hand, most of their cash income came either from the resale of a part of their incomes in kind, or from the sale of produce from the small private plots they were allowed to retain. In either case, these sales took place in open markets, where prices were not controlled.

During 1941–43 the Germans occupied areas producing normally a large part of the country's farm surplus, and rationing was established in the cities. The Government in this way lost a considerable part of its ordinary turnover tax revenue and, despite a doubling of income taxes, had to resort to inflationary borrowing from the State Bank in 1942–43. Thus there was at least a quadrupling of the note issue. The prices in the free markets rose to a peak, in early 1943, sixteen times as high as the 1940 level. This meant, in practice, that money flowed in large amounts to the hands of peasants who alone had goods for sale at these prices.

In early 1943, and again in 1944, the government sought and obtained very considerable sums as donations from collective farmers. In particular, I recall publicity given to Ferapont Golovaty, a collective farm president from the vicinity of Saratov. His contribution in 1943 was enough to pay for a fighter plane. This plane was shot down during the year, and the following year he contributed enough to buy another. One very curious feature was this: the price of a fighter plane, in fixed prices, in early 1943, was only a few times the open-market price of a cow in Kuibyshev, where I was at the time. The distortion of the price system was then at its greatest and led to extremely curious results.

Under wartime conditions, the government could rely on direct controls to a greater extent than in ordinary times. The fact was that the collective farm system did lead to relatively steady deliveries of grain and other staples to the cities, so that the troubles over the disappearance of grain, which were a continuous source of concern in the 1920's, did not reappear during the war, when conditions might have been expected to be worse; however, the flow of money into the rural areas would have led to considerable trouble about incentives under any conditions but those of wartime. For instance, the financial incentive for peasants to seek jobs in factories would have been much less in wartime conditions, even though the government might well have wished it otherwise. Likewise, the incentive to work for the collective farm, as compared to the incentive to work individual plots, would have been greatly reduced.

The government sought to control the problems arising from the combination of food shortage and inflation by a dual price system. Beginning in the spring of 1943, it revived a policy of the early 1930's and opened a set of urban stores selling unrationed goods at prices approximating those of the open market. It gradually reduced these prices and thus forced down the open market prices, which were directly competitive. This policy could work because the budgetary balance was improving and because the advance of the army into the food-surplus areas made the supply situation better (despite the damage done to these areas by war). By the end of 1945, free market prices, though five times as high as before the war, were only at one-third the peak of 1943. The original postwar economic policy, as embodied in the 1946–50 Five Year Plan, anticipated that (just as in 1934–35) prices in the open market could be brought down to the level of prices of rationed goods, so that rationing could be abolished fairly soon. As events turned out, the supply of consumer goods (including food) was not increased fast enough to make this change possible, and at the end of 1947 a currency conversion took place. This resolved the problem by making largely worthless the accumulated cash holdings of the rural population.

The wartime experience of the U.S.S.R., and the experience of the European satellites of the early 1950's, suggests that the institutions associated with compulsory deliveries of agricultural output perform certain tasks well. When farm operations are mechanized, as is notably the case in grain farming, the collective farm system does make the farm surplus relatively independent of other economic conditions. When bread makes up the bulk of the urban diet, the Soviet arrangements do in fact provide important sources of money and goods and thus tend to accelerate the course of industrialization.

Soviet experience also suggests, however, areas where collectivized agriculture and the pricing which goes with it work less satisfactorily. The system, as it was built up in the U.S.S.R., was designed to reduce the amount of labor per acre farmed, and consequently permitted considerable increases in the area under cultivation; however, increases in the acreage cultivated do not yield proportional increases in output if the new land has lower yields than the old. In fact, increases in acreage have tended increasingly to occur in areas which are relatively subject to drought, since these are now the principal areas open for expansion.

Soviet agriculture has also relied very heavily upon mechanization and in particular upon the use of tractor-drawn equipment. Such equipment is almost irrelevant in the breeding of livestock and is relatively less useful in crops other than grain and sugar beets. In other countries, a considerable part of the investment in equipment in recent years has gone into equipment other than tractors and combines. In the United States and Canada, for example, milking is very largely done by machine, and electrical equipment is an important source of farm power. Finally, a considerable increase in output has taken place because of increased yields, and these are in considerable degree due to the use of fertilizers and pesticides.

It is strikingly true of Soviet agriculture, however, that the use of electrical power and of chemicals has been very slow. There is a strong contrast between the mechanization of ploughing and harvesting in grain, and the situation as regards animal products generally. There is a strong contrast between growth in mechanical traction on the one hand and growth in the use of electricity and chemicals on the other. As a result, the Soviet diet relies much more heavily on starches than one would expect of a developed country. Fresh meat and vegetables are scarce in the U.S.S.R., as compared with other developed countries.

Several sorts of explanation can be given for this state of affairs. The first runs in terms of the organization of agricultural labor. Nove[1] has shown, for instance, that labor productivity, in the most mechanized grain operations, is much lower than abroad because of the elaborate bookkeeping which goes on to make sure that grain is actually used for collective farm uses, instead of being diverted to the personal uses of the farmers. He and others have maintained that the collective farm is unable to organize effectively the relatively labor-intensive operations associated with growing vegetables and raising livestock.

On the basis of this sort of explanation, policies which increased the productivity of labor in these areas might be expected to raise total output. Why, then, has rural electrification, for example, been so slow, and why has the development of fertilizers and pesticides been so small? The sort of answer which must be given here runs in terms of the strategy of economic development. Soviet doctrine has maintained that the development of capital goods industries must be given priority. If an investment program merely raises agricultural output, it will presumably be of relatively little concern. The grain crisis at the time of collectivization, it is true, led to an exception, since tractors had to replace horses and since large-scale farming had to replace small-scale. But in the general course of Soviet policy since collectivization, it would not really have been thinkable to devote industrial resources to investment in agriculture.

A third kind of explanation, which is partly consistent with these, runs in terms of prices. When the authorities can enforce compulsory deliveries or procurements, they can secure minimum supplies of most items. In some years, indeed, these deliveries were calculated on the basis of quotas based on acreage, so that some farms had to purchase animals from other farms (more or less illegally) in order to have animals to deliver. But it was ordinarily

[1] A. Nove and R. D. Laird, "A Note on Labor Utilization in the Kolkhoz," *Soviet Studies*, Vol. IV, 1953, pp. 435–42.

possible to make good a shortage on one account by an excess on others. Thus in fact farms had a tendency to deliver those items for which prices were relatively favorable, and not those for which prices were lowest.

This meant, in particular, that minimum amounts of meat would be delivered. Moreover, the fact that the retail price of food includes a substantial turnover tax means that collective farms and their members alike have a strong incentive to make sales directly at the retail level. The fact that free market prices arise whenever there is a shortage of goods at the retail levels tends to divert goods (and money) from the state, particularly at those times when the state needs them most.

In the late 1940's agricultural policy was influenced by what had become classical agricultural policy. Acreage was increased, and continuous efforts were made to increase yields by exhortation. Output increased, as was to be expected, for in the war-devastated areas it took time to regain prewar yields, while output in the rest of the country was maintained at the increased levels achieved during the war. The focus of publicity centered for a time on long-term measures to increase yields in relatively dry areas, through afforestation and irrigation. In retrospect, two important new policies were introduced, one of which was abandoned after Stalin's death.

The first new policy involved the consolidation of collective farms and the expansion of state farms. As of 1940 the average collective farm consisted of eighty-one households. The size of the household is not known but can hardly have been less than five persons, which suggests that somewhere in the neighborhood of 400 persons may have been attached to the farm. As of 1959 the average rural community contained about 2,500 persons. (A community here is defined as an area having a village soviet.) Thus the average village contained several times as many persons as the average collective farm. In 1950, the policy of consolidation was announced. In the space of a year the number of collective farms was reduced by the order of one-half. The managerial aspects of such a policy are fairly simple. Soviet administration deals much more effectively with small numbers of large organizations than large numbers of small ones. This is because the large amount of information which it requires about individual enterprises makes control slow and cumbersome when many units must be regulated.

Moreover, in a collective farm of ninety families, it is highly probable that family ties will be strong, so that some internal resistances to outside management can develop. Moreover, effective farm management is hard to train and keep because of the tendency for the better-educated village population to move into the cities; and in the postwar years, moreover, there was a shortage of male labor because of wartime deaths.

On the other hand, the larger the collective farms the greater was the stress put on extensive agriculture. This was associated with increased mechanical energy and did not of itself do anything to raise yields or provide resources for raising the level of productivity of livestock, dairy, or vegetable operations. The Soviet government had always taken the position that state farms were a more desirable form of social organization than collective farms, and it undertook the expansion of state farms simultaneously with the consolidation of collective farms; but state farms (except when run as demonstration farms) had ordinarily been more successful in grain and other single crop, large-scale operations, which could be run as factory-type operations, and less successful in operations which depended upon intensive operations.

Waste was at this time the perennial problem of agriculture. This led to a statistical problem which caused considerable controversy in English-language economic literature. Until 1935, Soviet literature distinguished with some precision between the biological yield—the crop actually in the field—and the barn yield—the crop actually harvested and stored on the farm. After 1935, Soviet literature conspicuously failed to distinguish between the two. Soviet production statistics became suspect, since there were grounds for believing that the barn yields before collectivization were being compared with the more recent biological yields. There were also grounds for believing that harvesting losses (which are always higher with mechanized than nonmechanized processes) were in fact unusually high in the U.S.S.R. The issue was full of political consequences. As Baykov pointed out, if the Soviet Union were in fact reporting biological and not barn yield in the early 1950's, then Soviet per capita food consumption at that time must be below the levels of 1910–30. Unfortunately, Baykov held that this was an absurd conclusion. In 1954, Malenkov vindicated Baykov's critics, of whom Jasny was not the least vehement, declaring that it was time to stop the "pernicious practice" of reporting only biological yields.[2]

After the currency conversion of 1947, the Soviet government undertook to lower retail prices, which were fixed at almost double the 1940 level. For several years, an annual reduction of prices, including food prices, took place every March first, with considerable fanfare. Clearly, the continuation of this policy for any length of time required the expansion of farm output; but despite considerable efforts, the successive reductions of food prices became smaller and smaller, so that the last such general reduction occurred in 1954, and those of 1952 and 1953 were very small indeed.

The question of what to do about agricultural organization in the broadest sense was first raised by Stalin in 1952; earlier public postwar discussions are quite specific, are aimed basically at managerial techniques on the farm, and do not consider agriculture as a part of a larger system. The publication of Stalin's *Economic Problems of Socialism* was particularly significant, because it discussed the farm problem in the context of the entire economy. The fact that its proposed solution has been discarded does not diminish its interest.

The most startling feature of this work was the fact that it changed a basic tenet, expressed, for instance, in the *Short History of the Communist Party*. There it had been categorically stated that the question of class conflict had been finally resolved by the 1917 revolution. In contrast, Stalin stated that the existing collective farm system presented a fundamental problem, which was perhaps less extreme than the class struggle he associated with capitalist economies but which was nonetheless basic. Stalin attributed this conflict to the fact that the output of collective farms belonged to the farms, so that the state appeared as an outside customer. He contrasted this with the situation in state enterprises, where the state, as owner, could dispose of the output as it wished. The difficulty arising from this fact lay in the power of the collective farms to influence the prices at which they traded with the rest of the economy.

It may seem hard to understand why Stalin should have taken

[2] Alexander Baykov, *Postwar Economic Developments in the USSR, Bulletins on Soviet Economic Development* (University of Birmingham), No. 8 (May, 1953), pp. 29–45, especially p. 39. *Pravda*, August 9, 1953; December 16, 1958.

this position, since compulsory delivery prices had been almost unchanged for twenty years; but in fact the other prices in the system had not been changed. Moreover, the tendency of the farms and their members to try to sell at the highest price possible, given multiple pricing, meant a continuous administrative supervision of the physical process of handling farm output, the magnitude of which we can guess at from the accounting procedures of the individual collective farms, the wholesale and the retail trading systems.

Stalin's proposed solution was couched in political terms: to raise the collective farms to the level of national property and to speed up the transition to communism (the ultimate goal of the Soviet state) by introducing "direct exchange" in the rural areas to take the place of money. The details of the proposal were never exposed in full administrative detail. It appeared that the entire output of collective farms was to be assigned to the state and that collective farm members were to be assigned consumer goods (including, apparently, food) in special rural stores. In effect the system seemed either to abolish the use of money in the rural areas or to involve the use of a special type of money, usable only in rural areas. It is likely that this money, indeed, would have been usable only on the farm to which a farmer belonged.

The mechanics of the proposal, by the way, bear a curious resemblance to some features of Edward Bellamy's utopian novel, *Looking Backward*. Bellamy, however, maintained that his system would be a natural and pleasant one. It is of some interest to readers of utopian literature to speculate about the problem of introducing projects of major reform, in the light of this resemblance; for Bellamy thought people would like a nonmonetary system, while Stalin's tone suggests he anticipated the sort of resistance he had met in 1930.

After Stalin's death, the *Economic Problems* dropped from current discussion. After some years, disagreement began to be expressed with many of the propositions it contained. Certainly Soviet agricultural policy has tended along lines which differ in important ways from those prescribed; however, it is clear that the problem stated in the *Economic Problems* is one which the present government has recognized. In this case (as in many others) we find that a publication which appears to be merely an exercise in Marxist dogmatics is actually the formulation of a real problem.

Likewise, economic "anti-Stalinism" has real problems in mind. When real problems exist, we must expect practical men's actions and proposals to have important elements in common, even when they disagree.

Thus there have been important areas of continuity in the technical aspects of Soviet farm policy. For instance, the tendency to increase the average size of collective farms has continued. The tendency to emphasize state farms has continued. A considerable new effort was made to expand farm acreage, by settling large numbers of people in the semi-drought regions east of the Volga. Investment in farm machinery, especially large-scale tractor-drawn machinery, has continued. In all these respects, the Soviet Union has maintained its traditional line of attack.

Table 8–1 gives an impression of the organizational changes in Soviet agriculture. Comparing 1960 to 1940, it is clear that the sown acreage of collective farms was declining in the late 1950's,

TABLE 8–1

THE NUMBER AND SIZE OF SOVIET AGRICULTURAL ENTERPRISES, 1940–60

	1940	1950	1955	1960
1. *Collective Farms*				
Number	236,900	123,700	87,400	44,900
Acreage under collective sowing (million hectares*)	117.7	121	149.1	123.1
Total head of cattle (millions)	20.1	28.1	26.9	36.3
Average households per farm	81	165	231	383
Average acreage sown (hectares)	492	967	1,702	2,745
Average head of cattle...	85	224	308	807
2. *State Farms*				
Number	4,159	4,988	5,134	7,357
Sown acreage (million hectares)	11.6	12.9	25.9	67.2
Total head of cattle (millions)	2.5	2.8	3.3	14.4
Average number of workers	330	351†	409	745
Average acreage sown (hectares)	2,800	2,600	5,000	9,000
Average head of cattle	592	562	652	1,957

* One hectare is 2.47 acres.
† This figure is estimated. Until recently only "workers" were reported; now only total persons working are reported. The 1940 total is reported in *Narodnoe Khozyaistvo,* but not the 1950 total. It has been assumed that from 1940 to 1950 the total changed in the same proportion as workers.

so that by 1960 it was only 5 percent above 1950. Thus the entire increase in area under cultivation has (again on balance) occurred in state farms. The average acreage sown per collective farm was five times as large in 1960 as in 1940, and the average number of households had almost quintupled. State farms had about six times as much acreage under cultivation in 1960 as in 1940, so that for the two kinds of farm taken together, acreage had risen almost 50 percent.

This change, of course, tends to lead to Stalin's goal of making agriculture as a whole more like state industry. It does so by confining growth to the state farm sector, where factory-type methods are supposed to prevail. It also does so by increasing the size of collective farms until individual family ties among members are necessarily very much less close. Instead of moving toward a barter system of trade between agriculture and the state, however, Soviet policy of the 1950's actually moved toward a strengthening of the monetary ties between agriculture and the rest of the economy.

There have been important changes, however, in the agricultural pricing system. The compulsory deliveries and payments in kind to machine-tractor stations ceased in 1958, so that money income of collective farms rose, as did the importance of the state as a source of money income. Table 8–2 shows that the value of sales to the state by collective farms in 1960 was about eleven times as high as in 1940 and about five times as high as in 1950. The total

TABLE 8–2

TOTAL MONEY INCOME OF COLLECTIVE FARMS AND FARMERS
(BILLION RUBLES, AT CURRENT PRICES)

	1940	1950	1955	1960
Total	2.07	3.42	7.56	13.31
Sales to the state	.91	2.15	5.52	10.86
Crops	.69	1.81	3.76	6.13
Animal products	.22	.34	1.76	4.73
Sales from "*kolkhozy* trade				
procedures"	.73	.91	1.57	1.60
Crops	.45	.58	.84	1.05
Animal products	.28	.33	.73	.55
Other income	.52	.45	.78	1.03
From livestock	.10	.10	.30	.20
From subsidiary enterprises...	.42	.35	.48	.83
Total collective farm money income per household from collective farm activity (rubles)..................	110.7	168.5	382.1	780.7

increase in income from this source was about 10 billion rubles, out of a total increase in collective farm money income of about 11 billion rubles. In consequence, the state's share in total collective farm income rose from about 45 percent in 1940 to 65 percent in 1950 to over 80 percent in 1960; in particular, sales of livestock to the state accounted for only about 10 percent of collective farm income in 1940 and 1950, but accounted for over one-third of the total in 1960.

This change reflects very considerable changes in the prices paid to collective farms by the state. Table 8–3 gives data compiled by Jasny. There is no reason to suppose any very marked increase in costs over this period. Even in 1962, according to Jasny, these prices were still somewhat below production costs. The conclusion is quite simple. One reason for continuing difficulty in the supply of livestock products to the state has been that the farms sold these goods at a loss. In the circumstances, it is hardly surprising that farms should have tried to divert goods away from the state and into the more profitable free markets.

TABLE 8–3

PROCUREMENT PRICES PAID TO COLLECTIVE FARMS, 1953-62*
(1952 = 100)

	Pigs	Cattle	Milk	Eggs	Wool
1953	453	338	202	126	107
1954	786	476	289	135	146
1955	806	464	303	152	158
1956	976	508	334	155	246
1957	1151	604	362	169	285
1958	1156	1147	404	297	352
1959	1181	1226	404	310	353
1962	1435	1628	444	341	353

* Naum Jasny, "The Failure of the Soviet Animal Industry," *Soviet Studies*, XV (October, 1963), p. 213.

It is possible to get some further idea of the increasing importance of income from the state to the rural community by comparing retail trade in rural areas with trade on the collective farm markets. The money income of collective farms must be used in part to pay operating costs and taxes, so only part of it is available to be distributed as money income to members. These members, moreover, derive part of their money income from selling goods which they produce as individuals. Moreover, some (perhaps most) rural money income is earned by wage-earners on state farms and other state institutions in rural areas. It is not possible to obtain complete data on these various kinds of transactions; however, Table 8–4 indicates a number of important tendencies.

TABLE 8–4

SOME INDICATIONS OF RURAL SPENDING, AND SOURCES OF INCOME, 1940–60
(BILLIONS OF RUBLES, EXCEPT AS NOTED)

	1940	1950	1955	1960
Total retail trade, state and co-operative stores*	15.0	31.7	45.3	74.4
Trade in rural areas	5.2	8.7	13.3	18.9
Sales on collective farm market				
Total	2.5	4.3	4.9	4.2
Through open market	2.5	4.3	4.4	3.4
Through co-operatives	–	–	.5	.8
Sales on market by farms	.73	.91	1.57	1.60
Sales on market by farmers	1.77	3.39	2.83	1.80
Sales of individuals to state and to co-operative and state stores	–	.20†	.80	3.30
Total money income of farmers and other individuals from preceding two sources	1.77	3.59	3.63	5.30
Apparent money income after taxes of rural population from payments by state and collective farms‡	3.4	5.1	9.7	13.6

* State and co-operative retail trade, less collective farm market transactions handled by the co-operative store system.
† Wild guess.
‡ Retail trade in rural areas, minus preceding row.

It is clear from this table that rural spending per capita is relatively small. In 1940 rural retail sales were only one-third of the total, though two-thirds of the population was rural; in 1960, when half the population was rural, about one-quarter of the trade was in rural areas. Of course, the rural population is relatively self-sufficient in food, and of course some urban sales are made to farm people; but the difference in living standards is an important one. The problem to be resolved is the source of rural money income. This may arise either from the farmer's membership in a collective farm, his employment at a state farm, or his own earnings as an independent seller.

Reference has been made to the open market in the war years. In recent years, collective farms have been increasingly led to provide supplies for sale on the open market through the co-operative store system. These sales have been at prices midway between those of the ordinary stores and the true open market prices. The existence of such trade serves to control open market prices; while all collective farm market transactions seem to have been stable at 4 billion or 5 billion rubles a year, the transactions at uncontrolled prices seem to have dropped by about one-third over the past decade.

In particular, it would appear that collective farms now sell more and that their members, as individuals, sell less than formerly. In 1950, the farms sold only one-quarter of the total; in 1960, they sold 40 percent of the turnover. Thus individuals' incomes from this source have fallen. To offset this, the state and the retail trade system have increased their purchases from individuals, so that on balance over the past decade there has been a slight increase in the direct money earnings of individuals from the sale of their output. This increase is small: an increase of 1.8 billion rubles from 1940 to 1950 and a further increase of 1.7 billion rubles in the next ten years.

On the other hand, total rural spending rose by 3.5 billion rubles from 1940 to 1950 and by 10.2 billion rubles from 1950 to 1960. This increase must have come overwhelmingly from earnings received from collective and state farms in the past decade. About half the increase of 3.5 billion rubles in retail spending between 1940 and 1950 and 8.5 billion of an increase of 10.2 billion rubles in the following decade came from these sources.

These figures tell us nothing directly either about the "terms of trade" between city and farm, or about the rural standard of living. They do, however, indicate that the rural people have become much more dependent upon their position in state or collective farms, and much less dependent upon their status as "private businessmen" in the past ten years.

In this sense the Soviet regime has taken measures to weaken the role of the open market in agricultural life which was so evident in wartime. The existence of a channel whereby goods sold through the co-operative system are in direct competition with the free market is, of course, a system of multiple pricing. Moreover, so long as the state has direct control over the growing state farm sector, the state is in a position (should need arise) to hold down free market prices by diverting a part of other output to this purpose. There is no practical way of detecting, of course, how much of this trade represents bona fide sales by farms, and how much represents price-maintaining operations from state stocks. We may ultimately have information on the success of this system if information becomes available for 1963–64; for in 1963 the harvest was very bad and open market prices would have risen if not held back by the new mechanisms.

The new mechanism, of course, is a substitute for the barter-type system advocated in Stalin's *Economic Problems*. Instead of attempting to segregate the farm system from the urban community, it has increased the importance to the farm population of money income originating from socialized agriculture. This approach is, of course, an attempt to do two things: first, to control the level of open market prices by having continual state intervention in this market and, second, to give collectivized agriculture a major role in supplying the rural population with money income.

The apparent danger in the system is that the control of prices in the open market may require too many resources, for the state can force down open market prices only by diverting goods from the regular system of urban stores; however, the urban manifestation of a situation leading to high open market prices is apt to be an excess of purchasing power. Open market prices are in any case, however, above the ordinary retail levels; therefore, if the state sells more at these prices, it absorbs more urban purchasing power than it otherwise would and tends to restore stability, at least in a short-term disturbance such as a crop failure.

The changes in Soviet agriculture over the past decade may or may not have increased the output of Soviet agriculture and the standard of living of the Soviet consumer. Whether they have or not is a question which may be left to the statisticians; but they have been addressed in part to a real problem of incentives and to a real potential for economic disequilibrium, a dramatic manifestation of which occurred during the second world war.

Chapter 9 CAPITAL FORMATION

The Soviet Union, since about 1930, has been engaged in a major effort to expand its industrial plant. Indeed, the whole process of economic planning has been associated with construction programs. It is therefore natural that a discussion of investment in plant should be an important part of any discussion of Soviet economics. This investment process, of course, affects all sectors of the economy; so in a sense it does not matter which aspects are discussed first. Let us first examine construction enterprises—that is, the people who actually carry out the work of building new plants. Then we shall see the role of those who are to use the new capacity. Some of these are existing enterprises (when expansion of existing plant is in question). Some of them are ministries and economic councils (where wholly new enterprises are formed). Finally, we must consider the interests of the government, since increases in plant and equipment represent increases in the unified fund of state property, to which reference has already been made.

Some Soviet enterprises are concerned with building and installing new equipment. These will be called construction enterprises. Their current output is associated with gross investment, of course; but economics generally, and Soviet economics in particular, makes a clear distinction between output for current use and output for the expansion of fixed assets, which is a major part of gross investment. Soviet institutions reflect quite sharply this theoretical distinction.

In March, 1960, there were 9,752 construction enterprises (not counting the construction departments which are attached to some large producing enterprises, and construction organizations associated with collective farms and other co-operatives). Of these,

1,628 were attached to ministries of the U.S.S.R., 3,224 to economic councils, 3,651 to the ministries of the republics, and 1,249 to local government. The construction industry is thus widely scattered in terms of its administrative organization. It is clear that the conditions in individual enterprises vary enormously. Considerable discussion has taken place over how to "rationalize" this industry, but there seems to be no way to avoid having many small organizations. Thus in 1960, 35 percent of all enterprises performed work of less than 1 million rubles, and 39 percent performed work of between 1 million and 2 million rubles.

Some Soviet construction enterprises are geographically localized. That is, they are prepared to perform many types of building, but only in a certain locality. Others are functionally specialized. That is, they build only a certain kind of facility—railroads, power plants, metallurgical plants, and so on—but will build the plant anywhere in the country. There have usually been ministries of construction attached to the union government and republican governments to cope with the less specialized forms of construction. The ministries and economic councils have divisions which operate specialized enterprises. In some cases, large enterprises with fairly long-term expansion programs have their own construction departments, which may in this context be treated almost as if they were separate enterprises. Construction work is diffused throughout the economy, and construction enterprises exist in many forms, corresponding to the structure of organization of current output.

The construction enterprise operates on the basis of contracts, just as producing enterprises do. It has the equivalent of a production plan, which tells it how much it is supposed to build in any period. The typical construction enterprise will be working on more than one project at any time; and to complete its plan, it must perform a certain total amount of work. In this respect, it has many elements in common with building firms in other countries. An important problem in building generally is to keep personnel busy. The successful builder is one who is able to shift his employees from one project to another, so that they are kept busy even if unexpected snags arise in individual projects. The builder's customer, in the Soviet Union as elsewhere, is irritated and perplexed by the builders who take people off his project and return them to it in apparently erratic fashion. This fact means that the building industry in the Soviet Union is under the same sort of continuous criticism that builders receive elsewhere.

In some cases, it is possible to schedule construction work with some precision. For the construction of very large power plants, such as the various hydroelectric power plants on the Volga, special construction units are created. Building of these plants involved basically the moving of very large amounts of earth, the laying of very large amounts of concrete, and the installation of specified numbers of generating units. In this case, a contract would coincide with the builder's plan, and it would be relatively easy to organize the work. But in most cases, such ideal conditions do not hold.

The principle that construction should be kept distinct from current output has been interpreted to mean that funds accruing from current output should not be used to finance construction, and funds allocated for construction should not be used to finance current output. If this principle were not observed, producing enterprises could expand their plant even if the government did not wish them to do so; and enterprises which were supposed to expand could use their investment funds to cover operating losses, so that intended construction work would not in fact be carried out.

In order to prevent either of these undesirable events from occurring, the construction enterprises are required to keep their current bank accounts in a special Construction Bank. Until recently there were separate investment banks for industry, agriculture, trade and communal (i.e., local) enterprises. These were similar in structure and have now been merged. Payments into a construction enterprise's current account may come only from another account in the Construction Bank. The accounts from which payments for construction are made receive funds in accordance with the rest of the investment operation, and the Investment Bank can determine relatively easily whether too many funds are being allocated to construction work. We shall also see that the control process makes it relatively easy to ensure that at least enough funds are available to finance construction.

The construction of new plant is based upon a *Plan for Capital Works*, which is analogous in construction to the *Production Plan* which governs current operations. No construction work is authorized unless it appears in the list of projects accompanying the *Plan for Capital Works*. If such work is authorized, the Construction Bank will open a special account for it and permit payments, on the basis of a contract, to a construction enterprise.

A particular project listed in the *Plan for Capital Works* will also have designated sources of funds. The most important source of funds is the state budget—that is, tax revenue. Tax revenue has not yet been discussed, so at this point we must accept on faith that the Soviet Union has taxes, some of which are devoted to construction. The taxes are paid to the Ministry of Finance, which then allocates them to ministries and economic councils. These in turn form contracts with building enterprises and use the funds (which are deposited in the Construction Bank) to pay for the construction work.

Not all investment funds come from the state budget. Some of them come from producing enterprises. A part of an enterprise's profits may be allocated to new construction. Moreover, the enterprise regularly allocates a part of its income to a depreciation account, and some of these funds may be made available for construction. In either case, as we have seen, enterprises are required to make regular payments of depreciation funds and of profits into special accounts. If the enterprises are actually financing construction work, these special accounts will be in the Construction Bank. In either case, the producing enterprises will be required to furnish regularly enough funds to meet the payments they are supposed to be making for new construction on their premises.

Naturally, the description which has been given here is somewhat idyllic. In any particular period, literally thousands of enterprises may fail to deposit funds on time; they may exaggerate their profits if they wish to speed up construction on their own premises (borrowing from the State Bank to conceal what they are doing); construction enterprises may in fact operate very inefficiently, and so on. If, however, economic conditions in the country are relatively good, these disturbances will be marginal. If they are not good, then construction operations are only one of many kinds of operations which will be disturbed. The foregoing description applies to the principles under which the construction process should operate, and it approximates reality only in part.

It should also be stressed that while the Construction Bank supervises the expenditure of funds, it does not provide technical inspection of the projects. It is up to the agency contracting with the construction enterprise to ensure that the contract terms are met. The bank cannot claim an expertise in seeing whether a power plant (for instance) is built according to contract specifications.

That task belongs to the ministry, economic council, or enterprise which will operate the new facility.

One feature of the foregoing discussion must be strongly emphasized. In none of these steps is there any borrowing. Enterprises expand if they have profits or depreciation funds or a budget appropriation. New plants are created if there is a budget appropriation. In any case, the funds are essentially state funds; if there were borrowing, the state would be paying itself interest. Soviet thought regards this possibility as ridiculous and wrong. Enterprises are creatures of the state and operate parts of a single fund of state property, rather than assets which are in any sense their own; however—and this *however* is particularly important in agriculture—co-operative enterprises do own their fixed assets. Consequently there is no reason why the state should make grants to them to finance construction. Co-operatives may expand using their own retained profits, but they have no source of outside funds; therefore, the Construction Bank does make investment loans to co-operatives (especially collective farms). Here an interest rate of 2 percent is normally charged, and the loan must be paid off in a stated period (usually ten years). This interest charge is low and does not serve as a rationing device, as interest charges generally do. The Soviet government does not approve of such a use of interest charges and claims that this rate is mainly to cover the bank's costs.

The agricultural and trading sections of the Construction Bank, then, do make loans. The funds which they lend come in part from repayments on earlier loans. In addition, the Investment Bank ordinarily receives a budget appropriation extending its loanable funds.

This system of investment finance has important repercussions on the behavior of individual producing enterprises. As long as the marginal physical productivity of plant is positive, the enterprise will wish to expand. By expanding plant, given a fixed labor force, the enterprise can increase total output and also the average productivity of labor. Since the enterprise sells at a fixed price, its revenue will increase; and since the additional plant does not add to costs, its profits will also increase. The amount of plant which enterprises will wish is then greater than what it would be if there were a cost attached to expansion. Consequently, one may expect that (in a technical sense), there will always be a capital shortage in the U.S.S.R. It is this capital shortage which makes it necessary to have a *Plan for Capital Works*. For any plant, this plan will indicate a maximum amount which may be spent on expansion in any period.

Moreover, the wage structure of Soviet industry dictates that available funds shall be used in a rather special way. There has been a good deal of attention given in recent years to the fact that Soviet engineers are highly paid relative to unskilled labor. The differences between engineers' pay and the pay of ordinary labor is greater in the U.S.S.R. than in the West. Even before the second world war, as Bergson showed, the differentials between skilled and unskilled labor were great and rising. Galenson's studies show a continuation of this trend. Indeed, the combination of rapid industrial advance and a rapid influx of untrained farm labor to the cities would suggest such a trend.

In the circumstances, the pattern of machine utilization in the Soviet bloc may be expected to be rather different from that in the West. Clark[1] has described the Nowa Huta plant, built by the U.S.S.R. in Poland. At this plant, the blast-furnace operations (which require skilled labor) are as highly mechanized as in comparable U.S. plants. Such operations as cleaning slag from the floors of the open-hearth furnaces are performed by unskilled labor using picks and shovels; the comparable U.S. operation uses a bulldozer. So in a Soviet assembly-line enterprise, parts may be carried to the line by unskilled labor. This selective pattern of mechanization is very much in accord with our expectations, given the structure of Soviet wages.

Ministries and economic councils have the problem of allocating fixed amounts of budgetary funds for construction purposes. On a broader scale, the government as a whole must allocate funds among the various claimants. It has ruled out the possibility of using an interest rate as a device for limiting the demands for funds placed upon it. It therefore has the problem of selecting those projects which are to appear in the *Plan for Capital Works* and of appropriating funds to them. The problem is one of central interest to economists generally, and Soviet economists and engineers have intermittently discussed it also.[2]

---

[1] M. Gardner Clark, Report on the Nowa Huta Steel Plant named after Lenin, near Cracow, Poland (Ithaca, N.Y.: Cornell University, School of Industrial and Labor Relations, 1957).

[2] Gregory Grossman, "Scarce Capital and Soviet Doctrine," *Quarterly Journal of Economics*, 1953.

As the problem of investment decisions is usually formulated, it makes no difference whether the economic unit making the decision is using its own funds or acquiring funds from elsewhere. This is true because it is presumed that the cost of using one's own funds can be measured by the return one would have obtained by investing them elsewhere. In a perfect market, the return the unit gets on lending its funds should approximate the cost of borrowing. Moreover, under perfectly competitive conditions, borrowers and lenders can make their own operations as large or as small as they wish without affecting interest rates. It is in this context that investment decisions are usually discussed.

In the case of Soviet state-owned enterprises, however, additions to plant and equipment are costless, in the sense that there is no interest payment and also no repayment of principal. The only obligation undertaken by the enterprise is to make depreciation payments. As long as the new plant increases the value of enterprise output by an amount exceeding the value of the plant (over its entire lifetime), the enterprise will wish to make the expansion. Moreover, it will be a matter of indifference to the enterprise whether it pays for its expansion from budget funds or from its own profits. This is true because enterprises which do not use their profits for expansion (or other approved purposes) must pay them into the state budget. The enterprise will probably find it easier to get permission to use its own profits than it will to get additional funds from outside; therefore, it may be presumed that there will in fact be a tendency for more profitable enterprises to expand more rapidly than less profitable ones. This would be true even if there were no particular reason for the enterprise to select more profitable expansion programs in preference to less profitable ones.

In many cases, it must be quite difficult to keep enterprises from illicit investment. Thus any plant in the metal trades may be tempted, if it has any profit at all, to use some of its workers to make odd bits of equipment and machinery in their spare time. Some work of this sort is necessary in any event, since Soviet plants tend to make their own parts rather than to buy them. It is consequently difficult for Soviet authorities to restrict hidden investment of this sort, although they can limit it drastically by the separation of current output from construction, as has been described.

It is in this connection that Soviet price policy becomes especially important. A distinction has been made between the prices received by individual factories and the industry-wide prices which are paid by buyers. The former prices are set close to the cost levels of the individual producers, while the latter reflect industry-wide costs and the government's interest in subsidizing or making profits from the industry in question. The profits made by the individual enterprise depend basically on whether its operating costs are greater or less than those which the government thinks it is capable of having.

Let us consider the Urals city of Tagil, near which are two steel plants. The Nizhny-Tagil steel plant is small, old, and probably high-cost. The Novo-Tagil plant is large, new, and probably low-cost. If the former has skilled managers and the latter is run by unskilled ones, however, the old plant will show a profit, and the new one will not, even though the costs of the old plant are far in excess of those of the new plant. In these circumstances, it by no means follows that the profitable plant should be able to invest and the unprofitable plant unable to invest. That is because the industrial selling agent makes a loss on the sale of output from the high-cost plant and a profit on the sale of output from the low-cost plant.

Let us take another possibility. Suppose the two plants had basically the same costs and differed only in size. It would not follow that the smaller should be expanded if it were the more profitable; for if the two plants use different mines (as in fact they do) and the smaller plant operates a smaller deposit, expanding it would merely lead to the exhaustion of its materials supply within the lifetime of the new equipment. Granted what is known about the future, it could be said that present rates of profit or cost are not guides to future rates of profit or cost.

Soviet economics has argued that the goods produced in the U.S.S.R. are sold either to the state (for defense, welfare, investment) or to consumers. It does not make sense to say the state makes a profit selling to itself. Consequently investible funds arise basically from transactions between the state sector and the consumer sector. If the state were to invest in such a way as to maximize profit in this sense, it would have to invest in consumer goods industries; however, the problem the Soviet economy has faced has been to develop the capital goods industries. Thus the Soviet financial problem is to transfer investible funds from the profitable sectors of the economy to those in which investment must take place. These investible funds may take the form of profits. If so, the profits must largely be taken away from the enterprises which earn them; however, it is possible to prevent these funds from appearing as profits. This may be done by introducing a turnover tax, which puts into the state budget money which has never formed a part of the revenue of enterprises, even though it originates in connection with the distribution and sale of consumer goods.

It is important to note that this view of the turnover tax assumes that consumer goods prices are fixed. Changes in the turnover tax, given these prices and an output plan, merely redistribute funds between the enterprises' profit accounts and the state's budget revenue. Thus the Soviet position is that the turnover tax is in fact a part of profits and hence investible funds. Western economists say the turnover tax is a tax on consumers just as a sales tax is; but this analysis is based on the supposition that a change in turnover tax must affect retail prices, which Soviet economics denies.

Soviet investment policy has concentrated construction in the capital goods industries, where prices have been kept low and hence profits have been kept small. It has used funds originating in the distribution of consumer goods and has therefore had to keep the enterprises in such industries from making profits which they could invest.

There still remains the problem of selecting among projects. Soviet engineers and economists who must make detailed proposals for railroad lines, power plants, steel mills, and so on are keenly aware of the problem and have at intervals proposed various criteria. They have suggested, for instance, that of two projects having equal productive capacity, that one should be preferred which promises the lowest costs over its lifetime, that the project which pays for itself most quickly should be preferred, and so on.

This Soviet literature has been discussed by Hunter, Grossman, Kaplan, and others. They have shown that it originates in the engineering profession and has generally been attacked by Soviet economists on the grounds that directly or indirectly it introduces profit as a criterion for investment, by creating a synthetic interest rate of some sort to replace the interest rate which is lacking in the Soviet economy. For example, a rule which says that projects should not be introduced unless the savings from cost reductions will cover the cost of the plant in ten years is equivalent to saying that the plant must be able to pay a 10 percent charge per year on its new investment.

An example of the kind of problem involved is the question of whether to build steam or hydroelectric power plants. In the early 1950's, several extremely large power plants were built along the Volga, and others were proposed. Such plants are enormously costly, but their operating costs are extremely low. Since their expected life is very long, they can certainly be economic, as experience elsewhere has shown. More recently, the Soviet government has decided in favor of steam plants rather than other hydroelectric plants on the ground, basically, that they would have shorter pay-off periods. Here is a case, then, in which the Soviet government has reversed itself and has come to act as if there were an interest rate.

There are other cases, however, in which it is clear that major projects have been carried out, even though it was unlikely that they would be profitable. In part, such projects have been made possible by the use of convict labor. Thus the Moscow-Volga canal, the Pechora coalfields, the Karaganda coalfields, some of the post-revolutionary railroads built in Central Asia and Kazakhstan, and so on, were built using convict labor. Presumably their costs would have been considerably higher if free labor had been used. In other cases, different subsidies existed. Thus the West Siberian steel industry was built originally to use iron ore from the Urals. This ore was hauled a distance of 1,500 miles by rail. It was argued that this would be economic, since the freight cars in question hauled coal in the opposite direction and would otherwise return empty; however, in order to make this system pay, extremely low freight rates were fixed, so that if the railroad in question was not subsidized from the budget, losses had to be recovered on other kinds of freight. It is not clear what form the subsidy arrangement actually took. In fact, the Siberian steel industry ultimately found that it was more economic to use local ore of poor quality than Urals ore of good quality.

It may be argued that any major program of regional development involves a risk. Such a program should sometimes be undertaken even if it involves temporary subsidization, because in the long run external economies will occur, which will then make the proposition economically justified. This proposition is perhaps a valid one, but the Soviet government in such cases has preferred to argue that objective necessity (or political considerations) required the project and that it was wrong in principle to call attention to the elements of subsidy which might be involved.

The Soviet government has been in the position of wishing to perform as much construction as possible. Its enterprises also have an incentive to expand, since they consider capital goods as free commodities. There is thus some tendency for "overinvestment" in the Soviet economy. It is sometimes the case that investment causes too much "strain" on the economy. But the terms *overinvestment* and *strain* are ill-defined notions. It is therefore of some interest to spell out what the overall consequences of investment programs are and to see precisely what may happen to make the government reduce its investment at certain times. It is also useful to consider what the upper limits to an investment program may be.

The first aspect of an investment program in the U.S.S.R. is that it is associated with an increase in the urban population. Consequently, as industrial capacity rises, so must the total supply of all urban services; therefore, even if the objective of the government is mainly to expand the capital goods industries, in fact it must also provide the housing, utilities, stores, and services to supply the workers in these industries. Table 9–1 is extremely interesting in this respect. For even in a period like 1946–50, housing construction accounted for one-fifth of all investment. The three last items—transportation, housing, and trade and services—provide no "goods" at all, but about 45 percent of all investment has gone into these categories. This is true even though some of these sectors —notably housing and trade—have been sectors in which Soviet performance has notably been worst. Consequently, the total amount of investment generated by a unit of investment in industry far exceeds in general the cost of the factory itself. It seems to be the case that a part of the Soviet government's troubles from "overinvestment" has come from its tendency to underestimate the total investment generated by individual projects.

It is necessary to put in a warning about Table 9–1. It is based upon the deflation of value figures by a price index. Both the value figures and the deflator are imperfectly understood and are hence suspect, but the general orders of magnitude are revealing for the purposes to which they have here been applied.

TABLE 9–1

CAPITAL INVESTMENTS, BY SECTORS OF THE ECONOMY,
IN "COMPARABLE PRICES"

(Billion Rubles)

	1946–50	1951–55	1956–60
Total	41.4	79.2	149.3
Industry	17.2	34.4	48.0
Capital goods industries	15.1	31.1	40.4
Consumer goods industries	2.1	3.4	7.6
Housing	8.3	15.7	34.8
Trade, services, and social services	6.1	9.9	21.7

The construction industry, in turn, will be inclined to do easiest things first. If its output plans are increased, and its resources are not, its tendency is to start more projects than it finishes, doing the easy parts of each project and letting the more difficult parts wait. There is, of course, always some unfinished construction in progress; but when pressure on the construction industry increases, unfinished projects become more numerous. Thus the value of unfinished construction projects rose from 85 percent of the annual rate of construction work in 1950 to 101 percent in 1953, at a time when industry seemed in general to be having trouble finishing its plans. Thereafter, it declined to 69 percent in 1960, corresponding to what seemed an "easing" of economic conditions. Hence when investment plans tend to be "excessive" in terms of the construction industry, there is a tendency for the press to complain about costs, about delay in completing projects, about "dissipation of resources" among too many projects, and so on.

Second, there is an intimate connection between an investment program and the state of construction enterprises. The *Plan for Capital Works* is after all the output plan of the construction industry. If the industry is not capable of increasing its output beyond a certain level, or if its costs rise with output, then allocating larger funds in the capital works plan will not lead to corresponding increases in the output of the construction industry.

There are really two aspects to this problem. The first is that construction is in part based on individually designed projects, so that the concept of a fixed price is not as meaningful in construction as in industry or agriculture. The second is that often the way a building enterprise chooses to fulfill its production plan can be inconvenient to the state.

Soviet enterprises, like others, have become more mechanized.

This means that the cost of equipment has increased relative to the cost of construction and installation of equipment. This is true even though there is reason to believe that construction costs have tended to rise relative to machinery prices. Thus in 1940, actual building operations represented 77 percent of investment, in 1950 only 60 percent; and in the 1950's they fluctuated between 59 and 63 percent of the total, ending at 63 percent in 1960. It is still the case, however, that construction is the largest part of investment costs. Construction is hard to standardize, and it is therefore hard to fix prices for construction work.

One way that this has been done is to standardize building designs. In 1951 23 percent of all construction work was done to standardized designs. In 1961 63 percent of the total was standardized. In housing construction, 93 percent of all designs were standardized; sectors other than industry used standardized designs for about 75 percent of their work, but industrial products were only 42 percent standardized. One may suspect that new Soviet housing may lack in variety; however, the general standardization outside of industry has unquestionably made it easier to establish contract prices to which building enterprises may be held.

It is nevertheless the case that most industrial construction (and until recently most construction) has been done on a basis which made price control relatively difficult. It is reasonable to suppose that in these circumstances there will be a tendency for excessive construction costs. The ministries and economic councils which are waiting for new plant will be inclined to allow costs to rise in periods when the construction industry is working under pressure. This is because the money spent comes from "someone else" (i.e., the budget), and they need to get the plant completed to get along with production.

The points made so far are concerned with narrow problems. If the Soviet government underestimates the investment in housing and services induced by an industrial construction program, or if it otherwise plans investment too great for the construction industry to handle readily, it will create technical difficulties in that industry as well as delays for those who intend to use the finished plant. But too great a capital works plan can lead to difficulties in other sectors as well.

In particular, the investment program is one of the two main consumers of machinery. The other is the armaments program. The two programs are of course interrelated, since a part of the investment program builds armament plants. Increased armaments programs divert some machinery plants from the current output of capital goods and a part of the construction industry from the production of civilian plants. Likewise, given a total level of machinery output, the larger is capital investment, the less will be current armament output. The larger is investment in civilian industry, the less will be armament output and plant construction taken together.

Hence the size of the investment program is influenced at any time by the short-run military policy of the U.S.S.R. (which determines the current armament output level) and the long-run military policy (which determines the level of investment in armaments plants). Throughout Soviet history, military considerations have been very important and have helped to determine the general configuration of investment programs. Military considerations explain to a considerable extent why the metallurgical and machinery industries have been so extremely important in investment plans generally; for if the U.S.S.R. were to have large armed forces and simultaneously to expand industrial output, investment in the machinery industry would have to be very large indeed.

The size of the investment program also affects the consumer sector. It may be assumed, from the data on farm incomes already given, that the diversion of labor from farm to city increases total money income, since city labor has a higher standard of living than farm labor. If the labor flowing into the cities were employed in consumer goods industries, it would correspondingly increase the value of consumer goods manufactured. On the other hand, if labor is employed in the manufacture of capital goods or in construction, then no additional supplies of consumer goods will be forthcoming.

In a market economy, one would expect such a situation to lead to an increase in prices. If prices are fixed, however, the tendency for demand to rise more rapidly than output produces shortages rather than price increases. The problem of the authorities is to offset this tendency without diminishing the flow of labor into urban occupations. This problem explains in part the continuing preoccupation with agricultural mechanization; for if machinery can replace labor on the farm, then the output of agriculture can offset the outflow of labor. Food output represents a large part of retail purchases (58 percent in 1950, 57 percent in 1960); and if it is produced by machine rather than labor, the total markup available to the state is increased.

Moreover, this problem explains in part the Soviet preoccupation with labor productivity. If labor productivity rises, then the consumer goods industries can supply more goods to meet increased demand, even if the quantity of labor and plant they employ is constant; however, the larger Soviet investment programs are, under any given set of conditions, the more resources must be diverted from the consumer goods industries, and the greater will be excess demand for such goods at a given set of prices. During the 1930's, the Soviet government was willing to allow retail prices to rise. During the war, it allowed open market prices to rise. After 1947, however, a serious attempt was made to return to the prewar price level. This was not fully successful, but prices were in fact stable for almost a decade after 1953. The maintenance of such stability does depend in considerable part upon the limitation of investments.

There is even evidence that the size of investment programs may be influenced by agricultural conditions. Thus the bad harvest of 1963 is said to have caused reductions in investments. Some of these declines are technical declines in agricultural investment. Thus if the harvest is bad, construction of storage facilities may easily be postponed, and increases in livestock population (which are treated as an investment) may not occur. But there are reasons why nonagricultural investment might also decline in such a situation. A decline in food production means a decline in turnover tax collections on food and hence a decline in budgetary income. It may prove easier to reduce investment expenditure than other expenditure. Unless some expenditure is reduced, personal expenditures must drop without corresponding declines in personal income. It cannot be expected that personal willingness to spend will decline because of the crop failure. Consequently, it would be reasonable to expect increases in excess demand for consumer goods and shortages of such goods, unless something is done.

Clearly it would be possible to multiply examples of this sort, illustrating the close connection between investment programs and the rest of the economic system. The important conclusion to be reached is that we may trace in the Soviet economy, as in other economies, the consequences of changing investment programs. In the Soviet case, investment does not seem to be governed by a profit motive but rather by the effort to expand output of heavy industry. The lower limits of the process have not proved important, but the upper limits have. These upper limits can be seen to have been reached at some periods of Soviet history, when inflation, of a special Soviet sort, has taken place. It would appear that in recent years the government has been concerned not to have it recur, and we can in principle follow a number of statistical indicators which show the degree of success it has had in avoiding it.

Chapter 10 FISCAL AND MONETARY POLICY

The economic functions of the Soviet state are of two kinds. As was seen in Chapters 3-6, the state intervenes in the operations of enterprises by fixing their marginal cost and revenue functions, and by defining plans, the points at which steps in these functions occur. Later chapters will discuss the problem of coordinating the plans of the individual enterprises in such a way as to produce optimal (from the state's viewpoint) results. These aspects of state activity are of course of great interest, but they do not exhaust the economic role of the state.

A major part of state economic activity occurs because the state buys large quantities of goods and services on its own account, raises large sums through taxes, and through its direct operation of the banking system, determines the volume of credit and hence the money supply. Those aspects of state fiscal policy which affect capital formation have already been discussed. This chapter treats fiscal and monetary policy as a whole, combining the budget and banking systems into a single "state sector" in contrast to individuals and enterprises.

In this three-sector analysis of the Soviet economy, it is hardly to be expected that state transactions with households can be discussed independently of state transactions with enterprises or of enterprise transactions with individuals. Nowhere is this more apparent than in discussions of the turnover tax, the largest single item of state revenue. In form, the tax is a difference between the price paid by buyers of consumer goods (consumers, wholesalers, or retailers of consumer goods) and the price received by sellers of consumer goods (retailers, wholesalers, or manufacturers). As such, it is analogous to an excise tax. It is customary, in courses on purely competitive markets, to show that part of an excise tax is paid by sellers, and a part by buyers. The relative shares of the tax burden are then shown to depend on the price elasticities of supply and demand.

It is customary for Soviet economists to argue that the tax is paid exclusively by enterprises. They argue that retail prices would be unaffected by changes in the turnover tax, so that only enterprises are affected. In contrast, western Sovietologists usually argue that changes in turnover tax affect retail prices without affecting enterprise receipts. The Soviet position would be correct if quantities supplied were unaffected by prices (i.e., marginal revenues). In Chapters 4 and 6, this was shown to be untrue. The western position would be correct if quantities demanded were unaffected by prices (i.e., marginal costs). The buyers in question are households; non-Soviet households are not thought to have perfectly inelastic demand curves.

This issue, as a theoretical problem, is not very interesting, but it has important practical ramifications. Soviet economists assert that the turnover tax is in its effect a tax on enterprise profits, so that it represents a part of the flow of funds between the state and enterprises. Western economists assert that it is in effect a tax on consumers, so that it represents a part of the flow of funds between

TABLE 10–1

THE ROLE OF THE BUDGET IN ACCUMULATION, FOR SELECTED YEARS, 1940–61 (IN BILLION RUBLES)

	1940	1950	1955	1958	1959	1960	1961
Profits	3.3	5.2	12.6	20.1	23.0	25.2	26.8
Turnover tax	10.6	23.6	24.2	30.5	31.1	31.3	30.9
Accumulation	13.9	28.8	36.8	50.6	54.1	56.5	57.7
Paid into budget	13.1	28.2	25.7	45.7	49.0	51.7	52.8
Retained by enterprises	.8	.6	1.1	4.9	5.1	4.8	4.9

the state and households. In either case, the turnover tax is a part of state revenue, and hence a source of investible funds. It is convenient to use the Marxist expression "accumulation" to refer to the sum of profits and turnover tax.

Table 10–1 shows that for the last generation at least 90 percent of accumulation has ended up in the budget. Even if the turnover tax is treated as an excise tax—that is, as a tax on consumption—about 75 percent of profits (accumulation minus turnover tax) is paid into the budget. It is notable, however, that the turnover tax and profits have not changed at the same rate. From 1947 to 1955 turnover tax revenue was held almost constant at levels close to 24 billion rubles a year. After three years of increases, the tax was stabilized at about 30 billion rubles in 1958–61. In contrast, profits have risen steadily by 1 billion to 3 billions annually since 1950. By 1961 profits were about five-sixths of turnover collections, while in 1950 they had been only a little more than one-fifth as great.

The periods of stability in turnover tax collection coincided with the two big price adjustment policies of the postwar period. The first was the period of retail price reduction of 1947–54. The second was the period of increase in prices paid to collective farms after 1952. Both of these policies would have led to decreases in turnover tax revenue if there had been no changes in quantities. Virtually nothing is known about Soviet decisions on price changes, but those who suspect that Soviet bureaucracy seeks simple rules may find in these facts some support for their thesis: prices were cut and output increased in such a way as to hold turnover tax payments constant.

TABLE 10–2

SOVIET BUDGET REVENUE, BY MAIN CATEGORIES, FOR SELECTED YEARS, 1940–61 (IN BILLION RUBLES)

	1940	1950	1955	1958	1959	1960	1961
Total Budget Revenue	18.0	42.3	56.4	67.2	74.0	77.1	78.0
Turnover tax	10.6	23.6	24.2	30.5	31.1	31.3	30.9
Profits taxes on state and co-operative enterprise	2.5	4.6	11.5	15.2	17.9	20.4	21.9
Taxes on individuals	.9	3.6	4.8	5.2	5.5	5.6	5.8
Social Insurance taxes	.9	2.0	2.6	3.3	3.6	3.8	4.2
Borrowing	1.1	3.1	3.7	1.1	1.5	.9	.8

Table 10–2 makes it clear that budget revenue is overwhelmingly influenced by these sources of income. Indeed, the two are almost the only sources of unencumbered income. The Social Insurance taxes are virtually committed in advance by the government's various social welfare programs, and since 1958 the revenue from borrowing is in the form of savings accounts. These represent

liabilities of the government. While they are not likely to be drawn upon, they are virtually sight liabilities.[2]

Half of all profits originate in industry (Table 10–3). The rest are scattered throughout the economy. Trade and supply (this is the system of *snab* and *sbyt* wholesale brokers administering the materials balances) jointly account for only about one-sixth of all profits. It is not possible to give a more precise account of profits; and turnover tax data, by industry and sector of the economy, are not available.

TABLE 10–3

PROFITS IN THE SOVIET ECONOMY, BY SECTORS, FOR SELECTED YEARS, 1940–61 (IN BILLION RUBLES)

	1940	1950	1955	1958	1959	1960	1961
Total	3.3	5.2	12.6	20.1	23.0	25.2	26.8
State enterprises†	3.1	5.0	12.0	19.3	22.1	24.4	26.1
Industry†	1.7	3.2	6.7	10.7	12.5	14.0	15.3
Agriculture and procurements	–.1	–.2	.4	.5	.6	.1	.3
Transport and communications	.7	1.1	2.3	3.5	3.9	4.4	4.7
Construction	*	–.5	*	.8	.9	1.1	1.0
Supply	.1	.1	.6	.9	1.0	1.2	1.0
Trade	.3	.4	1.1	1.3	1.4	1.3	1.2
Other	.4	.9	1.0	1.6	1.8	2.2	2.5
Consumer co-operatives	.1	.2	.5	.8	.9	.8	.7
Producer co-operatives†	.3	.4	.7	.6	.6	–	–

* Losses of less than fifty million rubles.
† In 1960 producer co-operatives became state enterprises. Soviet statistics published before the merger listed their profits under "co-operatives"; beginning in 1960, the producer co-operatives are added to industry. In this table, the figures for industry and for state enterprise include producer co-operatives; the amounts thus included are also recorded under their proper heading.

TABLE 10–4

PRINCIPAL CATEGORIES OF STATE BUDGET EXPENDITURES FOR SELECTED YEARS, 1940–61 (IN BILLION RUBLES)

	1940	1950	1955	1958	1959	1960	1961
Total Expenditures	17.4	41.3	54.0	64.3	70.4	73.1	76.3
Expenditure on the economy	5.8	15.8	23.3	29.0	32.4	34.1	32.6
Social and cultural resources	4.1	11.7	14.7	21.4	23.1	24.9	27.2
Defense	5.7	8.3	10.7	9.4	9.4	9.3	11.6
Administration	.7	1.4	1.2	1.2	1.1	1.1	1.1
Expenditures on state loans	.3	.5	1.4	.4	.7	.7	.8

[2] From 1935 till 1958 the government regularly borrowed about as much as it collected in income taxes. The lending was only quasi-voluntary and was conducted as a payroll deduction plan. Lottery winnings took the place of an interest coupon. There was no legal market for the bonds thus issued, but the Soviet press has complained that "speculators" bought them at considerable discounts and were, in some cases, able to live on their lottery winnings as if they were coupon-clipping capitalists.

When Table 10–4, showing the principal categories of budget spending, is taken into account, it is possible to arrive at two interpretations of the role of the budget. If the turnover tax is considered a tax on consumers, then, in 1961, for instance, households paid 56.1 billion rubles to the government and were paid almost all of the 27.2 billion in social-cultural expenditures, plus a relatively small part of the expenditures on the economy and defense, plus most of the administrative expenses and the expenditures on loans. On balance, then, the government would have reduced individual purchasing power by perhaps 15 billion rubles and increased enterprise purchasing power by almost the same amount. If the turnover tax is considered a tax on profits, then householders paid about 25 billion rubles to the government, receiving about 40 billion rubles in exchange.

It should make some difference whether the Soviet government transfers 15 billion rubles from households to enterprises or whether it makes a transfer of the same order of magnitude in the opposite direction, but one cannot clearly distinguish in principle which interpretation is the better. In the circumstances, the following statement seems in order: The main function of the budget is thus the reallocation of funds within the economy. The budget itself ordinarily shows a surplus which has run in the range of 2–4 billion rubles a year in recent years (Table 10–5), including sums borrowed through the savings bank system and the former subscription system. This means that on balance the budget takes small but not negligible sums from households and enterprises.

TABLE 10–5

THE SOVIET BUDGET SURPLUS, FOR SELECTED YEARS, 1940–61 (IN BILLION RUBLES)

	1940	1950	1955	1958	1959	1960	1961
Revenue	18.0	42.3	56.4	67.2	74.0	77.1	78.0
Less: borrowing	1.1	3.1	3.7	1.1	1.5	.9	.8
Tax revenue	16.9	39.2	52.7	66.1	62.5	76.2	77.2
Expenditures	17.4	41.3	54.0	64.3	70.4	73.1	76.3
Tax surplus or deficit	−.5	−2.1	−1.3	1.8	2.1	3.1	.9
Cash surplus	.6	1.0	2.4	2.9	3.6	4.0	1.7

The reallocation process in the budgetary system involves mainly budget receipt of turnover tax and profits and budget expenditure on the economy, welfare programs, and armaments. The detailed reconstruction of these accounts will not be undertaken here, but a few observations are in order.

First, there is some overlapping of accounts. If an armaments plant sells its current output, the sale will be recorded as a defense expenditure. If an armament plant is to be built, this will be recorded as an expenditure on the economy (the plan for capital works is the most important single component of this class of expenditure). Expenditures on science are part of the education account of social and cultural expenditures. A particular research project will, however, appear under defense, if the Ministry of Defense makes a contract with a research institution; it will be a social and cultural expenditure if that institution finances it under its own appropriation; and it will be a nonbudgetary outlay if it is financed by an enterprise from retained profits.

Second, budget expenditures in a program are not the same as total national expenditures on that program. In the case of social and cultural expenditures (Table 10–6), about 90 percent of all expenditures go through the budget. The main nonbudgetary funds here seem to be (1) research funds spent by enterprises and (2) tuition expenditures paid by individuals. The Soviet health spending contrasts with the British in that there are no private hospitals and virtually no private practice; the contrast with the U.S. (where only veterans receive government medical service) is even greater. In the case of expenditures on the economy, it must be remembered that Soviet enterprises are on *khozraschet* (as explained in Chapter 3), so that only their transactions with the budget are recorded. In contrast, the total revenue of the U.S. (and until recently the British) postal service appears as budget revenue, and the total expenditure is a budget expenditure. Some items are in part but are not entirely budget-financed. The detailed breakdown of expenditures on the economy is not as complete as for social and cultural expenditures, but some data on planned expenditures are available (Table 10–7).

The budget is not the only means at the disposal of the state for influencing the economy. In addition, the banking system is available. The Construction Bank does lend funds to collective farms; a part of its free resources at any date come from the repayment of principal on such loans and from time deposits of collective farms. But effectively the Construction Bank is most easily considered an arm of the budget, for increases in its loanable funds are obtained from budget appropriations.

The State Bank is the most useful part of the banking system,

TABLE 10-6

BUDGETARY AND NONBUDGETARY SOURCES OF FUNDS FOR SOCIAL AND CULTURAL PURPOSES, SELECTED YEARS, 1940–61 (IN BILLION RUBLES)

	Total							Budget							Nonbudget						
	1940*	1950	1955	1958	1959	1960	1961	1940	1950	1955	1958	1959	1960	1961	1940*	1950	1955	1958	1959	1960	1961
Education ...		6.6	8.1	10.4	11.5	12.6	14.0	2.3	5.7	6.9	8.6	9.4	10.3	11.3		.9	1.2	1.8	2.1	2.3	2.7
Science ...	.9	n.a.	n.a.	2.4	2.8	3.3	3.8	n.a.	.5	.8	1.7	2.0	2.3	2.7	.4	n.a.	n.a.	.7	.8	1.0	1.1
Other	5.7	n.a.	n.a.	8.0	8.7	9.3	10.2	n.a.	5.2	6.1	6.9	7.4	8.0	8.6	.5	n.a.	n.a.	1.1	1.3	1.3	1.6
Health		2.6	3.7	5.0	5.5	5.9	6.1	.9	2.1	3.1	4.1	4.5	4.8	5.0	.5	.5	.6	.9	1.0	1.1	1.1
Social insurance ⎱	3.8	4.8	8.8	9.4	9.8	10.8		.5	1.3	1.7	2.4	2.7	2.8	3.2 ⎱	.3	.5	.2	.1	.1		0
Social care ⎰	(combined)							.4	2.2	2.6	6.2	6.6	6.9	7.6 ⎰							
Total		13.0	16.5	24.2	26.4	28.3	30.9	4.1	11.7	14.7	21.4	23.1	24.9	27.2		1.3	1.8	2.8	3.3	3.4	3.7

(Note: in the original, "Social insurance" and "Social care" are joined by a brace; the Total and Nonbudget figures are given as a single combined entry, while the Budget figures and the 1961 column are shown separately.)

* Figures for nonbudgetary expenditures are not available.

TABLE 10–7

BUDGETARY AND NONBUDGETARY EXPENDITURE ON THE ECONOMY, FOR SELECTED YEARS, 1950–63 (IN BILLION RUBLES)

	1950	1955	1958	1959	1960	1961	1962	1963
Total								
Total expenditures on the economy	n.a.	33.5	41.3	48.4	52.2	56.4	56.6	63.2
Capital construction	13.6	16.1	19.9	22.4	26.2	29.5	30.7	33.8
Additions to enterprises' "own" working capital..	1.7 ⎫	⎫	⎫	⎫	2.8	3.3	3.1	3.6
	⎬ 17.4	⎬ 21.4	⎬ 26.0					
All other expenditure ...	n.a. ⎭	⎭	⎭		23.2	23.6	22.8	25.8
Budget								
Total expenditures on the economy	16.4	22.2	25.7	30.9	32.8	33.9	32.5	34.5
Capital construction	10.7	10.9			18.0	19.5	19.7	20.4
Additions to enterprises' "own" working capital..	.7 ⎫	⎫		⎫	1.1	1.1	1.1	
	⎬ 11.3			⎬ 14.8				
All other expenditure ...	5.0 ⎭			⎭	13.3	11.7	13.0	
Nonbudget								
Total expenditures on the economy	n.a.	11.3	15.6	17.5	19.4	22.5	24.1	28.7
Capital construction	2.9	5.2			8.2	10.0	11.0	13.4
Additions to enterprises' "own" working capital..	1.0 ⎫	⎫		⎫	2.2	2.0	2.5	
	⎬ 6.1			⎬ 11.2				
All other expenditure ...	n.a. ⎭			⎭	10.3	11.1	12.8	

since it has the ability to expand or contract credit. This means that it may offset or reinforce actions by the budgetary system which, as we have seen, affect the funds held by enterprises and households. To understand the mechanism involved, it is convenient to look at the form of the balance sheet of the State Bank. This form, by the way, is not the same as the structure of the statistics on the Soviet banking system. That is because the statistics refer to the entire banking system and are, moreover, incomplete.

Assets	*Liabilities*
Float	Float
Short-term loans	Current accounts of enterprises and institutions
	Note issue
	Accounts of the Ministry of Finance
	Savings Bank System
	Budget accounts
	other

The balance sheet of the State Bank has not been published since 1935. It is possible, however, to arrive at very rough estimates of the orders of magnitude of the balance sheet of Soviet banking as a whole, since total credit issued and also a variety of miscellaneous data are available for a number of years (these are given in Table 10–8). The entry "other State Bank liabilities" includes the note issue but presumably also includes other items as well. In particular it should include a major item: the cash balance of the Ministry of Finance—that is, of the budget system. This account apparently is subject to various accounting changes—for instance, those occurring in connection with the revaluation of assets in various sectors of the economy. Several such revaluations have occurred in the 1950's and 1960's and involve technical changes in various accounts. Where *changes* in the note issue are concerned, it seems to be more possible to arrive at rough estimates of the changes in the note issue (Table 10–9). This table, of course, does not indicate the *level* of any of the accounts.

The "float" arises in connection with payments among enter-

TABLE 10–8

A PARTIAL STATEMENT OF THE BALANCE SHEET OF THE SOVIET BANKING SYSTEM, FOR SELECTED YEARS, 1940–61 (IN BILLION RUBLES)

	1940	1950	1955	1958	1959	1960	1961
Assets							
Long-term credit	.8	2.0	3.0	4.0	4.2	3.8	4.1
Short-term credit	5.6	17.3	21.1	33.2	39.6	42.7	47.4
Total	6.4	19.3	24.1	37.2	43.8	46.5	51.5
Float	1.9			6.9	7.6	8.3	9.6
Other credit	4.5			30.3	36.2	38.2	41.9
Total	6.4	19.3	24.1	37.2	43.8	46.5	51.5
Liabilities							
Float*	1.9		[5.5]§	6.9	7.6	8.3	9.6
Deposits of enterprises and institutions	2.1	3.8	5.5	6.9	6.8	7.1†	
Savings deposits	.7		5.3	8.7	10.1	10.9	11.7
Other Investment Bank liabilities‡	.7	2.3	3.7	4.5	5.0	4.0	
Other State Bank liabilities	1.0		[4.1]§	10.2	14.3	16.2	

* See text.

† Assuming that the increase in deposits of enterprises and institutions was equal to the increase in the deposits of "the economy." The latter can be inferred from data on current assets and cash as a percentage of current assets.

‡ Total assets of the Investment Bank are equal to long-term credit, plus short-term credit to construction enterprises. The deposits as recorded in this table include current accounts of construction enterprises and investment accounts of collective farms, which are held in the Investment Bank. These figures are obtained by subtraction (the 1955 and 1960 figures include some guesses).

§ Wild guess.

prises. From the bank's point of view, collecting on a draft involves (1) acquiring a draft, (2) making an advance to a seller, (3) collecting a liability from the buyer's bank branch, (4) collecting from the buyer's account. Consequently, the accounts representing drafts in process of collection and loans made on the basis of these drafts must have corresponding liabilities accounts. Not much is known about these accounts; but at the end of 1961, advances on drafts

TABLE 10–9

APPARENT CHANGES IN SOVIET DEPOSITS AND NOTES
1956–61 (BILLION RUBLES)

	1956	1957*	1958	1959	1960	1961
Increases in total credit	4.6	2.6	5.9	6.5	2.8	5.0
Less budget surplus (before borrowing)	1.2	[1.5]	1.8	2.1	3.1	.9
Total	3.4	[1.1]	4.1	4.4	−.3	4.1
equals Increases in savings accounts	1.1	1.7	.7	1.3	.9	.8
Increases in current accounts	11.8	−.4	2.3	−1.1	.3	
Apparent increases in note issue	−9.5	−.2	1.1	4.2	−1.5	

* For some reason, the 1957 budget results have been suppressed, and it is necessary to guess at the results.

were 9.6 billion rubles, or about 20 percent of total short-term credit in the economy. If these accounts behave like the float in other countries (there is no reason why they should not), they are subject to short-term variations of a fairly random sort and are of minor economic importance.

The short-term loans other than the float are the main instrument of the State Bank. The bank, by expanding credit, can offset the effect of an enterprise's payment of profits to the budget; by contracting credit, it may offset permission to retain profits granted to an enterprise; and if the bank chooses to, it can supplement budget policies which add funds to or take funds from the current assets of enterprises.

When the State Bank issues a loan, it increases correspondingly the enterprise's current account; when an enterprise repays a loan, its repayment is charged against its current accounts. These are at any moment both grants and repayments of credit; the net change in credit is immediately associated with a like change in current accounts of enterprises. On the other hand, when enterprises make payments to the budget, their cash is reduced; and when they sell to budget institutions, their cash is increased.

It might appear that the budget and banking system between them can fairly well control enterprises' activities, since budget procedures make it possible to vary the amount of profit retained by enterprises; and, given profits, enterprises may acquire purchasing power only if the State Bank is willing to increase its loans. It would appear that by simultaneously reducing the amount of profits retained by some group of enterprises and the amount of loans granted these enterprises the state can effectively contract their resources. Conversely, it would seem that by allowing enterprises to retain profits, or by expanding loans to them, the state can effectively expand their resources.

There are, however, some practical limitations to this apparent omnipotence. These are the monetary counterparts of real problems which have already been discussed in part. It has been observed that enterprises in general make payments by draft; however, in one important case, where wage payments are involved, enterprises pay in currency (State Bank notes). Likewise, enterprises in general receive income in the form of drafts; but retail stores have revenue in the form of currency. Thus, while enterprises' "cash" transactions involve entries in bank accounts, households' "cash" transactions involve receipts or payments of currency. In some sense, then, the Soviet economy has two kinds of money, one used by enterprises and one by individuals. There is a parity rate of exchange between them, but in fact conversions occur only when households have economic contacts with the socialized sector.

Generally speaking, any change in the activity of producing enterprises (whether they are in industry, construction, agriculture, or whatever) means a change in wage payments by these enterprises and hence an increase in the note issue. Any increase in retail sales, or taxes, or deposits in savings accounts means that notes are paid to enterprises or the state, and the note issue is correspondingly reduced.

Suppose that there is an increase in construction, with no change in the supply of goods to retail stores or in taxes. Then wage payments in construction will rise, while the rest of the system will be unchanged. The rate of putting notes into circulation will rise, while the rate of taking notes from circulation will not; thus the note issue will rise. This is basically the situation discussed in connection with agriculture. In terms of monetary theory, a rise in money income leads to an equal rise in cash balances of households. In this case, free market prices rise to a level where the demand for notes is equal to the note issue. Alternatively, the income velocity, which is the ratio of retail sales to money income after taxes, would decline in household transactions with the state sector; therefore, there is excess demand for goods, which is the same as saying that forced savings occurs, or that actual income velocity of money is less than that desired by households.

Moreover, a situation in which the note issue is increasing because wage (and other income) payments to households are rising relative to retail sales and tax payments by households has an effect upon enterprises. Assume, to simplify matters, that the budget is exactly balanced. Then enterprises' cash resources are drawn because of the outflow of notes into circulation. Unless enterprises can increase these resources by borrowing, they will be forced to do one of two things. They may try to carry on their affairs with smaller cash balances than formerly (increasing the velocity of turnover of current accounts), or individual enterprises may try to convert a part of their inventories into cash.

If enterprises try to carry on with smaller cash balances relative to turnover, the probability of their having insufficient cash assets to meet particular drafts falling due must increase. In this case, the possibility of a "liquidity crisis" exists. The banking system has never been willing to allow any major difficulty of this sort to arise. The functions of the State Bank have been defined in such a way that this possibility is not really conceivable. In fact, then, the banks may be expected to allow increases in credit to offset the increases in notes, if the Bank feels that a genuine liquidity problem exists. The possibility here discussed is thus mainly of theoretical interest.

If one enterprise attempts to reduce its inventory as a means of raising cash, it can do so. For reasons familiar to monetary economists in general, a concerted attempt to do so will have a rather different effect; for when an enterprise reduces its inventory, it reduces its purchases relative to its sales. If all enterprises try to do this at once, the effect is to maintain cash balances constant (since only inter-enterprise payments are here involved) but to lower the level of purchasing generally (and hence of output). Such a change will indirectly affect the rate at which the note issue is growing, for lower output means lower out-payments of notes in the form of wages.

There is one case in which the State Bank made a major attempt to lower inventory. From 1948 (immediately after the currency conversion) until 1951, a major campaign was waged to induce enterprises to reduce inventories relative to output. (Since output was rising, it was apparently not realistic to consider absolute declines in inventory). During this period, there was a tendency for the inflow of currency into the State Bank to decline, since retail prices were being reduced. Consequently, anything which increased the supply of goods without correspondingly increasing wage payments would contribute to the stability of the note issue and would hence reduce the pressure upon the State Bank for additional loans.

Control of this section of the Soviet economic process is the object of the *Cash Plan* of the State Bank. This document is a reconciliation of the various documents which involve additions to the note issue (i.e., wages, state payments of pensions, and so on) with documents involving reductions in the note issue (i.e., retail trade and services paid for by consumers, income taxes, anticipated additions to savings accounts, and so forth). As a result of this reconciliation, it is possible to arrive at some evaluation of the consequences of the expected situation of the household sector, and of the impact of this situation upon enterprises. The cash plan is thus of assistance in determining the amount of bank credit to be issued in a given year.

The *Cash Plan*, however, may have further effects. If the bank feels that credit expansion should not be undertaken in excess of some amount, it can use the *Cash Plan* to indicate how retail trade plans, or wage payments plans, or pensions and taxes should be altered so as to control the increase in the note issue (or, equivalently, the expansion of credit).

Thus if a trial version of the *Cash Plan* shows a larger increase in the note issue than the State Bank would like, it may simply refuse to expand credit. On the other hand, it may equally well go to the proper authorities to try to obtain increases in the retail trade plan, or decreases in the plan for money wages, or readjustments in proposals for direct taxes or pensions. If in fact some of these changes were made, the observer might be tempted to say that the Soviet authorities preferred "nonmonetary" to "monetary" measures. In a sense this would be true, even though the decision to take them was the result of a monetary analysis.

Monetary economies are characterized by flows of money payments which "correspond to" flows of goods and services. Thus if I buy a package of cigarettes, I exchange money for cigarettes. Monetary economics asserts that there may be various kinds of connections between the two sorts of flows and seeks to arrive at workable rules for relating the flows. In the Soviet system, analysis is further complicated by a second dichotomy. On the one hand, there exist plans, which reflect the desires of the state. On the other, there exists reality, which is always somewhat different.

Suppose that the Soviet state undertakes a comparison between what it wants to happen and what is actually taking place. Then it will have to compare the state of individual parts of the economy. Suppose it considers retail trade; retail trade involves both a movement of goods from stores to consumers and a movement of bank notes from consumers to stores (and hence out of circulation). There is no reason *a priori* to say that one flow rather than the other is "wrong." Both must be; and the remedy must affect both flows in some suitable way. The fact that a remedy is "nonmonetary" does not mean it has no "monetary" aspects. The fact that a remedy is "monetary" does not mean that it has no "real" aspects. In order to separate the monetary from the nonmonetary aspects, it is convenient to schematize the various processes thus far presented. This will be done in the following chapter.

Chapter | THEORIES ABOUT SOVIET
11 | INCOME AND OUTPUT

If we were analyzing any economy except the U.S.S.R., it would probably be possible to use macroeconomic analysis to set up a model of the gross national product. This type of model has stimulated a great deal of interesting work on private enterprise systems. In such systems, it is plausible that the main variables—consumption, savings, investment, etc.—form a system of simultaneous functions whose behavior can be shown to replicate observable data in important respects.

It is doubtful that macroeconomic models of the Soviet economy can be constructed along lines analogous to those of private enterprise economies. A basic component of most models of private enterprise economies, for example, is a consumption function. A typical consumption function asserts that consumption varies with the national product (or at any rate with disposable income). In the Soviet-type system, it is as natural to consider consumption as a residual in output plans, so that the main problem to be resolved by a model is how income and cash balances are redistributed throughout the system in response to achieved investment plans. A main problem of models of private enterprise economies is the formulation of mechanisms capable of determining the level of investment, for variations in investment are almost universally held to be the dominant factor in income and output fluctuations. In the Soviet system, the main theoretical problem to be resolved is a statement of an upper bound for investment under given conditions, for a basic initial condition of models should be a predisposition of the state to maximize investment, subject to various constraints.

Consequently, macroeconomic theory should probably not be

constructed in terms of national product models. This is not to say that national product accounting is uninteresting. Indeed, for the formulation of certain identities in models, it may be essential; in international quantitative comparisons, national product calculations may be vital, and so on. But the national product is much less appealing as a theoretical construct in the study of Soviet economic processes than it is in the study of other economies.

The following discussion will therefore rely mainly on the concepts of intersectoral payments developed in the last three chapters. It is therefore useful to develop somewhat more formally the theory relevant to such systems.

The argument of Chapters 8–10 was presented in terms of a few macroeconomic variables. In each case, flows of income and expenditures through some sector of the Soviet economy were analyzed; and flows were related to levels or changes in levels of stocks (including stocks of money). In each case, an economic aggregate was shown to have transactions with a few other aggregates in a way which made it possible to define and name the main flows of payments within the economy. These flows may be represented by diagrams or by systems of equations.

The simplest flow to describe is that given in Figure 11–1, which was discussed in Chapter 10. Here the economy is divided into three sectors, households, enterprises, and the budget. In addition, the State Bank is represented as providing loans to enterprises. If we denote these four aggregates by subscripts H, E, B, and G and set X_{ij} equal to payments by sector i to sector j (over the range H, E, B, G), we have the following identities:

$$X_{HE} + X_{HB} + X_{HG} = 0$$
$$X_{EH} + X_{EB} + X_{EG} = 0$$
$$X_{BH} + X_{BE} + X_{BG} = 0$$
$$X_{GH} + X_{GE} + X_{GB} = 0$$

This system is describable as a system of identities, because all income earned by any sector is completely accounted for. If households do not spend their income (i.e., buy from enterprises) or make it available to the budget (as taxes, or as loans through the savings deposit system), they must hold it as currency (i.e., one of the elements of the State Bank balance sheet, and one of the conse-

FIGURE 11–1
THE FLOW OF PAYMENTS INVOLVING HOUSEHOLDS

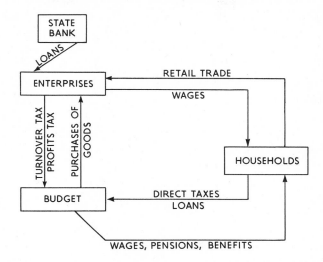

quences of bank credit). If enterprises do not pay out their cash receipts as wages or as taxes, they must repay loans or accumulate cash balances, and so forth.

Several observations must be made about this system of identities. The first is that net receipts of sector i from sector j are the same as net payments by sector j to sector i. We may therefore reduce the number of different symbols by writing this system in the form

$$
\begin{aligned}
X_{HE} + X_{HB} + X_{HG} &= 0 \\
-X_{HE} \phantom{+ X_{HB}} + X_{EB} + X_{EG} &= 0 \\
-X_{HB} - X_{EB} \phantom{+ X_{EG}} + X_{BG} &= 0 \\
-X_{HG} - X_{EG} - X_{BG} \phantom{+ X_{EG}} &= 0
\end{aligned}
$$

This system may also be written in the matrix-vector form

$$
\begin{pmatrix}
0 & X_{HE} & X_{HB} & X_{HG} \\
-X_{HE} & 0 & X_{EB} & X_{EG} \\
-X_{HB} & -X_{EB} & 0 & X_{BG} \\
-X_{HG} & -X_{EG} & -X_{BG} & 0
\end{pmatrix}
\begin{pmatrix}
1 \\ 1 \\ 1 \\ 1
\end{pmatrix}
=
\begin{pmatrix}
0 \\ 0 \\ 0 \\ 0
\end{pmatrix}
$$

From this method of writing, it appears that all the elements above the diagonal are positive and all below it are negative. This is not, of course, the case; but it is true that any element X_{ij} is equal to $-X_{ji}$, where X_{ji} is the corresponding element on the other side of the diagonal. Matrices having this property (if X_T is the matrix obtained by interchanging the rows and columns of a matrix X, then $X_T = -X$) are called skew-symmetric.

The second observation that must be made is that in this matrix of payments, every flow of payments is a *net* flow. For example, the transactions between enteprises and households include wage payments by the former and retail spending by the latter. It is important to notice, in this connection, that enterprises can be divided into two subsets: retail stores[1] and others. With minor qualifications,[2] retail stores receive payments from, and other enterprises make payments to, households. Consequently, the system just described is an aggregation of a system (where R denotes retail stores) having the matrix

$$\begin{pmatrix} 0 & X_{HE} & X_{HR} & X_{HB} & X_{HG} \\ -X_{HE} & 0 & X_{ER} & X_{EB} & X_{EG} \\ -X_{HR} & -X_{ER} & 0 & X_{HB} & X_{HG} \\ -X_{HB} & -X_{EB} & -X_{HB} & 0 & X_{BG} \\ -X_{HG} & -X_{EG} & -X_{HG} & -X_{BG} & 0 \end{pmatrix}$$

In this expanded system, X_{HE} and X_{HR} represent, respectively, (net) wages and (net) consumer spending; but, owing to macroeconomic regulations, net and gross come close to being the same.

It may also be observed that a quantity such as X_{HE} is obtained by summing operations involving a great number of enterprises and households. It would certainly tax human statistical resources to do so, but in principle any of the numbers—say X_{HE} —could be replaced by a block of numbers, in which each row would represent a particular household and each column a particular enterprise. Such disaggregation would not, of course, alter the skew-symmetric nature of the matrix nor the existence of a matrix equation of the general form given above.

Figure 11–1 is the most highly aggregated representation of income flows which has been discussed in this book. Several other sets of flows, however, have been treated. Thus Figure 11–2, which summarizes the schema in Chapter 8, divides the household and

---

[1] Strictly speaking, retail stores and service establishments.
[2] Households, for instance, make payments to public utilities which also sell to other enterprises; and retail stores pay wages to their employees.

enterprise sectors into collective farm and non-farm sectors.[3] This subdivision of two units appearing in Figure 11–1 reveals that this diagram conceals a number of economically meaningful relations. Figure 11–2 refers, of course, to the period since the machine-tractor stations were absorbed by the collective farms. Prior to that time, the MTS would have appeared in the diagram as a portion (to be separately designated) of the agricultural procurements system. In this sense, major institutional changes can alter the flow of incomes within the Soviet system and correspondingly change even macroeconomic systems of relations.

Figure 11–3 is a partial representation of the nonagricultural sector. It is "institutional" in the important sense that it lists the Construction Bank as a "financial intermediary," absorbing the "cash flow" (depreciation allowances plus retained profits) of enterprises and the investment appropriations from the budget, and releasing funds needed for the plan of capital works.

Both Figure 11–2 and Figure 11–3 are "sectoral." That is, they represent only a part of the flow of payments in the Soviet economy. Thus each corresponds to a particular submatrix of some skew-symmetric system. The points at which contact exists with the rest of the economy are indicated on these diagrams by double arrows. When they are combined, as in Figure 11–4, a closed system is obtained.[4] It is naturally of theoretical interest to consider the connection between such "open" characterizations as those corresponding to Figures 11–2 and 11–3, and those of closed systems such as that diagrammed in Figure 11–4.

It has been noted that a system of net flows of income amounts to a system of simultaneous equations, the matrix of which is skew-symmetric. That is, there is a system

$$XI = \Theta$$

where X is a matrix of net flows of income, I a vector of ones, and Θ a vector of zeros; but X may be written in the form of $X_1 - X_2$, in which X_1 and X_2 represent, respectively, incomes and expenditures. Thus, if we look at an element X_{ij} of X, it refers to the net payments by sector i to sector j, and consequently is the difference

---

[3] For purposes of this discussion, state farm personnel are treated like city workers, and state farms like urban enterprises.

[4] This system, of course, is closed only because international economic relations are disregarded. These are discussed in Chapter 12.

FIGURE 11–2

THE FLOW OF PAYMENTS ASSOCIATED WITH COLLECTIVE FARMING

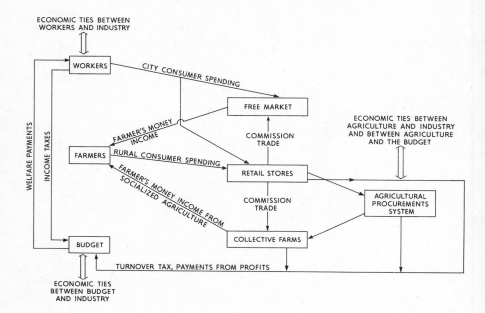

FIGURE 11–3

THE FLOW OF PAYMENTS ARISING FROM THE PROCESS OF CAPITAL FORMATION

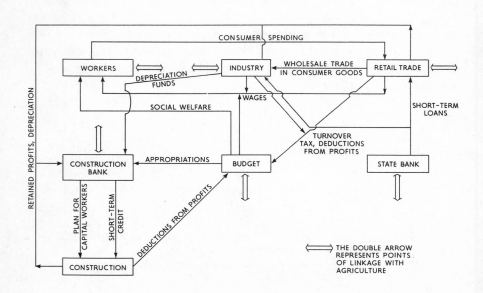

FIGURE 11–4

THE FLOW OF PAYMENTS IN THE SOVIET ECONOMY

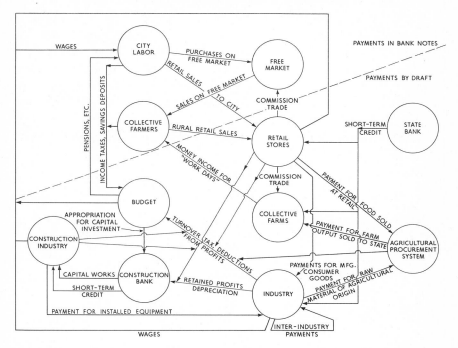

between X^1_{ij}, the gross payments by i to j, and X^2_{ij}, the gross payments by j to i. Soviet institutional arrangements tend to make it true at the macroeconomic level that if $X^1_{ij} \neq 0$, then $X^2_{ij} = 0$ and conversely; but there is no theoretical reason to insist on this generalization. Since the flow of incomes is closed (i.e., total expenditures account for total income), we may also write $XI = \Theta$ in the form

$$X_1 I = X_2 I$$

It is now possible to state formally the relationship between two systems of economic analysis. One of these is that developed in Chapters 8–10 and is based upon flows of net income. The other is that originated by Leontief in his *Structure of the American Economy*. The latter has found numerous applications in empirical studies of inter-industry relationships and is beginning to be used in Soviet bloc planning. The former is typically more often used in macroeconomic analysis, including monetary analysis.

A payment by a transactor i to another transactor j is the counterpart of a flow of goods or services from transactor j to transactor i. Some difficulty arises in this representation where the state is involved, because payments to the state are generally taxes, and it is generally the case that tax payments by an economic entity are not proportional to the services that entity receives from the state;[5] but this difficulty is resolved by a convention asserting that services (even unwanted ones) are taken to be proportional to tax payments. Consequently $X^1{}_{ij}$ may be set equal to $Q_{ij} P_j$, where Q_{ij} is the quantity of output (of goods or services) going from j to i and P_j the price of these goods and services.[6] Let us now define a number A_{ij}, which represents the average amount of j which i uses per unit of i's output. Then,

$$X^1{}_{ij} = P_j A_{ij} Q_i$$

where Q_i is the total output of i. It may be, of course, that A_{ij} is a function of Q_i; but in Leontief's hypothesis, it is a constant. We then have the identity

$$\begin{pmatrix} X^1{}_{11} \ldots X^1{}_{1n} \\ \cdot \cdot \cdot \cdot \cdot \cdot \\ X^1{}_{n1} \ldots X^1{}_{nn} \end{pmatrix} \equiv \begin{pmatrix} P_1 A_{11} Q_1 \ldots P_n A_{1n} Q_1 \\ \cdot \cdot \cdot \cdot \cdot \cdot \cdot \cdot \\ P_1 A_{n1} Q_n \ldots P_n A_{nn} Q_n \end{pmatrix}$$

$$\equiv \begin{pmatrix} Q_1 \ldots 0 \\ \cdot \cdot \cdot \cdot \\ 0 \ldots Q_n \end{pmatrix} \begin{pmatrix} A_{11} \ldots A_{1n} \\ \cdot \cdot \cdot \cdot \\ A_{n1} \ldots A_{nn} \end{pmatrix} \begin{pmatrix} P_1 \ldots 0 \\ \cdot \cdot \cdot \cdot \\ 0 \ldots P_n \end{pmatrix}$$

The matrix (A_{ij}) has elements which are all non-negative, and this circumstance enables us to derive some important mathematical results.

Likewise, $X^2{}_{ij}$ may be set equal to $Q_{ji} P_i$, where Q_{ji} is the quantity of output going from i to j and P_i the price of these goods and services. We define, as before, A_{ji} as the average amount of i used by j, per unit of j's output. Then

$$X^2{}_{ij} = P_i A_{ji} Q_j$$

Then we have the identity

---

[5] Thus childless persons help support state-owned schools, and political dissenters help support government programs they do not approve of. In this sense, parents and government supporters pay less for the services of the state than they receive.

[6] *Price* is taken to mean *average revenue of the seller*. It will be recalled that in the discussion of planning, we have stated that average and marginal revenue of the seller are functions of the quantity of goods sold and of the plan. These complications are provisionally disregarded.

$$\begin{pmatrix} X^2_{11} \ldots X^2_{1n} \\ \cdot \cdot \cdot \cdot \cdot \cdot \\ X^2_{n1} \ldots X^2_{nn} \end{pmatrix} = \begin{pmatrix} P_1 A_{11} Q_1 \ldots P_1 A_{n1} Q_n \\ \cdot \cdot \cdot \cdot \cdot \cdot \cdot \cdot \cdot \cdot \\ P_n A_{1n} Q_1 \ldots P_n A_{nn} Q_n \end{pmatrix}$$

$$= \begin{pmatrix} P_1 \ldots 0 \\ \cdot \cdot \cdot \cdot \cdot \\ 0 \ldots P_n \end{pmatrix} \begin{pmatrix} A_{11} \ldots A_{n1} \\ \cdot \cdot \cdot \cdot \cdot \\ A_{1n} \ldots A_{nn} \end{pmatrix} \begin{pmatrix} Q_1 \ldots 0 \\ \cdot \cdot \cdot \cdot \\ 0 \ldots Q_n \end{pmatrix}$$

We now return to the equation $X_1 I = X_2 I$. If we write as A the matrix of input-output coefficients $D (X_i)$ the diagonal matrix of which the $i'th$ diagonal element is X_i and as $V (X_i)$ the vector of which the $i'th$ component is X_i, then this equation may be rewritten

$$X_1 I = D (Q_i) A D (P_i) I = D (P_i) A_T D (Q_i) I = X_2 I$$

It is also the case that

$$X_1 I = V (\underset{j}{\Sigma} P_j A_{ij} Q_i) = V (\underset{j}{\Sigma} X^1_{ij})$$

$$X_2 I = V (\underset{j}{\Sigma} P_i A_{ji} Q_j) = V (\underset{j}{\Sigma} X^2_{ij}) ,$$

as is to be expected because total income is defined equal to total expenditures for all industries. Since these vectors have as components the value of the outputs of the respective industries, we may write

$$X_1 I = D (Q_i) V (P_i) = D (P_i) V (Q_i) = X_2 I$$

We thus arrive at the two input-output systems:

$$D (Q_i) A D (P_i) I = D (Q_i) V (P_i)$$
$$D (P_i) A_T D (Q_i) I = D (P_i) V (Q_i) ,$$

and these imply (since prices and outputs are non-zero), that

$$A V (P_i) = V (P_i)$$
$$A_T V (Q_i) = V (Q_i)$$

The first of these is a set of restrictions on the prices, the second a set of restrictions on the outputs of the various industries. A famous theorem by Frobenius proves that if the matrix A is irreducible[7] then apart from a scalar factor there is only one vector

---

[7] A matrix is irreducible if it is impossible, by permuting rows and columns, to put it the block-triangular form:

$$A = \begin{pmatrix} A_{11} \ 0 \\ A_{21} \ A_{22} \end{pmatrix}$$

If it were reducible, then the prices in the second block would not depend at all on

V (P_i) and one vector V (Q_i) which satisfies the corresponding equation. Thus the "structures" of prices and output are determined. The levels are not determined, since if V (P_i) satisfies the equation, so does the vector V (λP_i), where λ is an arbitrary number; and it is the same for V (Q_i). The constraint that the price of money is always equal to one does away with this element of uncertainty, however.[8]

Literature on input-output has generally been more interested in the system of equations in quantities than that in prices. This is particularly true of the Soviet literature, in which prices are officially considered as fixed numbers having no economic consequence. It is difficult, however, to accept one half of the input-output system while rejecting the other. It is also difficult to imagine how the system can generate changes in outputs without generating corresponding changes in prices. It would be necessary, to achieve this result, that the input-output coefficients (the elements of A) change in very special ways, the nature of which is simply not known; however, if the analysis in Chapter 6 holds, then price in the sense of average cost or revenue (as used here) is not the same as price in the sense of marginal cost, as used in that chapter. If the Soviet statement "Prices are fixed" has been correctly interpreted in that chapter, then the term *price* as used in this chapter should be replaced everywhere by *average revenue*. It has been asserted in Chapter 6 that the average cost function corresponding to a one-step marginal cost function is

$$\frac{1}{X} \int_{z \le X} dP\,(z) \;=\; \begin{cases} P_1 & \text{if } X \le X_1 \\[2mm] P_1 + P_2\,\dfrac{X - X_1}{X} & \text{if } X > X_1 \end{cases}$$

Here X_1 is the planned output; P_1 and P_2 are the marginal costs of below-plan and above-plan products. For the purposes of this chapter, then, we must rewrite the system, introducing second subscripts (i) to designate particular producers. Thus, the equation

---

the prices in the first block, and the industries in the first block would not use the output of industries in the second.

[8] It is also shown in the literature on matrices that the components of V (P_i) and V (Q_i) are strictly positive if and only if A is irreducible. That is, if the economy produces some of every commodity, and there are no free goods produced, the price and output structures are uniquely determined. Operationally, this definition is the only one possible.

$AV\,(P_i) = V\,(P_i)$ becomes

$$A\,V\left[P_{1i} + P_{2i}\left(\frac{X_i - X_{1i}}{X_i}\right)\right] = V\left[P_{1i} + P_{2i}\left(\frac{X_i - X_{1i}}{X_i}\right)\right]$$

If some of the X_i are below plan, then the terms

$$\left(\frac{X_i - X_{1i}}{X_i}\right)$$

drop out of the corresponding components of the vectors.

The vector of average costs is therefore a function of the legally fixed marginal costs (prices) but is the same as the vector of these prices if and only if all quantities are less than or equal to their respective plans. If this new equation is to be satisfied, then several possibilities exist: First, assume the prices corresponding to the below-plan situation (P_{1i}) and plans (X_{1i}) are given, and the prices corresponding to above-plan quantities (P_{2i}) are given. Then the restraints imposed by actual quantities (X_i) and the average costs implied by the input-output matrix amount to a determination (via the input-output matrix) of the "black market" (or above-plan) prices which will exist in a given situation. Second, assume the prices corresponding to the below-plan situation (P_{1i}) and to the above-plan situation are both given (so that the latter are not "black market" prices in the sense of being illegal). Then from a knowledge of the structure of output given by the transposed system $A_T\,V\,(Q_i) = V\,(Q_i)$, it is possible to infer the levels of planned output (X_{1i}) which must be set to obtain the given output structure. Third, assume both sets of prices given, as before, and plans also given. It then appears that there is only one set of outputs which will satisfy this set of equations. It is not obvious that this set of constraints should necessarily yield the same structure of outputs as those implied by the transposed system. Further work is needed before an adequate interpretation of this possibility can be made.[9]

The analytical structure so far used is the theoretical "closed" system used by Leontief. The more common empirical applications use an "open" system derived from this one by considering only

---

[9] In the extreme conditions which preceded the currency conversions in the satellites (for instance, Rumania) in the early 1950's, "commercial" prices were sometimes inadequate to satisfy demand, and a black market developed as a third level of marginal costs. It may be that this empirical situation corresponds to the working out of this third possibility: outputs are determined by the transposed system, and a third price level is determined by this system of equations.

the submatrix of A obtained by disregarding one or more rows, and the corresponding columns of A. The economic interpretation usually given is that there exist "final consumers" (e.g., the state, or the state plus households); for such consumers, input-output coefficients may be considered as subject to deliberate variations. In the conventional problem of planning[10] the "closed" system is replaced by an "open" system. That is, the problem of finding the solution to the matrix equation (E is the identity matrix)

$$(A_T - E) \, V \, (Q_i) = \Theta$$

may be replaced by the problem of analyzing the system

$$(A'_T - E') \, V' \, (Q_i) = V' \, (f_i) \, ,$$

which relates a vector of total outputs Q_1 to a vector of "final demands" f_i (demand by the state, or the state and households). It is necessary to put primes by the vectors and matrices. These are of smaller order than those of the closed system. Computationally, one assumes a vector of final demands and endeavors to find corresponding outputs. That is, one endeavors to determine the vector $V' \, (Q_i)$ from the equation

$$V' \, (Q_i) = (A'_T - E')^{-1} \, V' \, (f_i)$$

It is, of course, much more difficult to perform the numerical work than to discuss the principle. For planning purposes, it is important that the vector $V' \, (Q_i)$ not have any components exceeding the productive capacity of the corresponding industry, that the vector $V'(f_1)$ be optimal from the state's point of view, and so on. It would be presumptuous to attempt to deal briefly with the very large literature on this problem, and we shall return to the starting point of the discussion.

Economists have been skeptical of the hypothesis that input-output relations are indeed invariant with respect to changes in prices, the level of output, and so on. Indeed, economic theory generally formulates nonlinear production functions; but it is not now possible to obtain numerical results for systems of nonlinear equations involving large numbers of variables, so that input-output is extremely useful as a first approximation to an adequate hypothesis about inter-industrial relationships.

The analyses of input-output started out from the observation

---

[10] The most authoritative discussion of these problems that has been written with the Soviet-type situation in mind is that of J. M. Montias, *Central Planning in Poland*, (New Haven, Conn.: Yale University Press, 1962), especially the appendices.

that from the skew-symmetric matrix of net income flows X, it was possible to derive input-output flows by observing that the matrices X_1 and X_2 (such that $X = X_1 - X_2$) can readily be formulated in terms of the input-output analysis; but input-output analysis is based upon a linear relationship which is assumed to exist between a buyer's output and his (gross) purchases from each other seller. Thus his *net* purchases from any industry depend upon both his output and his trading partner's output, if the input-output hypothesis is valid.

But the input-output hypothesis is not the only one which could be made. It could be modified in such a way that the net purchases, rather than the gross purchases, were linear functions of the buyer's output. Thus we recall that the skew-symmetric matrix X, which appears in the matrix equation $XI = \Theta$, has elements X_{ij}, representing the net payments by sector i to sector j. These net payments may be considered as a net flow of goods or services from sector j to sector i. This flow may be valued in units of the seller's output: $X_{ij} = P_j Q_{ij}$. If the quantity (Q_{ij}) of goods moving (on balance) from j to i is proportionate to the buyer's total output, we may write $X_{ij} = P_j b_{ij} Q_i$, where Q_i is the total output of the *i'th* sector. Consequently we may write

$$\begin{pmatrix} X_{11} \ldots X_{1n} \\ \cdot \quad \cdot \quad \cdot \quad \cdot \quad \cdot \quad \cdot \\ X_{n1} \ldots X_{nn} \end{pmatrix} = \begin{pmatrix} P_1 b_{11} Q_1 \ldots P_n b_{1n} Q_1 \\ \cdot \quad \cdot \quad \cdot \quad \cdot \quad \cdot \quad \cdot \quad \cdot \quad \cdot \\ P_1 b_{n1} Q_n \ldots P_n b_{nn} Q_n \end{pmatrix}$$

Or, in more compact form,
$$X = D\,(Q_i)\,B\,D\,(P_i)$$
Since $XI = \Theta$,
$$D\,(Q_i)\,B\,D\,(P_i)\,I = \Theta$$
$$B\,D\,(P_i)\,I = B\,V\,(P_i) = \Theta,$$
and since $X_T = -X$,
$$-X_T\,I = X_T\,I = \Theta,$$
so that
$$D\,(P_i)\,B_T\,D\,(Q_i)\,I = \Theta$$
$$B_T\,D\,(Q_i)\,I = B_T\,V\,(Q_i) = \Theta$$

This system of simultaneous equations resembles that in the input-output system in one important respect: prices appear as solutions to a system of homogeneous linear equations, and quantities appear as solutions to a second system; the matrix of one system is the transpose of the matrix of the other system. The input-output hypothesis, together with propositions relating to the irreducibility of that matrix, is used to show the existence of a unique price and output structure for an economy, when closed systems are used. Only by opening the system is it possible to allow for variations in these structures. It is natural, then, to inquire about the uniqueness of the vectors $V(P_i)$ and $V(Q_i)$ in the system being discussed here.

It may be asserted that the price and output structures are not, indeed, uniquely determined under this hypothesis. X is the product of three matrices. Two of these, $D(P_i)$ and $D(Q_i)$ are non-singular: the only sectors of the economy which have income or expenditures are those which produce positive amounts of scarce goods. The rank of X is therefore equal to the rank of B. The rank of B is equal to the rank of B_T, so that the price structure is uniquely determined if and only if the output structure is uniquely determined. If the economy has n sectors and the rank of B is r, then there are $(n - r)$ linearly independent vectors V such that $BV = \Theta$. It is already known that one such vector exists, so that the rank of B (or of X) is not greater than $(n - 1)$. The question is: is the rank of B strictly less than $(n - 1)$?

There is a theorem[11] which states that the rank of a skew-symmetric matrix is always an even number. That means that if there is an odd number of sectors, $(n - 1)$ is even, and X could be of rank $n - 1$; but if there is an even number of sectors, $(n - 1)$ is odd, and X could be at most of rank $(n - 2)$. There is no economic meaning to an assertion that an economy must contain an odd number of sectors, and it would be unfortunate to have theoretical propositions as important as these depend upon this (economically) meaningless assertion. It must therefore be asserted that price and output structures are not uniquely determined by B; the hypothesis may be substituted that net flows of goods are linear functions of the seller's output. This hypothesis means that each industry allocates its output in fixed proportions among sellers.

An impatient reader, accustomed to the Leontief hypothesis, might exclaim at this point that he is not surprised that a linear hypothesis about net flows should yield an indeterminate set of prices, for Leontief's system would clearly make a given net flow a function of the level of output of both transactors. A more patient

[11] F. R. Gantmacher, *The Theory of Matrices* (New York: Chelsea, 1959), II, 12.

reader, however, would remember that much macroeconomic reasoning talks of net flows as if they were the only relevant ones. He would inquire in more detail about the matrix of net flows under the hypothesis being investigated.

The matrix (X_{ij}) of net payments is the difference between a matrix (X^1_{ij}) of gross payments by i to j and a matrix (X^2_{ij}) of gross payments by j to i. A term in this matrix may also be represented by $X_{ij} = P_j \, b_{ij} \, Q_i$, where b_{ij} is the net flow (quantity) of goods from j to i, per unit of i's output. This net flow involves i's goods moving to j, and j's goods moving to i; the unit of account, however, is units of j's output. Then we have to relate b_{ij} to the terms β^1_{ij} and β_{ij} which exist because of the fact that X_{ij} is the difference between two gross flows of payments and goods:

$$P_j \, b_{ij} \, P_i \equiv P_j \, [\beta^1_{ij} - \beta^2_{ij}] \, Q_i = P_j \, \beta^1_{ij} \, Q_i - P_j \, \beta^2_{ij} \, Q_i$$

The first term on the right, of course, is the same as that which formed the basis of the Leontief scheme presented above. That is, β^1_{ij} is the quantity of j used to produce one unit of i; but it is no longer the case here that $\beta^1_{ij} = \beta^2_{ji}$. It is thus necessary to interpret the second right-hand term. (In what follows the term *value* is used to denote the product of a quantity times its appropriate price.)

We may always write $P_j \, \beta^1_{ij} \, Q_i \equiv P_1 \, \beta^2_{ji} \, Q_j$, since the sales of i to j are the purchases of j from i. This means that

$$\beta^2_{ji} \equiv \frac{P_i/P_j}{Q_i/Q_j} \beta^1_{ij} \, ,$$

and it is no longer the case that β^2 is the transpose of β^1, as was assumed in the case of the Leontief hypothesis. Since

$$X^2_{ij} = P_j \, \beta^2_{ij} \, Q_i$$

is the total value of goods sold by i to j, $P_j \, \beta^2_{ij}$ is the value of such sales per unit of i produced. This product has more intuitive economic meaning than β^2_{ij}, since in fact allocations systems frequently are essentially pro rata arrangements.

It would follow, then, that (a) an allocations system which controls the net payments between sectors by making them linear functions of buyers' outputs does not uniquely determine the output structure, and (b) an allocations system which prorates output of each sector among different sectors does not uniquely determine the output structure. These results are obtained on rather general hypotheses. They do not specify, for instance, the degree of aggregation used in defining the sectors of the model. Thus they are useful statements about macroeconomic hypotheses as well as about general equilibrium systems (in which each enterprise is a sector).

In a discussion of the Soviet-type economy, the property that the output structure is not uniquely determined is a desirable one. The hypotheses discussed have pertained basically to the elements of matrices determining the flow of goods and services between pairs of sectors. Suppose that all sectors are grouped into one of two sets, according to whether they are part of the state (institutions) or not (enterprises or individuals). Then the proposition "There is a unique output structure" means "Given a set of non-state levels of output, the levels of state activity are uniquely determined." Actually, it seems more reasonable that a given set of non-state activities is consistent with a variety of state actions. Similarly, if a set of state actions be given, it may seem reasonable that some variation in the level of non-state actions is possible. The reasoning given above is annoyingly vague, because it does not specify the amount of "flexibility" in the system; but it is not yet possible to be more precise.

The importance of the proposition that some "flexibility" exists in the system lies in the fact that the state must decide which of the various courses of action open to it yield it the maximal welfare. The analysis in the first part of this chapter turns out, therefore, to be necessary, since technological and control restrictions may not be sufficient to provide a unique result. The state, then, is not simply a passive instrument whose actions are determined within the system. It has a utility function, and this helps determine the outcome of economic processes.

When analysis deals with some particular group of sectors and disregards others, it isolates some subsystem of the entire matrix of payments X. Thus the discussion of construction in Chapter 9 amounted to a partitioning of the system

$$XI = \begin{pmatrix} X_{11} & X_{12} \\ X_{21} & X_{22} \end{pmatrix} \quad \begin{pmatrix} I_1 \\ I_2 \end{pmatrix} = \begin{pmatrix} \Theta_1 \\ \Theta_2 \end{pmatrix}$$

where X is divided into blocks, such that the subscripts 1 and 2 denote, respectively, sectors having to do with and not having to do with construction. Then the subsystem

$$X_{11} I_1 + X_{12} I_2 = \Theta_1$$

is considered. Setting $-X_{12} I_2 = V_2$, we rewrite:

$$X_{11} I_1 = V_2$$

If the submatrix X_{11} is non-singular, then a unique relation exists between construction and the rest of the economy. Going over to the decomposition of X given above, we have

$$D_1 (P_i) B_{11T} D_1 (Q_i) I_1 + D_1 (P_i) B_{12T} D_2 (Q_i) I_1 = \Theta_1$$

$$B_{11T} V_1 (Q_i) = B_{12T} V_2 (Q_i) = V_2'$$

In such an "open" system as this, $X_2 (Q_i)$ will not be uniquely determined, since there may be more than one such vector mapped by B_{12T} into V_2'; but this is of no great importance, for it says merely that not every change outside the construction sector affects the level of construction activity. The important thing is that B_{11T} should be non-singular. This condition specifies a (unique) relation between a set of construction activities and the level of activities in the non-construction sector. Not all submatrices along the diagonal of X will be non-singular. This simply means that not all groupings of economic sectors can be accompanied by satisfactory economic analyses.

It is necessary, unfortunately, to conclude this rather lengthy discussion of the role of the state in the Soviet-type economy with two warnings. The first is that the discussion pertains to an isolated economy. Foreign trade has not been discussed, although it may be important. It is disregarded because things have become complicated enough as they stand. Second, the discussion has taken as data input-output coefficients and allocations rules—the elements of the matrices with which we have dealt; but every student of the Soviet economy knows that an important part of planning is devoted to the calculation of these numbers. In an important sense, the state tries to alter these matrices in a desirable direction. Indeed, much of the purpose of construction programs is summarized in the phrase *alteration of input-output relations*. Such changes should be explainable in economic terms, but they cannot now be so explained. We must be content at this time with explanations which are "short-run" in the Marshallian sense. That is, they take "techniques" (and production functions) as given, even though one main objective of planning is to change them.

Chapter 12 : PLANNING AND THE WELFARE OF THE STATE

It is now possible to discuss planning in the sense that most discussions conceive it: a set of coordinated orders designed to achieve some objective. Strictly speaking, this discussion will apply to a closed Soviet-type economy, one which has no relations with foreign countries. This artificiality is used for reasons of simplicity, since the discussion would otherwise become very difficult.

Plans are made by the government, and to suit the purposes of the government. The microeconomic discussion presented in the first six chapters took the enterprise as its point of reference, and it was unnecessary (even undesirable) to specify anything about the relations which might or might not exist among individual numbers representing input or output plans of enterprises; but the government does not prepare plans by selecting numbers at random. It wants some things to happen and other things not to happen.

It is natural to theorize about planning in terms of maximization: the state wishes to maximize some function, the arguments of which are quantities (stocks or flows) of goods. Such a statement of the problem is in accord with economics generally; however, the nature of the state's utility function is somewhat unfamiliar. To the extent that the state buys goods, it behaves like an ordinary consumer. The state buys by collecting taxes, and it may have preferences for collecting taxes from one source rather than another. This, formally, does not distinguish it from consumers, who can be assumed to have preferences as to the kind of work they do. In some respects, then, the welfare function of the state may be analogous to that of the ordinary consumer.

If the theory were limited to this type of hypothesis, the state would not absorb the entire national product, because at some level of budgetary income and expenditures the disutility of a ruble's worth of additional tax revenue would exceed the utility of a ruble's worth of additional budget spending. There would be no particular internal problems to interest the theorist; however, the Soviet state is interested not only in its own income and expenditures, but also in those of the rest of the economy. For example, imagine the choice between issuing editions of Alfred Marshall and of Karl Marx to be purchased by Soviet economists. Assume the two editions have identical cost functions, that they sell at the same price, are subject to the same taxes, and that libraries (which get revenue from the state) will not buy either. Imagine that m_1 copies of Marshall and m_2 copies of Marx have been sold, and ask whether the state has a preference between the pair $(m_1 + 1, m_2)$ and the pair $(m_1, m_2 + 1)$. From what we know of the Soviet system, the state will be happier with the second possibility than with the first, even though its own budget is unaffected, either on the income or the expenditures side.

Moreover, the Soviet state is interested not only in the total amount of a given commodity which is consumed, but also in the identity of the consumer. For many years, efforts were made to restrict the use of petroleum products to aviation, automotive transport, and agriculture. Thus the welfare of the state was affected if fuel oil was diverted from trucking to railroad use, or from transportation to domestic heating.

We may represent the Soviet economy as a set of pairwise flows of goods among the state (denoted by a subscript S) and economic units (denoted by subscripts $1, 2, \ldots, n$), and write these flows in the matrix form

$$\begin{pmatrix} X_{ss} & X_{s1} & X_{s2} \ldots X_{sn} \\ X_{1s} & X_{11} & X_{12} \ldots X_{1n} \\ X_{2s} & X_{21} & X_{22} \ldots X_{2n} \\ \cdot & \cdot & \cdot \quad \cdot \quad \cdot \\ X_{ns} & X_{n1} & X_{n2} \ldots X_{nn} \end{pmatrix}$$

where X_{ij} is the quantity of goods or services of type i going to producers of goods or services of type j per unit of time.

To theorize about the state's welfare function by analogy with the theory of the consumer is to say that this function has as arguments only the elements of the first row and column of this matrix. The foregoing paragraphs suggest that some or all of the remaining elements of the matrix are arguments of the state's welfare function. Since this latter group of arguments are also functions of the welfare functions of individuals and of enterprises, the welfare of the state and of individuals is related. The welfare of individuals is also affected by the actions of the state. To some extent this interde-pendence occurs because the state is a priority buyer of goods so that the residual available to consumers and enterprises depends on the size of the state budget, and to some extent independence oc-curs because consumers and households pay taxes; but the welfare of individuals depends on how the state spends its income. Given a level of budget spending, the welfare of individuals may be presumed to be affected by the allocation of spending between schools and forced labor camps—to take an obvious example. Thus the welfare of the state depends in part on the consumption of particular goods by particular individuals, and the welfare of indi-viduals depends in part on the composition and level of the state's consumption. This problem is known in economic theory as the problem of interdependent welfare functions.

In the sort of interdependent utility function we must use in the case of state planning, the state can alter a particular flow of goods (an X_{ij} in the matrix above) by changing a plan, even though the change in the flow will not necessarily be exactly equal to the change in the plan, and even though no changes in budgetary income or expenditures is involved. Consequently, the first-order equilibrium conditions must define optimality, not only with respect to items in the state budget, but also with respect to other (plan-affected) flows in the economy.[1]

It is convenient to use a notation differing from that in the matrix of flows given above. The state will be assumed to maximize a welfare function U ($x_1 \ldots x_r$, $y_1 \ldots y_s$), in which the terms x_i represent goods and services which the state buys and sells on its own account through the state budget, and the terms y_i represent other flows of goods throughout the economy. The first set thus corresponds to terms in the first row and column of the matrix, and the second set to the remaining terms in the matrix. This distinction

---

[1] I remind the reader of the discussion, in Chapter 6, of the effect of a change in plans on the actions of enterprises. Those who are willing, after Chapter 7, to accept the concept of aggregation in Soviet conditions may identify the flows in the matrix with inter-industry payments. Others will associate an X_{ij} with a payment between a pair of enterprises or between an enterprise and a kind of worker.

is convenient, because the budget involves an income constraint, while other flows throughout the economy do not.

The economic agents involved in the flows denoted by terms y_i are enterprises and (groups of) individuals. When they are enterprises, they are assumed governed by output-maximization rules such as those given in Chapter 6. When they are individuals, they are assumed to be governed by supply or demand functions of the sort familiar to economic theorists.

One point should be spelled out, although it then becomes obvious. Enterprises may be rewarded on the basis of their output, even if the state does not wish to have them produce very much. The state's main control over economic activity in a growing economy lies in its ability to allocate investible funds. It may very well reward a group of enterprises for producing a large output with a given plant, while refusing them the funds with which to expand. Moreover, even in the short run, as has been shown, the maximum amount which enterprises can produce depends upon the input and output plans which they are given by the state. By controlling the amounts which enterprises may purchase, these plans affect the level of output at which average cost equals average revenue. From the state's point of view, the problem is to obtain optimal results by suitable selection of the output maxima attainable by the individual enterprises. Thus the state seeks to maximize a utility function[2]

$$U\,(x_1 \ldots x_r,\, y_1 \ldots y_s)$$

subject to a budget constraint:[3]

$$0 = \sum_1^r \int df_i\,(z_i)$$

$$\begin{cases} |z| \leq x_i \\ z \geq 0 & \text{if } i \text{ is an expenditure} \\ z \leq 0 & \text{if } i \text{ is a revenue} \end{cases}$$

and also subject to the constraints that each y_i is a function of plans $\Pi_1 \ldots \Pi_s$ for each flow in the economy:

---

[2] We assume provisionally the existence of a real-valued utility function and shall discuss briefly below the possibility that this function is lexicographic (vector-valued).

[3] It is convenient to use the convention that quantities on the income side are of opposite sign to quantities on the expenditure side. The marginal functions $f\,(z)$ are taken to be step functions with a single point of discontinuity.

$$y_i = y_i \, (\Pi_1 \ldots \Pi_s)$$

Thus the state maximizes the function

$$G \equiv U \, (x_1 \ldots x_r, y_1 \ldots y_s) - \lambda \left[\sum_1^r \int df \, (z) \right] +$$

$$+ \sum_1^s \mu_i \, [y_i - y_i \, (\Pi_1 \ldots \Pi_s)]$$

Here λ and the μ_i are Lagrange multipliers. The state's problem is to select optimal x's and Π's—that is, an optimal budget and optimal plans allocating goods and services moving between pairs of enterprises, or between enterprises and groups of individuals.

It will be convenient to deal with the equilibrium conditions first under the simplified assumptions that the x_i are invariant with respect to the plans Π_k and that the y_i are invariant with respect to budget items x_k. This means that state budget income and expenditures can be altered at the margin without affecting flows among the other sectors. This assumption is certainly artificial and will later be removed. It gives us, however, the first-order equilibrium conditions:

$$0 = \frac{\partial G}{\partial x_i} = \frac{\partial U}{\partial x_i} - \lambda p_i \qquad i = 1, \ldots, r$$

where p_i is the marginal cost (or revenue) of the i'th commodity. (It will be recalled that the value of p_i depends on whether x_i is above or below the plan for x_i.) Likewise,

$$0 = \frac{\partial G}{\partial y_j} = \sum_{k=1}^s \frac{\partial U}{\partial y_k} \frac{\partial y_k}{\partial \Pi_j} - \sum_{k=1}^s \mu_k \frac{\partial y_k}{\partial \Pi_j} \qquad (j = 1, \ldots, s)$$

$$= \sum_{k=1}^s \frac{\partial y_k}{\partial \Pi_j} \left(\frac{\partial U}{\partial \Pi_k} - \mu_k \right)$$

This is a set of homogeneous equations in the variables $[\partial U/(\partial \Pi_k) - \mu_k]$. A sufficient condition for its solution is that $\mu_k = \partial U/\partial \Pi_k$. There arises the question of whether this solution is unique. If it is unique, and only then, the rank of the matrix $(\partial y_k/\partial \Pi_k)$ will be equal to s. Suppose that the rank of the matrix is less than s, then its transpose will also be of rank less than s. In this case, it will be possible to find a non-null vector $(d\Pi_1, d\Pi_2, \ldots, d\Pi_s)$ satisfying the equation.

$$
\begin{pmatrix} 0 \\ \cdot \\ \cdot \\ \cdot \\ 0 \end{pmatrix} = \begin{pmatrix} \dfrac{\partial y_1}{\partial \Pi_1} & \cdots & \dfrac{\partial y_1}{\partial \Pi_s} \\ \cdot & \cdots & \cdot \\ \dfrac{\partial y_s}{\partial \Pi_1} & \cdots & \dfrac{\partial y_s}{\partial \Pi_s} \end{pmatrix} \begin{pmatrix} d\Pi_1 \\ \cdot \\ \cdot \\ d\Pi_s \end{pmatrix}
$$

Consider an arbitrary equation of this system s, say the first:

$$
0 = \frac{\partial y_1}{\partial \Pi_1} \, d\Pi_1 + \frac{\partial y_1}{\partial \Pi_2} \, \partial \Pi_2 + \cdots + \frac{\partial y_1}{\partial \Pi_s} \, d\Pi_s
$$

The right side is the total differential of the function $y_1 \, (\Pi_1 \ldots \Pi_s)$. To say that it and all the other total differentials of the functions $y_k \, (\Pi_1 \ldots \Pi_s) \, (K = 1, \ldots, s)$ vanish is to say that in the neighborhood of equilibrium it is possible to alter all plans in the economy (other than those involving the budget) simultaneously, in such a way as to leave unaltered all the corresponding flows of goods in the economy. It may be that such a possibility is not inconceivable to a very advanced theorist, but in the present state of my knowledge it seems to me that this result should not be possible. If it is impossible, than the solution $\mu_k = \partial U / \partial \Pi_u$ for the equilibrium conditions must be unique.

A somewhat more complicated hypothesis about the connection between budgetary and nonbudgetary flows is the following: it is possible to alter nonbudgetary flows (the y_i) without affecting budgetary flows (the x_i); but changes in budgetary flows affect nonbudgetary flows. In this case the second set of constraints is altered to become

$$
\Sigma \, \mu_k \, [y_k - y_k \, (\Pi_1 \ldots \Pi_s, x_1 \ldots x_r)]
$$

The first-order equilibrium conditions then become

$$
0 = \frac{\partial U}{\partial x_i} - \lambda p_i + \sum_{k=1}^{s} \frac{\partial y_k}{\partial x_i} \left(\frac{\partial U}{\partial y_k} - \mu_k \right) \qquad i = 1, \ldots, r
$$

$$
0 = \sum_{k=1}^{s} \frac{\partial y_k}{\partial \Pi_j} \left(\frac{\partial U}{\partial y_k} - \mu_k \right) \qquad j = 1, \ldots, s
$$

In block-matrix form, this may be written

$$
\begin{pmatrix} 0 \\ \\ 0 \end{pmatrix} = \begin{pmatrix} E_r & \dfrac{\partial y_k}{\partial x_i} \\ \\ 0 & \dfrac{\partial y_k}{\partial \Pi_j} \end{pmatrix} \begin{pmatrix} \dfrac{\partial U}{\partial x_i} - \lambda p_i \\ \\ \dfrac{\partial U}{\partial y_k} - \mu_k \end{pmatrix}
$$

where E_r is a unit matrix of order r. This system admits of non-zero solutions (that is, $\partial U/\partial x_i \neq \lambda p_i$ and $\partial U/\partial y_k \neq \mu_k$ for at least one i or k) if and only if the transpose system

$$
\begin{pmatrix} 0 \\ \\ 0 \end{pmatrix} = \begin{pmatrix} E_r & 0 \\ \\ \dfrac{\partial y_i}{\partial x_k} & \dfrac{\partial y_i}{\partial \Pi_k} \end{pmatrix} \begin{pmatrix} dx_k \\ \\ d\Pi_k \end{pmatrix}
$$

has a non-null solution. The upper block, however, has a matrix (E_r) of rank r, so that dx_k must be null. The lower block, then, reduces to

$$
0 = \sum_{k=1}^{s} \frac{\partial y_j}{\partial \Pi_k} d\Pi_k \qquad (j = 1, \ldots, s)
$$

This condition is like that in the first case: it must be possible to alter plans for nonbudgetary flows (in the neighborhood of equilibrium) in such a way that no flow is actually affected. The extension of this reasoning to the most general case—where the zero block in the matrices above is replaced by the matrix $\partial x_i/\partial \Pi_j$—adds complication without adding interest.

From the point of view of applications, the relevant problem is often to explain how a change in government policy is related to changes in plans. This problem, indeed, is central to an explanation of Soviet actions.[4] By "a change in policy" is meant "a small change in the state's welfare function." This change displaces the equilibrium conditions

$$
\frac{\partial U}{\partial x_i} = \lambda p_i \qquad i = 1, \ldots, r
$$

$$
\frac{\partial U}{\partial y_j} = \mu_j \qquad j = 1, \ldots, s
$$

according to the rules

$$
p_i \, d\lambda = \sum_j \frac{\partial^2 U}{\partial x_i \, \partial x_j} \, dx_j + \sum_k \frac{\partial^2 U}{\partial x_i \, \partial y_k} \, dy_k \qquad (i = 1, \ldots, r)
$$

$$
d\mu_q = \sum_j \frac{\partial^2 U}{\partial y_q \, \partial x_j} \, dx_j + \sum_k \frac{\partial^2 U}{\partial y_q \, \partial y_k} \, dy_k \qquad (q = 1, \ldots, s)
$$

---

[4] If the Soviet government explicitly sought to maximize some utility function, then it would presumably attempt to carry out numerically the sort of operation which will be described here. Whether its procedures implicitly follow this procedure is a question which must be left to others.

The left sides of these two systems may, however, be expressed also as $d\left(\partial U/\partial x_i\right)$ and $d\left(\partial U/\partial y_q\right)$ respectively. Thus there is a system of equations which relates changes in marginal utilities to changes in the flows of goods (it is written in block form):

$$\begin{bmatrix} d\left(\dfrac{\partial U}{\partial x_i}\right) \\[2ex] d\left(\dfrac{\partial U}{\partial y_q}\right) \end{bmatrix} = \begin{pmatrix} \dfrac{\partial^2 U}{\partial x_i\,\partial x_j} & \dfrac{\partial^2 U}{\partial x_i\,\partial y_k} \\[2ex] \dfrac{\partial^2 U}{\partial y_q\,\partial x_i} & \dfrac{\partial^2 U}{\partial y_q\,\partial y_k} \end{pmatrix} \begin{pmatrix} dx_j \\[2ex] dy_k \end{pmatrix}$$

On the other hand, from Chapter 6, we may obtain the relationship

$$\begin{pmatrix} dx_j \\[2ex] dy_k \end{pmatrix} = \begin{pmatrix} \dfrac{\partial x_i}{\partial \Pi_j} & \dfrac{\partial x_i}{\partial \Pi_q} \\[2ex] \dfrac{\partial y_k}{\partial \Pi_j} & \dfrac{\partial y_k}{\partial \Pi_q} \end{pmatrix} \begin{pmatrix} d\Pi_j \\[2ex] d\Pi_q \end{pmatrix}$$

Consequently, if the two matrices of partial derivatives are non-singular, we have

$$\begin{pmatrix} d\Pi_i \\[2ex] d\Pi_q \end{pmatrix} = \begin{pmatrix} \dfrac{\partial x_i}{\partial \Pi_j} & \dfrac{\partial x_i}{\partial \Pi_q} \\[2ex] \dfrac{\partial y_k}{\partial \Pi_j} & \dfrac{\partial y_k}{\partial \Pi_q} \end{pmatrix}^{-1} \begin{pmatrix} \dfrac{\partial^2 U}{\partial x_i\,\partial x_j} & \dfrac{\partial^2 U}{\partial x_i\,\partial y_k} \\[2ex] \dfrac{\partial^2 U}{\partial y_q\,\partial x_j} & \dfrac{\partial^2 U}{\partial y_q\,\partial y_k} \end{pmatrix}^{-1} \begin{bmatrix} d\,\dfrac{\partial U}{\partial x_i} \\[2ex] d\,\dfrac{\partial U}{\partial y_q} \end{bmatrix}$$

In the particular case in which enterprises always carry out their plans exactly, the first right-hand matrix is the identity matrix. In cases in which plans are carried out with zero expected deviation, but random actual deviation, the expected value of the first right-hand matrix is a unit matrix also.

Needless to say, the practical aspects of calculating and inverting these functions is considerable. This aspect of the planning problem will be discussed at greater length in Chapter 13. For the present, it may be observed that to the calculation and inversion of the matrices in the last result there exist administrative measures in the U.S.S.R.: administrative agencies send draft plans to enterprises; enterprises send counterplans to the agencies; and agencies send final plans to the enterprises. If this system worked ideally, it would give the state an idea of what plans it would have to present in order to obtain optimal results.

The preceding discussion has been based on the existence of a real-valued utility function for the state. Unless such a function exists, economic theory is unable to define equilibrium conditions.[5] It has been shown that provided that (to use Chipman's terminology) utility functions are transitive, comparable, nonsymmetric, dense, directed, contradirected, and satisfy the axioms of choice and substitution, then such a function does exist. If it does not, then utility, at best, will be representable by a vector of (real) numbers. The nature of consumer equilibrium has not been explicitly explored for this case. Readers who feel that pointing out such esoterica is an attempt to reach self-annihilation through boredom may be reminded of the following problems:

1. Although the Soviet government has consistently claimed that the marginal utility of goods produced by state-owned industry infinitely exceeded that of goods produced by capitalist industry operating on Soviet soil, Lenin authorized both the New Economic Policy (NEP) and concessions to foreign mining companies.

2. Although the Soviet government has consistently maintained that the marginal utility of goods produced by collective farms infinitely exceeded that of goods (indistinguishable to the consumer) produced on the individual plots of collective farmers and city dwellers, Stalin during the second world war allowed both categories of citizens to increase their output of vegetables.

3. Although the Soviet government has consistently maintained that the marginal utility of goods designed to increase social consumption infinitely exceeded that of goods destined for individual consumption, the minister of finance at the 1948 session of the Supreme Soviet told several eastern cities that they would have to wait for additional public utilities—such as electric power and street-car lines—until some future date, because of financial complications (which could have been dealt with by increases in turnover tax, and consequent decreases in consumption).

In these examples, economic theorists would translate Soviet official doctrine as a lexicographic ordering of utilities—an ordering, that is to say, in which certain marginal rates of substitution became zero or infinite. Soviet practice, on the other hand, has frequently indicated that certain marginal rates of substitution which (in terms

[5] For a detailed treatment, the reader is referred to J. S. Chipman, "The Foundations of Utility," *Econometrica*, June, 1960.

of Marxist doctrine) were zero or infinite, in practice turned out to be nonzero and finite. The foregoing comments are designed only to suggest (on the basis of Marxist theory) that it is not reasonable to attribute real-valued utility functions to the Soviet State. There is also reason to believe (on the basis of Soviet practice) that such a real-valued function may (not unreasonably) be postulated.

Besides providing goods and services to the state, the Soviet budget maintains the agencies which enforce plans and regulations. Both plans and regulations are attempts to make sure that some activities are carried out and others are not. In the absence of state intervention, "speculators" would set up private businesses, and enterprises would carry out actions the state did not want. The prevention of both costs money. The cost of directing the economy into channels desired by the state presumably depends upon the discrepancy between the intentions of the state and the actions which the economy, left to itself, would take. It is not possible, as yet, either to discuss this problem in a very satisfactory way, or to ignore it.

It has been observed, for instance, that if the state wishes to evaluate the consequences of a particular allocation of resources, it must know the production functions of individual enterprises. In each enterprise, the ratio of marginal to average cost is different, and the effect of altering the total resources available to a group of enterprises depends on the individual reallocations made. It is possible that the cost of determining the optimal allocation exceeds the loss of efficiency resulting from suboptimal allocation. But even if it is worthwhile to make an attempt at optimizing resource allocation, it will be the case that costs to the budget vary in response to changes planned for enterprises.

Soviet macroeconomic regulations are essentially restrictions upon the nature of economic relations between classes of transactors. The theorist has no objection in principle to defining a matrix (X_{ij}) involving directed flows of goods and services between each pair (i,j) of transactors. Moreover, he is prepared to discuss systems in which all elements of this matrix differ from zero in principle; zero values may occur, because of the way the plans, prices, utility and production functions happen to exist, but these are not of particular interest in themselves. Soviet regulations, however, seem often to try to prevent certain kinds of transactions, and in particular, to prevent situations in which transactor i both sells to and buys from transactor j. Moreover, these arrangements tend to establish general rules applicable to large sets of transactors.

In particular, regulations may take the following form: Consider two sets of economic units, S_i and S_j. No member of S_i may sell to a member of S_j.[6] Or they may take the form: any purchases by a member of S_i from a member of S_j must follow a prescribed rule about marginal costs.[7] If the members of S_i and S_j were not inclined to perform the forbidden actions, then the regulation would be unnecessary. If they are inclined to perform the forbidden action, then enforcement of the regulation is necessary, and enforcement is expensive. It is natural to conjecture that the more actions a regulation prevents, the greater will be the costs of enforcement. Let us now explore some particular examples of such costs.

Suppose an enterprise seeks to maximize output, given a set of marginal revenue, marginal cost functions and plans. If two of its suppliers sell inputs which are indistinguishable (in that they have identical marginal productivity functions), the enterprise will prefer that input whose marginal cost is less. If the state is to ensure that the enterprise purchases the more expensive input, it will have to incur some administrative costs; and it is not unreasonable to suppose that the greater the difference in marginal costs, the greater will be the enterprise's incentive to break the rules. The greater, consequently, will be the vigilance needed by administrators.

But even if the marginal utility to the state of a sale by i to j exceeds that of a sale by k to j, the use of (budgetary) resources to ensure that i-j rather than k-j transactions occur may reduce direct state purchases of goods enough to reduce its total welfare. That is, it will be better for the state to accept the reduction in its welfare implicit in the k-j transactions in order to obtain the greater volume of direct purchases. In this sense, the level of utility which the state can attain is affected by the structure of (marginal) prices which enterprises may charge each other, and this structure is an element of budgetary costs.

In these examples, it turns out that some budgetary expenditures are incurred in order to determine what changes in output

---

[6] For example, enterprises are generally forbidden to make purchases from retail stores, or to sell directly to individuals. Collective farms may not sell directly to retail stores or individuals, and so on.

[7] For example, retail prices (wages) are uniform for particular commodities (trades) over considerable regions.

shall take place in individual enterprises; others are incurred in order to reduce to zero some element X_{ij} in a matrix of inter-sectoral payments; still others are incurred in order to maintain a particular step-function as the relevant one for some group of enterprises. In each case, maintenance of the regulation is of some advantage to the state, but it is not an absolute advantage. Even if it is not now possible to formulate the marginal utility and marginal cost associated with particular regulations, it is worth pursuing the analysis one step more.

It is known that at times of "stress" (e.g., the early 1930's, the second world war, the period of the Korean war) the Soviet government has increased the number and intensity of its direct controls; at other times it has reduced these. This situation, on the face of it is puzzling: if a discriminatory control system (or force) is expensive, one would expect it to be introduced at a time when goods are relatively plentiful rather than at a time when goods are relatively scarce.

We may formalize the problem by considering a case involving the state, and three enterprises, i, j, and k. Two of the enterprises, i and k, sell to the third, j. The state prefers to have j purchase from i rather than from k; the more it tries to divert j's purchases from k to i, the more it must give up budget goods (since regulation is expensive).

Suppose that the marginal utility to the state of goods sold by i to j is a rapidly declining function of the quantity thus sold, while the marginal utility of goods sold by k to j is a slowly declining function of their respective quantities. In this case, the effect of reducing all goods flows (as occurred in the initial phases of the second world war) is to increase the gain to the state from marginal diversions of j's purchases from k to i. Two cases are then possible: (1) the marginal utility of budget goods declines rapidly as quantities available increase. In this case, the state will not gain by diverting resources from the production of budget goods to the control of the flows from i to j and from k to j. (2) Marginal utility of budget goods changes little as quantity of budget goods increases. In this case, the gain to the state from using its resources to control the flows from i to j and from k to j will increase as total output decreases.

We may now reverse the problem, and consider an increase in the level of budget income and expenditure to be allocated between budget goods and regulation. Suppose the marginal utility of budget goods to be a given function of the quantity of such goods, and to be independent of the flows of goods from i to j and from j to k. Then as sales of both the i-j and k-j types increase, our assumed condition says that the state's gain from a marginal diversion from k to i declines. Whether or not the increase in output will lead to a strengthening or weakening of controls depends on whether the decline in the marginal utility of a ruble's worth of budget goods is greater or less than the decline in the marginal utility of preventing a ruble's worth of diversions.

Similar reasoning can be applied to the case where it is not the supply of goods which has altered (as in the foregoing), but where there is a "change in tastes." The beginning of industrialization in the late 1920's would be expressible as an increase in the marginal utilities of investment goods, and a decline in the marginal utility to the state of farm goods sold to the city population relative to that of manufactured goods sold to the city population.

It is necessary to suppose that the marginal utility of the kind of consumption favored by the control system declines relative to the less favored type of consumption as the quantity of both types of goods increases. If this is not so, there is no explanation of why controls become less general as output rises.

In concluding this discussion, we may observe that it is extremely hard in many cases to determine whether Soviet administrative policies change because of changes in the economy itself, or because of changes in the "tastes" of the state. Soviet official literature speaks as if all actions were designed to maximize the welfare function Lenin would have if he were still alive; and this attitude presumes that Lenin's tastes would have remained unaltered for forty years. Sovietologists strongly suspect, however, that some Soviet actions since 1924 would not have maximized Lenin's welfare function; that Lenin's tastes might have evolved over time, had he lived; and that quite possibly later leaders have had independent views of their own. In any event, as we shall see in the final chapter, there are disadvantages to considering "the welfare of the state" as being as well-defined as it has seemed in this chapter.

Nevertheless, it is useful to have considered the planning process as if the state were a monolith with given, unchanging tastes. It focuses attention on the relation between the state, on the one hand, and the rest of the economy on the other, and on the role of the state as regulator of the activity of enterprises and households.

Chapter 13 INTERNATIONAL TRADE

International trade raises very important problems of theory and of practice in an economy such as that of the U.S.S.R. It must, in its very nature, conflict with many of the central plans and regulations, since one of the partners in any trading transaction is not subject to Soviet law. If, for example, the Soviet Union has a regular export of timber to the London market (as has been the case for half a century), some Soviet organization must deal with British firms. These will ordinarily be unable to quote prices which are fixed, they may be unable to guarantee to accept deliveries in a regular quantity, and they will not wish to deal with Soviet government agencies as such, since these enjoy sovereign immunity from suit in ordinary courts.

Even if the trading partner has institutions like those of the Soviet Union (as do the European satellites), trade is complicated. A Czechoslovak machinery enterprise sells at prices established by the Czechoslovak government; it is subject to production plans, materials balances, and so on which are prepared by agencies which are not part of the Soviet administrative structure. Consequently, the Czech enterprise may be subjected to instructions which are inconsistent with what the Soviet enterprise or its Soviet administrative superiors might wish; and Czech business interests may be quite independent of those of its Soviet partner.

On the other hand, the Soviet government cannot allow its own enterprises to enter into foreign transactions as if these enterprises were private firms. If they could do so, they could perhaps thwart the intentions of the government, selling abroad goods which the government wanted at home and buying abroad goods which the government did not wish it to have. Consequently, the Soviet government has developed a special set of foreign trading institutions, aimed at isolating Soviet enterprises from foreign businesses and yet making possible international transactions.

Soviet foreign trade is a "monopoly of the state." This expression must be interpreted, just as we had to interpret the "single fund of state property" in talking of enterprises. Ownership of state enterprises is vested in the Ministry of Finance ordinarily; but the foreign trade monopoly is vested in the Ministry of Foreign Trade. The ministry, however, would have trouble trading aboard; for it is the agency of a sovereign power, and foreign courts could not entertain suits brought against it. The Ministry has therefore created special corporations, which actually carry on foreign trade. These are set up in such a way that they are, legally, on the same footing as private corporations, although they are owned by the ministry. It is they who actually buy and sell goods.

In some cases, the Soviet government has set up trading corporations in foreign countries. Thus the Amtorg Corporation was chartered under the laws of New York State. It could, I believe, conduct any sort of trade; but in fact it acts as buyer and seller for the Soviet government in the United States. Of course, when the Soviet Union was receiving Lend Lease aid from the United States during the second world war, the Soviet government could, and did, receive goods directly from the U.S. government, and Amtorg had very little, indeed, to do.

These foreign trade corporations are fairly numerous. Some of them import, others export, and a few do both. Most of them deal only in certain commodities, but some (like Amtorg) specialize regionally. Almost nothing is known directly about their internal operations, but we may guess fairly plausibly about some of their economic operations. For instance, we know that Soviet enterprises buy and sell on the basis of contracts at fixed prices. It would be contrary to the whole tenor of Soviet regulations for a foreign trading corporation to buy from or sell to Soviet enterprises on terms different from those applied to other Soviet enterprises. If it did, then enterprises would have a special financial incentive either to trade or to avoid trade with these corporations. We know, moreover, that imports and exports enter into the materials balances which are an important determinant of the allocations process. It is reasonable to conclude that the foreign trading corporations are in fact named in the materials balances and that enterprises trade with them as they would with other enterprises.

It is natural to inquire about the connection between the corporations which specialize by commodity and corresponding whole-sale *(snab* and *sbyt)* organizations. Some years ago, I attempted to determine whether such a connection existed. I found some grounds for suspecting that in the European satellites, at least, there was a connection. The Polish coal-exporting corporation, for ex-ample, might be either the regular coal *sbyt* organization itself, or a branch of it. The Romanian machinery-importing corporation might be either the regular machinery *snab* organization, or a branch of it. I could not reach any particular conclusions about the Soviet corporations. The point is, one suspects, a fine techni-cality. It does suggest that although legally the corporations are subordinate to the Ministry of Foreign Trade of their countries, they may have equally close business or administrative ties to the wholesale brokerage agencies which execute the materials balance plans.

Soviet enterprises keep their cash on deposit in the State Bank, and the bank is thus automatically informed of their operations. It is not surprising, then, to find that banking circles generally report that when a Soviet foreign trading corporation does business out-side the U.S.S.R., in foreign currency, it does not ordinarily have its own bank account but uses the accounts which the State Bank of the U.S.S.R. maintains in that country. In some cases, the Soviet government appears to own banks abroad—one such bank is said to exist in London and another in France.

The State Bank thus has a role in foreign trade operations. It is, of course, a government agency. (Its governor has the rank of minister.) It is therefore in a different legal position from the foreign trade corporations; but since it is a central bank, the cus-toms of central banking enable it to hold balances and conduct financial operations on the same basis as any other central bank.

When the Soviet Union exports, a Soviet foreign trade enter-prise buys goods from a Soviet domestic enterprise and sells goods to a foreign enterprise. (This enterprise will be a similar foreign trade corporation if the export is within the Soviet bloc; it will be a private corporation if the export is to a private enterprise economy.) When the Soviet Union imports, a Soviet foreign trade corporation buys from a foreign enterprise (of whichever kind) and resells to a Soviet domestic enterprise. The transactions with Soviet enterprises will be carried out in Soviet domestic prices; but the transactions with foreign enterprises will not be.

Any Soviet foreign trade corporation thus carries on transactions both in rubles and in foreign currency. The corporation does not, however, carry its own foreign currency balances but draws on or pays into the foreign currency balances of the State Bank. The corporation carries on its books the ruble value which its foreign currency balance would have if it were allowed to keep it. This sum, of course, is a liquid asset which can be used within the U.S.S.R., subject to other plans and regulations, of course.

A 10 percent increase, say, in the quantity of Soviet exports will mean a 10 percent increase in the value of payments by export corporations to Soviet domestic enterprises and a 10 percent increase in foreign exchange earnings. What is the effect on the cash position of exporters? This effect will depend on the price which Soviet goods command in foreign currencies and also on the price (in rubles) which the State Bank pays for these foreign currencies when exporters sell them. If foreign prices are low, or if the price of foreign currency is low, exporters will "lose money" on foreign trade in the sense that the rubles they receive from the State Bank will be less than the rubles they pay to Soviet domestic enterprises to buy the goods. The greater exports are, the greater will be this loss.

A 10 percent increase in the quantity of Soviet imports will mean a 10 percent increase in the funds which Soviet import corporations receive from Soviet domestic enterprises and also a 10 percent increase in the value of the foreign exchange which they must buy from the State Bank. If foreign prices are low, or if the price which the State Bank charges for foreign exchange is low, then importing corporations will "make money" on each unit of imports, and the more goods are imported, the more money the corporations will make.

We may look at three different financial measures of foreign trade: that of the domestic economy, that of the trading corporations, and that of the State Bank. If the value in domestic prices of exports exceeds the value in domestic prices of imports, this means that domestic enterprises are selling to foreign corporations more than is bought from them, so that foreign trade tends to increase the cash balances of the internal economy. Likewise, if the value in foreign prices of exports exceeds the value in foreign prices of imports, then the State Bank will be buying more foreign currency from export corporations than it sells to import corporations, so that its foreign exchange reserves will rise.

The foreign trade corporations are here in an intermediate

TABLE 12–1

The Effect of Exchange Rate Changes and Changes in the Trade Balance on the Cash Position of Foreign Trading Organizations, Assuming Similar Structure of Domestic and Foreign Prices

Trade Balance	Valued In		Foreign Trade Corporation Earnings and Payments at Various Exchange Rates								
	Domestic Rubles	Foreign Currency	Rate 3:1			Rate 4:1			Rate 5:1		
			Receipts	Payments	Net	Receipts	Payments	Net	Receipts	Payments	Net
1. Export Surplus											
Imports.........	50	200	50	67	−17	50	50	0	50	40	10
Exports.........	150	600	200	150	50	150	150	0	120	150	−30
Total.........					33			0			−20
2. Trade Balanced											
Imports.........	100	400	100	133	−33	100	100	0	100	80	20
Exports.........	100	400	133	100	33	100	100	0	80	100	−20
Total.........					0			0			0
3. Import Surplus											
Imports.........	150	600	150	200	−50	150	150	0	150	120	30
Exports.........	50	200	67	50	17	50	50	0	40	50	−10
Total.........					−33			0			20

situation. They pay out, on balance, to domestic enterprises, and take in, on balance, from the State Bank; but whether their cash situation improves or not will depend on how much the State Bank pays for each unit of foreign exchange. That is, it depends on the exchange rate.

Given a particular volume of trade, then, the impact on the cash position of domestic enterprises depends on how these goods are priced within the Soviet Union, the cash position of the State Bank depends on how they are priced in foreign countries, and the cash position of the trading corporations depends on both of these factors and the exchange rate.

If the structure of Soviet prices were the same as the structure of foreign prices, then analysis would be fairly simple. The State Bank would accumulate foreign exchange whenever domestic enterprises absorbed cash from foreign trade operations and would lose foreign exchange whenever domestic enterprises lost cash to foreign trade operations. In this case, if the exchange rate were properly fixed, the foreign trade organizations would exactly "break even," whatever the level of imports and exports might be. (If they had operating costs, one could introduce buying and selling rates to cover them.)

If, however, exchange rates are not at this optimal level, then the cash balances of the foreign trading corporations do depend on the balance of trade and on the rate of exchange. The way in which they are affected is illustrated by Table 12–1. Reading across this table, one may see the effect of a lowering of the exchange rate of the ruble for a given trade program. Reading down, one may see the effect of changes in trade, given an exchange rate. In each of the nine cases making up the table, the corporations' net position is the sum of the two numbers designated *net,* which arise, respectively, from import and from export transactions.

The situations analyzed in Table 12–1 are unrealistic because they assume Soviet domestic prices are proportional to prices in foreign countries. There is every reason to suppose that this is not the case. Soviet resource endowment is not that of other countries. If the Soviet Union were isolated from other countries and had a market mechanism, its prices would reflect the difference in resource endowment and would, therefore, differ from those in the rest of the world; but the actual Soviet price system is not a market system, and there is no reason to believe that administrative price fixing has

TABLE 12–2

SOVIET FOREIGN TRADE, 1950 AND 1955–61* (MILLION RUBLES, AT THE 1961 RATE OF EXCHANGE)

	Exports			Imports			Balance of Trade		
	Total	Within Bloc	Outside Bloc	Total	Within Bloc	Outside Bloc	Total	Within Bloc	Outside Bloc
1950..........	1615	1350	265	1310	1023	287	305	227	−22
1955..........	3084	2454	630	2754	2176	578	330	278	52
1956..........	3254	2461	793	3251	2452	799	3	9	−6
1957..........	3943	2974	969	3544	2543	1001	399	431	−32
1958..........	3868	2822	1046	3915	2918	997	−46	96	49
1959..........	4897	3711	1186	4566	3411	1155	331	300	31
1960..........	5006	3723	1283	5066	3478	1588	−60	−55	−5
1961..........	5399	3613	1786	5249	3452	1797	150	161	−11

* F.o.b. Soviet port or frontier for Soviet exports, f.o.b. port or frontier of exporter for Soviet imports.

caused Soviet prices to resemble world prices more closely than they would if the Soviet Union were an isolated market system.

The rest of this chapter will be concerned with several analytical problems involving Soviet foreign trade. It is convenient, however, first to include Table 12–2, which indicates that Soviet foreign trade rose substantially during the 1950's and that most of it is with other countries of the Soviet bloc. (For this purpose, Communist China is included in the bloc). Trade within the bloc, it may be noted briefly, is conducted on the basis of prices which are referred to as "adjusted world prices of 1950," so that in principle all trade is valued at these prices. Payments are made into clearing accounts in the State Bank of the U.S.S.R. Trade is on the basis of bilateral commodity lists, approved annually, and through 1963 annual bilateral balancing was the rule. The balance, in some cases, included Soviet credits; and the U.S.S.R., therefore, has shown export surpluses in its trade with the rest of the bloc. The credits are ordinarily earmarked for the purchase of sets of equipment needed for new factories. In some cases, in years when crops have been bad, credits have been earmarked for purchases of grain or other bulk foodstuffs. The principle of loans to aid balance of payments difficulties has not been recognized, and there is no record of loans to help the fiscal situation of governments. This trade is conducted in such a way as to fit in with Soviet bloc internal business practices. Thus, for example, enterprises producing for export consign their goods directly to the foreign enterprise or organization receiving them, and the draft covering payment is drawn on the suitable Soviet corporation, to be paid for out of its funds (and ultimately the bilateral clearing account).

The example in Table 12–1 may be expressed in general terms for an arbitrary foreign trade. Set:

C = the profit to foreign trade corporations
Q = quantities of goods
P = prices of goods
r = the exchange rate (the number of units of foreign currency per ruble)

The following subscripts will be used:

I denotes imports.
X denotes exports.
R denotes ruble prices.
F denotes foreign prices.

Then the foregoing argument shows that the profits of foreign trade corporations are

$$C = Q_I P_{RI} - Q_I \frac{P_{FI}}{r} - Q_X P_{RX} + Q_X \frac{P_{FX}}{r}$$

$$= Q_I \left[P_{RI} - \frac{P_{FI}}{r} \right] - Q_X \left[P_{RX} - \frac{P_{FX}}{r} \right]$$

If the structure of Soviet domestic prices differs from the structure of foreign prices, then there exist numbers a_I and a_X

$$\frac{P_{FI}}{P_{RI}} = a_I r \qquad \frac{P_{FX}}{P_{RX}} = a_X r$$

Thus the profits may be expressed in terms of Soviet prices:

$$C = Q_I P_{RI} (1 - a_I) - Q_X P_{RX} (1 - a_X)$$

Or they may be expressed in terms of foreign prices:

$$C = \frac{1}{r} \left[Q_I P_{FI} \left(\frac{1 - a_I}{a_I} \right) - Q_X P_{FX} \left(\frac{1 - a_X}{a_X} \right) \right]$$

Foreign trade will lead to zero profits if and only if

$$\frac{Q_I P_{RI}}{Q_X P_{RX}} = \frac{1 - a_X}{1 - a_I}$$

and more generally,

$$C \gtrless 0 \text{ if and only if } \frac{Q_I P_{RI}}{Q_X P_{RX}} \gtrless \frac{1 - a_X}{1 - a_I}$$

This inequality is expressed in terms of Soviet domestic prices. The corresponding statement, in terms of foreign prices, is

$$C \gtrless 0 \text{ if and only if } \frac{Q_I P_{FI}}{Q_X P_{FX}} \gtrless \frac{a_I (1 - a_X)}{(1 - a_I) a_X}$$

1. An increase in r means a decrease in the exchange rate of the ruble. Since

$$\frac{dC}{dr} = -\frac{1}{r^2} \left[Q_I P_{FI} \left(\frac{1 - a_I}{a_I} \right) - Q_X P_{FX} \left(\frac{1 - a_X}{a_X} \right) \right] = -\frac{C}{r}$$

Therefore

$$\frac{d \log C}{d \log r} = -1$$

Thus, decreases in the exchange rate mean directly proportional changes in the profits of foreign trade corporations, assuming the quantities of goods exchanged and prices are unaffected. Thus, if the corporations are making a profit, an increase in the exchange rate of the ruble will increase profits; if the corporations are making a loss, an increase in the exchange rate will increase losses. Only if corporations are exactly breaking even will profits be unaffected.

A proportionate decrease in the foreign currency prices of Soviet imports and exports obviously has the same effect on the profits of Soviet foreign trade corporations as an increase in the exchange rate of the ruble.

2. Suppose now that a choice is offered between identical foreign trade programs offered by two different countries. We denote the two proposals by adding 1 and 2 as superscripts to terms in P, a, and r, and investigate what is meant by the assertion, "It is more profitable to trade with country 1 than with country 2." Imports will be considered separately from exports.

a) It is more profitable to import a given set of goods from Country 1 than from Country 2 if:

$$Q_I \, P_{RI} \, (1 - a_I^1) > Q_I \, P_{RI} \, (1 - a_I^2)$$

Since $Q_I \, P_{RI}$ is positive and appears on both sides of the equation, the condition becomes:

$$(1 - a_I^1) > (1 - a_I^2)$$

$$a_I^2 > a_I^1$$

$$\frac{a_I^2}{a_I^1} > 1$$

This means that prices in Country 2 exceed those in Country 1, when both are converted into rubles. By definition:

$$P_{FI}^1 = a_I^1 \, r^1 \, P_{RI}$$

$$P_{FI}^2 = a_I^2 \, r^2 \, P_{RI}$$

So that:

$$\frac{a_I^2}{a_I^1} = \frac{P_{FI}^2}{r^2} \bigg/ \frac{P_{FI}^1}{r^1}$$

Therefore:

$$\frac{P_{FI}^2}{r^2} \bigg/ \frac{P_{FI}^1}{r^1} > 1$$

$$\frac{\overset{2}{P_{FI}}}{\overset{1}{P_{FI}}} > \frac{r^2}{r^1} = \frac{\text{units of currency 2 per ruble}}{\text{units of currency 1 per ruble}} = \frac{\text{units of currency 2, per}}{\text{unit of currency 1.}}$$

This inequality may be rewritten in the form:

$$\frac{\overset{2}{P_{FI}}}{r^2} > \frac{\overset{1}{P_{FI}}}{r^1}$$

Thus it will be more profitable to import from Country 1 than from Country 2 whenever the ratio of the prices of the goods in 2 to that in 1 is less than the (cross) exchange rate between 2 and 1.

b) It is more profitable to export a given set of goods to Country 1 than to Country 2 if

$$Q_X \, P_{RX} \, (1 - \overset{2}{a_X}) > Q_X \, P_{RX} \, (1 - \overset{1}{a_X})$$

$$(1 - \overset{2}{a_X}) > (1 - \overset{1}{a_X})$$

$$\overset{1}{a_X} > \overset{2}{a_X} /,$$

which is the opposite inequality from that in the case of imports. Hence also

$$\frac{\overset{2}{P_{FX}}}{\overset{1}{P_{FX}}} < \frac{r^2}{r^1}$$

Thus it will be more profitable for Soviet corporations to import from Country 1 than from Country 2 if

$$\frac{\overset{2}{P_{FI}}}{r^2} > \frac{\overset{1}{P_{FI}}}{r^1}$$

and more profitable to export to Country 1 than to Country 2 if

$$\frac{\overset{2}{P_{FX}}}{r^2} < \frac{\overset{1}{P_{FX}}}{r^1}$$

These results make it possible to carry on some preliminary analysis of Soviet foreign trade. It will be assumed that exporting corporations are given a list of quantities of goods which they are to export, and importing corporations a list of quantities of goods which they are to import. Soviet domestic prices are assumed fixed. The problem is to see how profits from foreign trade are affected by changes in prices in foreign countries. Foreign countries are assumed to be "capitalist," in the sense that they have market mechanisms and hence variable prices. It is also assumed that Soviet trade is not large enough to have an effect on prices in foreign countries.

Suppose now that two countries have convertible currencies and no exchange controls. Then, for their foreign trade to be competitive in world markets it is necessary that their exchange rates reflect the purchasing powers of their currencies.[1] For such countries,

$$\frac{P_{FI}^{2}}{P_{FI}^{1}} = \frac{r^2}{r^1} = \text{units of currency 2 per unit of currency 1}$$

To make this equality, it is necessary that the State Bank have rates for conversion of foreign exchange which preserve the cross-rates between the two countries which exist in the market. In fact, the State Bank does have a policy which maintains such cross-rates. Between such "hard currencies," then, it would be a matter of indifference (so far as their profits are concerned) with which countries the Soviet corporations traded.

Let us start from a situation in which the equality holds; let us suppose that Soviet foreign trade is equally divided between the two countries and that Soviet trade with each country is exactly in balance. Now let us suppose that prices in Country 1 rise more than those in Country 2, and that all prices rise in the same proportion within each country. It will now be the case that Soviet foreign trade organizations will increase their profits if they shift their trade in such a way as to import more from Country 2 and export more to Country 1.

For this situation to be possible, it is necessary that the countries in question (*a*) allow trade to shift, and (*b*) allow Soviet balances from its surplus with Country 1 to be applied against deficits in trade with Country 2. To make this matter a little more concrete, it is reasonable to suppose that as prices rose in Country 1, the country was inclined to increase direct controls over foreign trade. Such controls are not uniform but are apt to discriminate against exports to soft currency areas and against imports from

---

[1] Disregarding, for simplicity of presentation, the effect of persistent capital movements upon the balance of payments.

hard currency areas. This would mean that the trading partners of the U.S.S.R., in this situation, would be relatively willing to allow the reallocation of Soviet exports; however, Country 1 will not be inclined to allow the U.S.S.R. to use its earnings from increased imports from Country 2, since this will run counter to its attempts to improve its balance of payments.

This simple hypothetical example gives rise to a problem which is characteristic of those found in connection with Soviet foreign economic policy. Since the beginning of the cold war, the United States government has been concerned with trying to limit Soviet foreign trade and has therefore followed such trade very closely. Until about 1952, the discussion revolved mainly around Soviet attempts at trading with western European countries; during the rest of the 1950's, and since then, especial concern has been voiced over Soviet attempts to increase trade with Asia and Africa.

According to one interpretation, Soviet trade policy is essentially dominated by political considerations. The Soviet government aims at expanding trade wherever such trade will increase its political influence. In this view, as the number of new, independent, relatively weak, and neutralist governments in Asia and Africa grew, it was natural that the Soviet government should try to expand its trade and hence its political influence in these areas, into which penetration should have been relatively easy.

There is another interpretation, however. The western European countries managed generally to stabilize their internal prices at the time marked by the 1949 currency devaluations. Thereafter, price levels in Asia and Africa have tended to rise relative to those in European countries, so that their currencies have "softened" relative to European currencies. The observed shift in Soviet trade policy after 1952 or thereabouts would be explainable by the theory that Soviet foreign trade operations with Asia and Africa became increasingly more profitable, and those with Europe less profitable.

Those two hypotheses are linked, to the extent that governments which are new, relatively weak, and inexperienced tend to pursue more inflationary domestic policies than older, stronger, and more experienced governments; therefore, it would be difficult to find a way of deciding whether "political" or "economic" considerations had led to the shift in Soviet trade. This means that western writers are still free to use their a priori liking for particular kinds of causal explanations to take the place of analysis. Those who are in-

clined to ascribe "business-type" motivations to Soviet foreign trade
will be able to find evidence for their views.

3. It might be expected that Soviet exporting corporations
would try to obtain from domestic enterprises for export those items
for which Soviet domestic prices were low relative to world prices.
If they were able to do so, they would make greater profit on these
exports than they would otherwise; however, there is no particular
reason to suppose that such goods will be easier to obtain than
others. "Easy to obtain," in this context, refers to the problem of
obtaining an allocation in a materials balance. Some Soviet statements exist to the effect that when the Soviet government has
wished to speed the growth of an industry, because of pressing
"need" for its output, it has fixed the price low, subsidized the industry if necessary, and allocated its output. If this is generally true,
export corporations should find it relatively hard to obtain allocations of those goods which it would be most profitable for them to
export.

We cannot, of course, assume arbitrarily that foreign trade corporations seek to maximize "profit" or "cash balances." If they
did, it should be relatively easy to make a theory of Soviet foreign
trade. Actually, however, for much of Soviet history, foreign trade
seems to have been conducted along the following lines: (1) Soviet
imports should provide mainly goods which are needed in the
investment program and which cannot be produced readily in the
U.S.S.R. (2) A dependence on imports weakens the Soviet economy
politically, so imports of particular types of machinery should be
allowed only for the time needed for the U.S.S.R. to begin production of equivalent machinery. (3) Soviet exports should consist of
those goods which are least needed in the investment program.

In a developing market economy, such a program would tend
to take care of itself. The domestic prices of "most needed" goods
would rise, so that imports of such goods would also rise. The
domestic price of "least needed" goods would not rise, so that if
anything were exportable at all, it would be these; and pressure on
foreign exchange reserves would force the exchange rate to a level
where these "least needed" goods could be exported.

But where prices are fixed, and where distribution is controlled
by a materials balance, it does not follow that such a pattern of
trade would automatically be attained. It is true that wherever it is
very hard to obtain goods internally, importing corporations are

apt to try to import. Wherever goods can easily be obtained internally, exporting corporations are likely to be urged to export. In some cases, this phenomenon shows up quite clearly. Even in the early 1950's, when Soviet trade with Western Europe was very small, it was true that small batches of particular kinds of steel were regularly imported from and exported to Western Europe. Western Europe seemed to be treated as a sort of warehouse, and small-scale deliveries and withdrawals were used to smooth out Soviet production and allocation schedules.

It seems to be the case that the Ministry of Foreign Trade plans imports and exports and that the individual corporations receive these plans just as ordinary domestic enterprises receive plans. It is hard, indeed, to see how it could be otherwise, since otherwise foreign trading operations could not be fitted into domestic schedules of output, allocations, and investment; but where plans are prepared in terms of physical quantities, and the trading partners have market economies, physical planning may lead to foreign trade problems.

The classic case of this sort occurred during the First Five Year Plan in the early 1930's. The plan required large imports of machine tools and proposed to pay for them by exporting farm products. After 1929, the world depression began; one feature of it was that farm prices dropped much more sharply than prices of manufactured goods. Meanwhile, in 1930, the U.S.S.R. increased its investment program and collectivized agriculture. During collectivization grain output fell, partly because of difficulties of reorganization and partly because of bad weather, and a tremendous slaughter of livestock took place as a peasant protest against collectivization. Consequently, as the demand for imports rose, the supply of farm goods fell, and the terms on which they could be exported deteriorated.[2]

Over the past generation, the U.S.S.R. has become an industrial economy. All of our knowledge of industrialization suggests that manufacturing costs must have declined relative to agricultural costs, and one should expect drastic changes in the composition of

---

[2] One of the strongest criticisms of Stalin's policies is that he forced the export of food, on very unfavorable terms, at a time when there was an acute food shortage in the country. Again, in 1946–47, food exports were continued despite a crop failure. Echoes of this criticism still appeared in 1963, when there was a crop failure; this time Khrushchev decided to import grain and took political advantage of this decision to belabor his internal "Stalinist" critics.

trade; but exports of raw materials and fuel were two-thirds of all exports in 1913 and in 1939, and over half of the total in the late 1950's. Imports of this group were about half of the total in 1913 and 1938 and one-third of the total in the late 1950's. Soviet exports of finished goods go mainly to the satellites. In East-West trade, the decline of raw materials exports is even less striking.

Moreover, Soviet foreign trade is small, considering the growth in the country's output. Soviet sources claim that the volume of Soviet trade in 1961 was 2.7 times as great as in 1913, which is certainly a much smaller increase than the increase in total output. Again, the increase in trade with the West is much less than the increase in total trade. Assuming that prices in East-West trade changed in the same proportion as prices in trade within the bloc, then one would estimate roughly that the volume of East-West trade in 1961 was about 80 percent of the volume of all Russian foreign trade in 1913.

This situation contrasts strikingly with that of all other developed countries. In all other cases, the volume of foreign trade has risen sharply with output; moreover, most of the trade of industrialized countries consists of the exchange of finished goods with other industrialized countries. Industrialized countries other than the U.S., moreover, have largely stopped exporting agricultural products; and the U.S.S.R. has given clear indications that it has difficulty expanding agricultural production. In consequence, both the low level, and the commodity composition, of Soviet foreign trade are puzzling to the student of international economics. It is easy, but not very satisfactory, to blame the cold war for this pattern; for cold war considerations have not stopped Soviet foreign trade growth in cases where the Soviet government had commercially attractive offers to make in world markets. (Some may find the fact sad, but it is true.)

It appears likely that this very odd commodity structure of Soviet foreign trade reflects in part direct administrative controls. Soviet economic literature on these questions is rather scarce. What there is of it suggests that the Soviet government has what may be called a stereotyped reflex action to certain kinds of trade. It is automatically reluctant to export capital goods, especially machinery, on the grounds that such exports divert resources away from domestic investment. It has automatically hesitated to export oil and metals, on the grounds that they were scarce items of strategic value. It is automatically inclined to export grain, which is not used in investment; but since the second world war, the Soviet government has had to provide capital goods for the investment programs of its European satellites (and for a time Communist China). More recently, it has decided, on obviously political grounds, to provide a certain amount of equipment on credit to countries like India and Egypt. We can only guess, but a good guess would be that this form of trade has turned out to be more sensible on purely economic grounds than the Soviet government thought it would be. It would be in accord with our experience of industrialized countries generally that such changes would continue. Thus if (as was the case in 1963) the Soviet government decided to expand investment in chemicals and to reduce investment in metals, one would now expect it to try to export metallurgical and metal-working equipment. By now, it should be able to do so.

There may well be obstacles, however, to such a change in policy. Some of these are bureaucratic: officials who have for a generation been instructed that the acquisition of metallurgical and metal-working equipment was the main object of Soviet policy will find it difficult to adjust to a new formulation of economic priorities, and the adjustment of materials balances to allow for exports may prove a slow process. Some of the obstacles to shifts in exports may be technical, however. The structure of Soviet internal prices reflects in part the desire of the government to influence enterprises. Moreover, apart from such deliberate pricing, it is likely that a good deal of "inadvertent" price policy has occurred. Machinery production in the U.S.S.R. has tended to be concentrated in a relatively small number of large multi-product plants. The price of machinery in such plants depends to a considerable extent upon the actual decisions made about how overhead and joint costs should be allocated among the various kinds of output. Since Soviet industry has not competed in world markets, there is no reason why its treatment of overhead and joint costs should resemble that of enterprises in other countries.

Consequently, there is no particular reason why the domestic prices of Soviet machinery should reflect their relative scarcities, as compared to those of corresponding machines produced elsewhere. Where the price structure of the U.S.S.R. differs from that elsewhere, it might well be the case that export agencies would not find it financially feasible to export those particular kinds of machines which were currently in surplus owing to changes in investment plans. They presumably would not wish to subsidize exports. There might well appear to be a subsidy of exports in many cases, where past decisions about joint costs had led to relatively high domestic prices. The reallocation of such joint costs cannot be undertaken by an enterprise, or even an industry; and it is not in keeping with Soviet thought generally that domestic prices be revised in order to allow exporting corporations a bookkeeping profit on exports.

4. Suppose that foreign exchange rates are all given and, for simplicity, that the world consists of three countries: *U*, the U.S.S.R.; *S*, a satellite; and *R*, the rest of the world. Designate by $A < B$ the statement "The price in Country *A* is less than the price in Country *B*." Given exchange rates, this statement has meaning, provided it is not taken to mean that all or any enterprise in the world may freely decide to buy either *A*'s goods or *B*'s goods. For each commodity, one of the following statements will be true:[3]

1. $U < S < R$
2. $U < R < S$
3. $S < U < R$
4. $S < R < U$
5. $R < S < U$
6. $R < U < S$

If countries followed the policy of always buying goods in countries where the price was lowest, the U.S.S.R. would export goods in the first two categories, the satellite those in the next two, and the rest of the world those in the last two.

Suppose, however, that an iron curtain separates the U.S.S.R. and the satellite from the rest of the world and that within the Soviet bloc trade area, countries buy where goods are cheapest. In this case, the U.S.S.R. will export goods in Categories 1, 2, and 6; the satellite, those in Categories 2, 3, and 5. If the iron curtain is semi-permeable, so that some East-West trade takes place, some goods in Categories 5 and 6 will enter both U.S.S.R.-satellite trade and East-West trade. In this case, if prices in the three countries are independent of one another (so that they are unaffected by the volume of this international trade), it will be the case that the

---

[3] Strictly speaking, the inequality "less than or equal to" should be used here. It is simpler, for our purposes, to assume that commodities in different countries never have exactly the same price.

U.S.S.R. pays more for satellite goods than it does for comparable rest-of-world goods and that the satellite pays more for Soviet goods than for rest-of-world goods.

From the point of view of Soviet (satellite) foreign trade corporations, trade with the rest of the world would be more profitable than trade with the satellite (U.S.S.R.) for goods in Categories 5 and 6. In this sense, the existence of an iron curtain imposes a cost upon the foreign trade corporations. On the other hand, if the corporations resell internally at existing domestic prices, domestic enterprises will be unaffected by the existence of the curtain, with one important proviso: the quantities available for foreign trade within the bloc must be as great as those available from the rest of the world. If they are not, then the plans for consumption of goods in Categories 5 and 6 must be reduced. As was shown in Chapter 6, such reductions in plans will affect actual consumption (though not necessarily by the same amount).

The materials balance of each commodity within the U.S.S.R. and the satellite contains imports as a source, and exports as a use, of the commodity. The corresponding *snab* and *sbyt* wholesalers must obtain from or supply to the foreign trade corporations amounts of goods which *(a)* appear as parts of the domestic plans and *(b)* appear in annual bilateral trading plans between the U.S.S.R. and the satellite. Deviations from plan in one country will cause some deviation from plan in the actual volume of foreign trade; consequently they will also cause actual performance in the trading partner to deviate from plan. Actually there are more than two countries in the Soviet bloc, so that if deviations from plan are not in the same direction in all countries, above-plan performance in some countries may offset at least in part below-plan performance in others and reduce the amount of foreign-induced disturbance in the materials balances of all countries. If all countries, however, tend to deviate from plan in the same direction, such offsetting cannot occur. For instance, if there is simultaneously a drought in Hungary, Rumania, and the Ukraine, all grain exports of the bloc will tend to be below plan. If the Krivoi Rog iron mines (which supply iron ore to most of the satellites) deviate from plan, this will affect steel output and foreign trade of all bloc countries, and so on.

Since 1956, the bloc has asserted that 1950 world prices are the basis for trade within the bloc. Manifestly, the use of such prices will raise the revenue of bloc trading corporations on trade in Categories 1, 2, and 4 and reduce their revenue on trade in Categories 5 and 6. In fact, the trade in these last two categories will actually be conducted at a loss. If the corporations were guided by profit considerations, they would (given an iron curtain) simply stop intrabloc trade in those goods which were formerly supplied by the rest of the world. Such a policy would, of course, improve the position of the corporations at the expense of the internal economics of the individual bloc countries; so a loss by the corporations must be viewed as being at least partly offset by gains from additional sources of supply accruing to domestic enterprises.

The fact that such losses do occur does suggest, however, that it would probably be desirable, from the bloc's point of view, to allow deviations from strict adherence to world prices in intrabloc trade. It may be the case that relatively small departures from "world prices of 1950" could alter considerably the profitability of trade in commodities which it would be desirable on other grounds to trade. In fact, the unit values of goods for which country-by-commodity statistics exist do show considerable variation. Even though quality variations may account for a part of the differences, they do not appear to account for all of them.

The argument is often made that the U.S.S.R. discriminates against the satellites, paying them less and charging them more than western European countries. The evidence on this score relates in part to the early postwar period (1945–49) and was in part publicized by Yugoslavia after its break with the U.S.S.R. in 1948. At this time, of course, the U.S.S.R. was still officially treating some countries (East Germany, Hungary, and Romania) as conquered enemies and had not undertaken major commitments to aid in developing any of them. Moreover, conditions were sufficiently confused and data-collecting methods sufficiently poor to make conclusions uncertain. I am personally inclined to believe there may be a good deal of truth to the assertion.

More recently, however, attempts have been made to show that such discrimination existed in the late 1950's. Here, the unit values of Soviet trade statistics have shown that the U.S.S.R. charged the satellites more and (with less certainty) paid them less than Western Europe. The relevance of this assertion, however, is challenged by studies of Bulgarian trade statistics. Bulgaria is too small and weak to discriminate against anyone, yet Bulgaria

charged the U.S.S.R. more and paid it less than did Western Europe
in a majority of cases for which data are available.[4] The relevant test,
then, seems to lie in a comparison of Soviet-satellite and inter-
satellite trade. It has not yet been possible to make such a test. The
tests used so far merely reflect the fact that the Soviet bloc would
gain, at least in the short run, by trading more with the West and
less with itself. This fact is what we should expect from the
numerous statements to the effect that intrabloc trade in principle
is more desirable than East-West trade. The advantages are formulated mainly in terms which stress that bloc countries are led to
produce and export goods they would otherwise import. This
result, as we should expect, is achieved at a cost.

5. A somewhat artificial demonstration will now be made to
relate imports to domestic availability, using the concepts found
in Chapters 4 and 6. It will be assumed that each commodity is
produced by a single enterprise in each country, so that proper
cost functions for the "industry" are certain to exist. It will also
be assumed that the objective of the ministry regulating the enterprise is to maximize total availability of goods (imported or home-
produced). The ministry sells all goods at price p and buys imports
at a price $r \neq p$. Effectively, then, it has two costs to consider: the
cost of imported goods and the cost of domestic goods. This approach differs from that discussed in Chapters 4 and 6 in that it
compresses the enterprise and its ministry into a single unit, which
receives a foreign trade program from outside. The earlier discussion treated the enterprise as separate from the ministry and assumed it received orders from the latter.

Let the total available be x, imports x_F, and output $(x - x_F)$.
The domestic price is p, the import price is p', and the total cost of
producing $(x - x_F)$ units is $C (x - x_F)$. Then it is necessary to
maximize availability:

$$G = x - \lambda\pi (x, x_F)$$

where π is the profit function,

$$y = px - C (x - x_F) - p'x_F$$

[4] See Horst Mendershausen, "Terms of Trade between the Soviet Union and
Smaller Communist Countries, 1955–57," *Review of Economics and Statistics*, 1959,
pp. 108–18; *idem*, "The Terms of Soviet-Satellite Trade: A Broadened Analysis,"
ibid., 1960, pp. 152–63; Franklyn D. Holzman, "Soviet Foreign Trade and the Question of Discrimination," *ibid.*, 1962, pp. 134–47.

and is zero when output is maximized. Suppose an increase in the import quota x_F. The two equilibrium conditions are:

$$\frac{1}{\lambda} = \frac{\partial y / \partial x_F}{\partial x / \partial x_F} \quad \text{and} \quad \frac{1}{\lambda} = \frac{\partial y}{\partial x}$$

The total differential of the profit function is

$$0 = \frac{\partial y}{\partial x} \, dx + \frac{\partial y}{\partial x_F} \, dx_F$$

$$= \left(p - \frac{\partial C}{\partial x} \right) dx - \left(p' + \frac{\partial C}{\partial x_F} \right) dx_F$$

$$= \left(p - \frac{\partial C}{\partial x} \right) dx - \left(p' - \frac{\partial C}{\partial x} \right) dx_F$$

This last result follows because (given total usage) a decrease in imports has the same effect on production outlays from an increase in output. Thus

$$\frac{dx}{dx_F} = \frac{p' - \partial C / \partial x}{p - \partial C / \partial x}$$

In Chapter 4, we saw that marginal cost exceeds price. Therefore, the denominator is negative. If $p' \leq p$, the numerator is certainly negative also, so that dx/dx_F is positive. On the other hand, if import prices are high enough (specifically, if they exceed marginal cost) an increase in imports will decrease domestic availability.

Domestic output is $(x - x_F)$, and therefore the change in output is related to the change in total availability by the equation:

$$\frac{dx}{dx_F} - 1 = \frac{d \, (x - x_F)}{dx_F}$$

$$= \frac{p' - p}{p - \partial C / \partial x}$$

The denominator, as before, is negative, and we have the result: an increase in imports will be associated with increases in domestic output if import prices are below domestic prices. If import prices exceed domestic prices, domestic output will fall as imports rise.

This responsiveness depends on both import and domestic prices. Thus both availability and output increase more (decrease less), the higher import prices are, and the lower domestic prices are.

If the authorities are free to accept or reject an import quota, then the problem is resolved formally by redefining the profit function:

$$y\,(x) = \begin{cases} px - C\,(x - x_F) - p'x_F & \text{if } p' \leq p \\ px - C\,(x) & \text{if } p' > p \end{cases}$$

With this specification, imports will never occur if they have "bad" effects, either on total availability or domestic output.

If x_F is negative, then an export quota rather than an import quota is involved. Moreover dx/dx_F and $d\,(x - x_F)/dx_F$ refer to the consequences on domestic availability and on output, respectively, of *decreases* in the export quota. It is a straightforward matter to work out the details of this analysis.

The preceding discussion has differed from that in Chapters 4 and 6 in one respect: it has been assumed that domestic and foreign trade in a particular commodity were handled by a single agency which sought to maximize domestic availability of that commodity, given a foreign trade plan. The earlier discussion made a distinction between an enterprise and the regulatory agency (ministry) or economic council; and the early discussion in this chapter distinguished clearly between domestic enterprises and agencies on the one hand and foreign trade corporations on the other. If it is true (as it seems to be) that corporations, although owned by the Ministry of Foreign Trade, are in an important sense arms of the *snab* and *sbyt* wholesalers, then this procedure is not a bad approximation to the actual state of affairs.

5. It has so far been necessary to assume that import and export quotas are plans which are externally imposed on operating agencies. This assumption is necessary to a theory which disregards uncertainty in general and in particular the uncertainty which arises because those who execute plans have some say in the formulation of plans. Particularly in the case of foreign trade, some further comment is needed.

A plan, as we have said, is an order of the form "Produce at least x units." It must be issued by an agency to another agency. Once an import or an export plan exists, it becomes an order to the domestic enterprises of both partners to the trade. If trade is conducted on the basis of annual bilateral agreements, then presumably both governments must consent to the issuing of the plan in their names. If multilateral agreements existed, all governments would have to agree. It is natural to ask how agreements of this sort are reached.

It would be easy to answer the question in either of two circumstances. In the first case, there would be an international agency capable of giving trade plans to all the national governments. In the second case a branch of the Soviet Planning Commission would give trade plans to all the satellites. It does not appear that either of these courses is followed. As political leader, and as the largest industrial producer, of the bloc, the U.S.S.R. must be assumed to have greater influence (in some sense) than the other countries. Yet the way in which this influence is exercised is relatively obscure. Whatever the substance of international economic relations within the bloc, the form is that of sovereign states which negotiate bilateral commitments both annually and for longer periods. Thus a foreign trade plan enters the economy only when both partners agree to its contents.

Since 1949, a Council for Economic Mutual Assistance has existed within the Soviet bloc. Very little is known about it, except that it has occasional meetings which issue rather cautious press releases. This state of affairs is extremely revealing, given what was said of Soviet organizational practice in Chapter 2. The meetings of the council are "legislative"; and while a secretariat is believed to exist, there is no record of any action taken by it. If the council were more than a discussion group, and if it had power in its own right, then it seems likely that secretariat actions, rather than council actions would be newsworthy.

Generally speaking, when nothing is known about the activities of some Soviet organization expert opinion is sharply divided. One group will say that the absence of information is a sign that nothing is happening. The other will say that so much is happening that security regulations have been imposed to conceal the fact. Consequently, the preceding paragraph is bound to annoy those experts who take the latter view.

It is reasonable to infer the relative insignificance of the Council (for the point of view of its ability to issue plans binding upon the individual countries) at least through 1963.[5] But once a bilateral trading agreement is in force, the mechanics of foreign trade within the bloc are simple, and not very different from the mechanics of domestic transactions. A variety of statements exists

[5] In 1963–1964, the Western press interpreted Romanian government and party statements as expressing opposition to Council attempts to direct Romanian investment programs.

in several languages, to the effect that a domestic enterprise making goods for export within the bloc uses procedures almost identical with those it uses on domestic shipments. That is, it ships the goods directly to the foreign buyer. When the goods are shipped, it draws a draft on the export corporation, as if it were the buyer, and ordinary payments procedures seem to be followed. The export corporation is then reimbursed by its bank, which in turn receives automatically a credit in the ruble clearing accounts maintained by the State Bank of the U.S.S.R. This operation seems to have been resolved into a clear procedure.

However, to take a simple step further, the clearing accounts were apparently all bilateral through the end of 1963. In 1957-8 and again in 1963 the Council declared its intention of making it possible to transfer a surplus in one clearing account to offset a deficit in another. Such transfers have undoubtedly been made in the past, but it seems clear that they have been one-time clearing transactions, and have never been automatic.

If there were any general plan for international trade within the bloc, it would be absurd to insist on bilateral balancing. It would, of course, be necessary to have a means of ensuring that any exporting country allocated its shipments according to the plan, and it would be necessary to ensure either that for each country exports matched imports or that credit arrangements existed. However, there would be no reason why these calculations should be carried out on a bilateral basis, as apparently they are.

One explanation for this state of affairs is probably that the effort to unify clearing prices has so far been unsuccessful. The available data on unit values of goods in intrabloc trade support this view. If prices are indeed subject to negotiation, then of course a ruble clearing surplus in one bilateral account may represent quite a different amount of goods than will a ruble clearing deficit in another bilateral account. Even if they wished to, foreign trade corporations cannot entirely neglect their profit and loss positions, if only because they must obtain budget funds or loans to meet deficits. Trade may be possible at one price and not at another, if only because the corporations have limited funds; and it may be desirable to have trade at a "special" price in preference to no trade at the "standard" price.

Another explanation, however, is based upon the relation between domestic and international availability. If domestic and international prices are given, then any agency which could plan international trade would indirectly plan the availability of goods within each country. This proposition follows from the results of the preceding section. It may be argued that indeed it may be the objective of the Soviet government (or of all bloc governments) to have a single plan for the entire bloc; but in that case, it would be relatively inefficient to start from a plan for foreign trade. This is true because an individual country, confronted only with an externally imposed foreign trade plan, may still be able to alter the level and composition of domestic consumption by suitable manipulation of its domestic plans and regulations. If there were sufficient agreement on domestic plans generally, however, a satisfactory international trade plan should then be relatively simple to obtain.

It will be recalled that in preparing materials balances within a country it has proved very difficult to decide how much of a particular input any enterprise needs, given the anticipated time-path of its output. Moreover, where several enterprises are involved, each has its own production function, so that a country's total requirement depends on the allocation of output among the enterprises. Thus the export surplus or import needs of a country depend upon the way its total output is divided among producers. The domestic planners, therefore, must have information about each producing unit before they can issue any plan.

The same sort of result would follow, with redoubled force, for planning on an international basis. If each country had only one enterprise producing each particular commodity, then an international agency planning foreign trade would have the same difficulties that the domestic agency has in preparing a materials balance. That is, it would really have to have the same access to the enterprises which the domestic planners have.

If there are several enterprises producing a particular commodity in each country, the attempt to plan international trade becomes even greater. This is true because the export surpluses and import requirements vary with the reallocation of resources among enterprises. It is therefore in principle necessary for the agency planning foreign trade to have access to the information about individual enterprise in all countries.

Given the nature of the problem, it is not surprising that the Council of Economic Mutual Assistance should be composed of representatives of national planning commissions rather than of the national foreign trade ministries; but if economic planning is (as the Soviet planning literature insists) the expression of the national government's economic desires, then the existence of a genuine international economic plan seems to require that the individual national governments have no individual economic desires in the areas covered by the international plan. In this sense, the achievement of such a plan would seem to imply the relinquishment of an important attribute of national sovereignty.[6]

International economic relations among independent countries with Soviet-type economies therefore must be conducted on a bilateral basis. This result should not be surprising in the light of modern thinking on international economic relations. Free trade and convertibility can exist among a group of market economies only when each member government is prepared to allow events in foreign countries to have domestic consequences. In the "pure" gold standard case, this means that a depression abroad must be allowed to reduce domestic prices, and a foreign inflation to raise domestic prices. The much more complicated international arrangements of the present day require ultimately that domestic monetary authorities limit their domestic actions in such a way as to avoid undue losses in foreign exchange reserves and that they respond to foreign developments in suitable ways.

The entire effort of national planning in the Soviet sense is to increase the power of the national government over its internal affairs. In order to do so, it must have means of isolating its economy from the rest of the world, so as to increase its freedom of internal action. In the circumstances, it is not surprising that the conduct of international economic relations should become inherently more difficult.

To say what has just been said does not mean that the Soviet bloc will never obtain a central planning mechanism. To say this would imply a forecast that national governments within the bloc will be able to retain their present powers. Likewise, it does not mean that the Soviet bloc will never achieve a multilateral payments mechanism. To say this would imply the forecast that the national governments will be prepared to relinquish a part of their present controls over their internal economies. I am not prepared to make either forecast. The purpose of the present discussion is

---

[6] In fact, this seems to have been the point insisted on by Romania in 1963–1964.

merely to clarify the reason for the state of affairs within the Soviet bloc in the postwar period.

6. Foreign trade operations have an effect upon the operations of the fiscal and monetary authorities. This effect may be discussed in terms of the profit and loss position of the foreign trade corporations. These earn money by selling exports to foreigners and imports to domestic enterprises; they pay out money when they buy imports from foreigners and exports from domestic enterprises. Their transactions with foreigners, of course, affect the foreign exchange position of the central bank. This may be taken as "external," in the sense that foreign money cannot be used internally, and foreign prices differ from domestic prices; however, the corporations do have to buy and sell foreign exchange (in transactions with their bank); and they do have to pay their bills, whether incurred in foreign or domestic currency.

Consider a situation where the foreign exchange position of a country remains fixed. This means that receipts equal payments, when these are valued in the "foreign" prices used in international trade. But domestic prices are different, and there is no reason why the corporations will receive the same amount of money from the sale of imports that they pay for exports. If they "lose" money, then the cash balances of domestic enterprises will increase. If they "show profit" the cash balances of domestic enterprises will fall. Since enterprises normally pay out a part of their cash receipts in the form of wages, one would expect the note issue to change in the same way as the current accounts of enterprises.

Therefore, the foreign trade balance (valued in domestic prices) has an internal monetary effect. Moreover, the profits or losses of corporations, as here defined, may entail some action by the budget or bank. It might be that the corporations will borrow to cover deficits, and repay loans when they have profits. In this case, a trade deficit will have the same domestic effect as an increase in bank credit, and a surplus the same effect as a decrease in bank credit.

This possibility, however, implies that the authorities are willing to allow such effects to take place. Actually, increases and decreases in credit, given fixed levels of output, tend mainly to alter domestic surpluses or shortages of goods. Internal shortages of goods will be matched by excess cash balances of enterprises. In order to prevent international trading operations from increasing such balances, the authorities may prefer to subsidize the losses of foreign trade corporations from tax revenue, and not allow the corporations to borrow from the State Bank. Such subsidies neutralize the effect of foreign trade on the domestic money supply. The price of this neutralization, however, may be that investment programs are affected by the foreign trade program.[7]

If a country sells abroad on credit, as the U.S.S.R. does, the effect is to increase the domestic spending of corporations relative to their domestic revenue. In this sense foreign loans are inflationary, for they tend (unless offsetting measures are taken) to add to the money held by enterprises and individuals. Similarly imports financed on credit would be deflationary.[8]

It might be held that since foreign transactions may be prevented from having internal monetary effects, they are indeed of no monetary consequence. But this statement would assume that the fiscal authorities recognized foreign trade effects as they occurred, and took prompt action to neutralize them. In fact, the authorities may well not do so, since the measures they would have to take may interfere with the attainment of other objectives, such as retail price stability, the construction program, and so on. Indeed, from published accounts, there is no particular awareness on the part of Soviet bloc governments of the connection between international and domestic economic affairs on the macroeconomic level.[9]

7. To conclude: the foreign trade of the U.S.S.R. is conducted in such a way as to minimize the contact of Soviet enterprises with

[7] If turnover tax rates were flexible, investment programs would be unaffected. But from 1954 until 1963, it was government policy to hold retail prices stable, so that in fact only the profits tax was flexible. But an increase in the profits tax means mainly a decrease in self-financed investment. If taxes as a whole are constant, and budget spending on foreign trade increases, domestic investment will be the main casualty.

[8] In the period following 1945, reported Soviet budget revenues included sizable reparations payments (from East Germany, Finland, Hungary, and Romania). It is also possible that there was some repatriation to the U.S.S.R. of profits earned by "jointly owned" corporations operating in these countries. These payments appear to have ended in the early 1950's. Later, the U.S.S.R. extended credits abroad to the satellites, including eventually Cuba and Communist China, and to several other countries, notably Egypt, India, and Indonesia. It is not known whether these loans were treated as budget expenditures, or whether the State Bank was ultimately the source of the funds involved.

[9] A reader of the manuscript of this book, who must remain unnamed, has commented: "Equating Bulgaria and the U.S.S.R. is like equating Denmark and the U.S.A.: If Denmark builds three apartment houses, the import bill skyrockets, reserves fall, the discount rate goes up, machine guns appear on the roof of the central bank;

other countries, and to minimize the effect of foreign events on Soviet behavior. Trade from the domestic point of view is conducted on the basis of quantitative plans, and domestic prices show no tendency to move in response to foreign prices. Within the Soviet bloc, there is a tendency toward having a single price for all international transactions in any one commodity, but variations do occur. Given prices, foreign trade in a commodity may theoretically be expected to have an effect upon domestic production, and foreign trade as a whole has a monetary effect, unless this is deliberately offset. Thus foreign trade has internal economic repercussions, even though these work themselves out rather differently from the way they work themselves out in a private enterprise or market economy.

---

stiff upper lip; see-saw economy. The United States? It can generate a domestic housing boom without the faintest impact on external balance. Away from the effete East Coast, whoever heard of the balance of payments? What, dear boy, is a proper construct of the Bulgarian economy? It consists of three interdependent groups: (*a*) mountain brigands who fire on passing travelers, using ancient, long-barreled muskets cherished since the Turkish border wars; (*b*) people in the flatlands who, while largely sedentary, are engaged in horse stealing, which doesn't necessarily add to national wealth but makes for higher turnover; and (*c*) violinists and other musicians adept at hitting some gosh-awful seventeen-stringed monstrosity tuned in diminished sixths. There is also the State, recruited from groups (*b*) and (*c*), who persecute group (*a*). The difficulty about analyzing trade in the planned economy is that the U.S.S.R. is a special case (which we have looked at for too long). The smaller countries are not now carbon copies of the Soviet blueprint, if they ever were. Besides, the sheer size of the Soviet land mass carries with it an abundant and varied resource endowment, which makes for relative self-sufficiency. The U.S.S.R. can obtain many benefits of the division of labor, without the 'bother,' so to speak, of foreign entanglements." My preoccupation with theory may tend to make readers ignore considerations like these.

Chapter 14   UNFINISHED BUSINESS

The foregoing chapters made a start at formulating an economic theory of the Soviet-type economy. The first six chapters presented the economic theory which is relevant to output-maximizing enterprises, and the general equilibrium theory which should accompany such microeconomic analysis. Chapters 7–12 constructed the elements of a macroeconomics suitable to Soviet conditions, by defining some of the principal flows of income and funds and by formulating the role of fiscal, monetary, and international factors in an economy apparently dominated by direct controls. There is still a number of theoretical problems which are not yet resolved and which must ultimately be resolved if economists are to have an adequate model of the Soviet-type economy.

Given the material at our disposal, economists might be inclined to dynamize the analysis carried out in the foregoing chapters. It would be a relatively simple matter, in principle, to assume that the state prepares its plan for any period on the basis of output performance in the preceding period, and that the output of enterprises in one period reacts to plans prepared in the preceding period. Such a dynamization would have current output depending upon output in the two periods preceding; or, alternatively, it would have current plans depending upon the plans made in preceding periods. Dynamization of this sort will not, however, be attempted here. Even if it were formally successful, the formal results would not be very interesting, because it would be difficult to show that they were relevant to Soviet conditions. The task of dynamization must be preceded by an exploration of the economic implications of the Soviet state structure. It will turn out that a good deal of work remains to be done before these implications can be expressed in terms suitable for an economic theory. In this sense, the present work must be described as incomplete.

The reader will have noticed that, in most of the discussion, the state has been assumed to present to enterprises the arbitrary plans. Very little has been said to characterize the structure of plans. In Chapter 10, it was assumed that the state had a utility function, in much the same sense that individuals have utility functions, for purposes of economic theory. It is a commonplace in economic-theory courses that it is the family rather than individuals which makes economic decisions in ordinary market behavior and that to treat the family as an individual bypasses a number of important problems pertaining to welfare economics in a small group. The Soviet state, even under the most Stalinesque leadership, is much less a unit than the family. Its welfare function, if such exists, might be expected to be correspondingly difficult to describe. It is worth considering in detail why in principle the methods of Chapter 10 should be considered as only an inadequate first approximation of those which are really needed.

A variety of reasons, more or less subtle, could be advanced to explain why the state should not be considered a "monolith" for theoretical purposes. One reason, which in itself is sufficient to enable us to discard such a hypothesis, is simply that the Soviet economy is so large as to make this approach untenable. We need only very simple data to introduce the problem.

Table 14–1 is a very rough estimate of the number of "primary" economic units in the U.S.S.R. which are subject to plans. Enterprises are certainly among these. It is not completely clear, of course, what the proper definition of *enterprise* should be. The table lists 40,000 collective farms, as of 1962. These farms are amalgamations of the 225,000 farms which existed in 1949; there is some reason to believe that the new farms are "holding companies" and that older farms, which may now be designated *brigades,* are still the relevant operating units. Moreover, as of 1962, there were several hundred thousand quasi-industrial operations conducted by collective farms on a somewhat autonomous business basis, and a decision must be made whether to treat them as separate industrial operations or as parts of farms. Probably the list of enterprises is on the short side, but it will do for illustrative purposes.

We have not discussed institutions in detail, mainly on the grounds that they were not particularly interesting from the economist's point of view but resembled rather the post office, police department, or school of other countries because of their financial and operational dependence upon higher administration. Their activities, however, often have economic consequences; and the state must issue to them even more detailed instructions than it gives to enterprises. Institutions, then, are among the economic entities for which plans must be issued.

TABLE 14–1

ROUGH ESTIMATE OF THE NUMBER OF ENTERPRISES AND INSTITUTIONS
IN THE U.S.S.R., 1962 (IN THOUSANDS)

Enterprises	1175
Retail stores	603
Industry*	250
Catering	163
Repair and workshops*	100
Collective farms	40
Construction	10
State farms	9
Institutions	518
Schools	227
Libraries	132
Cinema	121
Medical	27
Newspapers and journals	11
Total	1693

* In 1954 there were 12,000 state enterprises (large-scale and small-scale) plus 28,000 industrial producer co-operatives. These have since become state enterprises. In recent years 800 to 1,200 industrial enterprises have been built or rebuilt annually.

If it were possible to plan 1.7 million economic units simultaneously, or even 1.2 million enterprises, it would be possible for the state to select for the economy as a whole plans which would optimize some welfare function. Such a method of planning would require the solution of a corresponding number of equations, and it may be stated with certainty to be beyond the range of human computing capacity as of 1964. Indeed, apart from an assertion of this sort, it is obvious, from Soviet discussions of planning procedures, that no attempt at planning in this sense is attempted. Instead, planning goes through tiers of administrative agencies. The "bottom" level supervises enterprises directly; the "top" consists of the head of government and party; in between are agencies, each of which supervises a group of lower agencies and each of which is supervised by a higher agency. The State Planning Commission is two tiers below the head of the government; its head is only one tier below him.

This fact is imposed by theoretical and technical considerations. The Soviet government has never prepared a plan by assigning preference values to a variety of hypothetical "results" to a productive process. In part, this is because it rejects the possibility of doing so (since it is Marxist and does not admit the role of constrained optimization in economics). In part, this is because it is like other governments and does not wish to surrender its freedom of choice (even of inconsistent choice) in favor of mathematical elegance. Even if it wished to behave as economists say it should, however, it couldn't solve its problem rigorously (for there are too many variables to handle).

Hence, a theory of how Soviet planning works must take into account the existence of an administrative structure in the planning process. Given the present state of administration and of computational techniques, the number of agencies (we shall now use this term to include enterprises, institutions, and agencies) which a given administrative unit can effectively supervise is limited. If one agency can effectively supervise ten subordinates, then it will require one agency and ten subagencies to supervise 100 enterprises.

The number of subordinates which can effectively be controlled by a single superior unit will be referred to as the *span of control*, a term used in the literature on public administration. The number of enterprises and the span of control determine the number of tiers in an administrative system. Thus, if the span of control is n, the State Planning Commission can supervise n ministries[1] (to retain Soviet terminology) operating n^2 chief administrations, n^3 divisions, n^4 sections, and n^5 enterprises. Reasoning in the opposite direction, if there are N enterprises, then the span of control must be $N^{1/2}$ if the administrative system has two layers (the Planning Commission and Ministries), $N^{1/3}$ if the administrative system has three layers, and so on.

There are roughly 1.7 million Soviet enterprises. In a two-tiered administrative system, the span of control would have to be 1,305; in a three-tiered system it would be 119; in a four-tiered system, 36; and in a five-tiered system, 15. A government may elect to operate many or few tiers of agencies; but if it chooses to have too few, it assigns to each agency more subordinates than it can effectively

[1] The pre-1958 system described here has been altered, so that regional economic councils for most enterprises replace functional ministries; but the number of tiers in the administrative system does not seem to have altered.

supervise. Some studies have shown that the span of control of an individual is likely to be not greater than ten. The Soviet system, with its five tiers, is probably at the outer limits of an effective span of control.

If increasing the number of tiers in an administrative system decreases the span of control and hence increases the effectiveness with which a given agency can supervise its subordinates, then it would seem a simple matter to improve the efficiency of an administrative hierarchy: simply add more tiers. Another element intervenes, however: the larger the number of steps between the State Planning Commission and the enterprises, the greater the probability that an order issued by the commission will never reach the enterprises and the greater the probability that a piece of information about enterprise operations will never reach the commission. Suppose that an agency in an administration executes an order by performing an unambiguous action, and suppose each agency obeys a proportion P of all orders it receives. Then in a t-tiered administrative system, P^t will represent the proportion of orders from the top which will actually be carried out by the enterprises. Table 14–2 shows that this proportion declines rapidly as the number of administrative tiers increases.

If the Soviet system be taken as containing five tiers (as seems to be the fact), then any appreciable failure to obey orders is greatly magnified. A subordinate who does 95 percent of what he is told may seem reasonably obedient; but a chain of such subordinates, disobeying independently, will lead to only 77 percent effectiveness of command at the enterprise level. This circumstance doubtless helps to explain the stress on discipline and obedience in Soviet administrative literature. The existence of many administrative tiers also affects the flow of information to the Planning Commission. The numbers in Table 14–2 may also be used to show how much

TABLE 14–2

THE RELATION BETWEEN THE NUMBER OF ADMINISTRATIVE TIERS AND
THE EXECUTION OF ORDERS BY ENTERPRISES

Percent of Orders Executed at Each Level	Percentage of Planning Commission Orders Executed by Enterprises if the Administrative System Has				
	2 Tiers	3 Tiers	4 Tiers	5 Tiers	6 Tiers
.95	90	86	81	77	74
.90	81	73	65	59	53
.80	64	51	41	32	26
.70	49	34	24	17	12
.60	36	21	13	8	5

useful information generated by enterprises will reach the commission, assuming that administrators pass various proportions of it to their superiors.

Suppose, now, a given administrative structure—that is, a given span of control S and a given number of tiers t. Then the work of an administrator consists in receiving plans from his superior, preparing plans for his subordinates, seeing that his subordinates do what they should, and reporting the results of his work to his superior. Most of the planned actions of economic units such as enterprises can be expressed in numbers, representing output, labor employed, costs, profits, taxes paid, inventory, and so on. To make things simpler, suppose that every action may be represented by a number. A plan is a set of numbers, and a report on what happened is a set of numbers. For every number in one of these documents, Soviet planning literature tells us that the following steps are taken:

1. A plan is drafted by a superior and sent to a subordinate.
2. The subordinate examines the plan, prepares a counter-plan, and returns it to the superior.
3. The superior studies the counter-plan and sends a revised (and final) plan to the subordinate.
4. The subordinate executes the plan.
5. The subordinate reports to the superior what he has done.
6. The superior studies this report and starts the process over again for the next period's plan.

The sixth step is basically a return to the first, so that there are really five separate actions involved in each plan period. If a plan contains n individual items (the enterprise's work is characterized by n numbers) and the span of control is S, then the administrator makes $5nS$ decisions per planning period, each decision involving selection of a number for a planning or a performance document.

In the U.S.S.R., there exist monthly, quarterly, and annual plans of operational significance.[2] Let us suppose that the monthly plans alone were to be planned and to be carried out by enterprises, and see the number of decisions which would be required monthly by individual agencies, assuming spans of control implied, for Soviet conditions, by various numbers of administrative tiers. A tabulation is given in Table 14–3.

An official located at an arbitrary point in a five-tiered Soviet administrative system who handled plans—each consisting of five

[2] Chapter 2 explained why Five Year Plans were not operationally significant in this sense.

TABLE 14–3

THE EFFECT OF THE SPAN OF CONTROL AND THE NUMBER OF PLANNING INDICES
UPON THE MONTHLY DECISION RATE OF SOVIET ADMINISTRATORS

Number of Administrative Tiers	Span of Control	Monthly Decision Rate, Assuming the Number of Indices in a Plan Is				
		1	5	10	25	50
2.............	1305	6525	32,625	65,250	163,125	326,250
3.............	119	595	2,975	5,950	14,875	29,750
4.............	36	180	900	1,800	4,500	9,000
5.............	15	75	375	750	1,875	3,750
6.............	11	55	275	550	1,375	2,750

numbers—would go through the following steps each month: he receives a five-number draft plan from above; he sends upward a five number counterplan; he receives a five-number final plan, and he sends upward a five number report; he sends downward fifteen five-number plans; he receives from below fifteen five-number counter-plans; he sends fifteen five-number final plans; and he receives fifteen five-number reports. A message traveling downward in his system must be disaggregated. For every number coming down to the official, fifteen numbers must be sent to subordinates. Messages traveling upward are condensed. Fifteen numbers reaching our official from below produce one number to be sent upward.

Our official may be quite well acquainted with the numbers sent by his immediate subordinates. Suppose, however, that he wishes to find out why their performance is of a particular sort. He must then investigate the $15 \times 15 = 225$ agencies two tiers below him, which is a much more tedious operation. Otherwise, he may be unable to determine whether deficiencies are concentrated in a few of these agencies, or whether they are diffused throughout the entire set. It will be impossible for him to be as well informed about the 225 agencies two tiers away as he is about his fifteen immediate subordinates. (Otherwise, the number of tiers could be reduced.) It is partly for this reason that Soviet enterprise management has the divided responsibility that was discussed in Chapter 3. If ministries and economic councils, the Communist party, the labor unions, the Ministry of Finance, and so on each transmit a few facts, then this apparent redundancy may increase markedly the chance that vital information will travel the entire route (in either direction) between enterprise and the Soviet government.

Textbooks on business management used in Soviet institutions of higher education, and manuals published for the use of accountants and planners in the Soviet Union, make it abundantly clear that Soviet enterprises report far more than fifty numbers pertaining to their current operations. Some of these reports are used for audit purposes—they serve to keep management honest; but if we took literally the assertion that the planning-counter-planning procedure just outlined involved the serious consideration by administrative superiors of all the numbers prepared by sub-ordinates, we should conclude that the "representative agency" (to use a Marshallian expression) makes in the order of 5,000 decisions per month, or perhaps 200 per working day.

Suppose that this is indeed the case, and imagine an agent of the American Central Intelligence Agency who is dropped by para-chute into the Soviet planning apparatus. The function of this agent is to creep stealthily into agencies at night and surreptitiously to change all the numbers in the official correspondence. Let us imagine him a statistician at heart, so that he changes them at random by percentages which are normally distributed with mean zero and standard deviation of five. He would thus prepare false tables, with true averages but with otherwise scrambled data.

Economic theory suggests to us that this agent would intro-duce nonoptimality into the operations of the economy. If the plan is carefully designed, so as to lead to maximum welfare of the state, then these changes would cause misallocation of resources; more-over, until the agent was caught red-handed, it might be impossible to detect the fact that he was at work, since his activities would tend to leave totals unchanged. Furthermore, the agencies would be so busy manufacturing 200 numbers apiece per day that until the auditors came around months (perhaps years) later, they would not have the time to see what was being done.

George Orwell's novel, *1984*, is the only discussion of this prob-lem; and of course literary discussions do not wholly satisfy the scientist. Orwell's vision is of the official sitting in his office, with-out contact either with the leadership (indeed, Big Brother may not exist at all) or with reality. His function is to process documents. When random events intrude from the outside, not merely is his present activity, but also his past, altered. Orwell suggests, of course, that nothing really happens at the bottom levels—enterprises may exist no more than Big Brother. With due respect to the brilliance of this book as satire and as social commentary, one cannot but point to two circumstances which have so far rendered it unsatisfactory as a representation of Soviet processes. First, it appears that Soviet enterprises do exist and that the actions of administration do have an effect upon real things.[3] Second, it is not possible for higher administration to be out of contact with reality, as long as other, more or less unfriendly, powers exist. The Soviet government might wish to follow the Chinese example and consider the United States to be a "paper tiger"—but as long as American armaments function mechanically and are manned by people who obey American orders, it behooves the Soviet government to be able to meet real arms with real arms. (In contrast, Orwell's wars are not real wars, for no country in his system is ever victorious or ever defeated.)

Orwell nevertheless points to an important economic fact. A great deal of the planning work of the state is performed by agencies which have documents both as inputs and outputs. Documents which move upward in the administration are condensations, and documents which move downward in the administrations are expansions. The Soviet government (that is, the premier and his immediate deputies) can, within the limits of their span of attention, make individual plans for enterprises and observe the performance of individual enterprises. This means that the planning process is within their control to the extent that they can intervene in the normal administrative processes, thereby disrupting them. In a properly functioning administration, such intervention should be unnecessary.

Let us formalize the problem, in its simplest form. We assume that the Soviet economy consists of (a) the premier, (b) one administrative agency, and (c) two enterprises and that the only plan relates to output. Then the procedure in month m is as follows:

1. The premier sends a number $N_1(m)$ to the agency.
2. The agency sends numbers $n_1(m)$ and $n_2(m)$ to the enterprises.
3. The enterprises send numbers (counter-plans) $r_1(m)$ and $r_2(m)$ to the agency.

[3] For example, during the winter of 1944–45, I was commuting daily into Moscow on the Yaroslavl Railroad. At one time, the freight yards at Losinoostrovskaya were filled with hundreds of freight cars, which did not change their position from one week to the next. One day the newspaper *Gudok* carried a detailed criticism of this particular yard and this particular delay of valuable cargo (much of it Lend Lease). Forty-eight hours later the yard was a vast expanse of bare tracks. Reality did reach a higher agency, and action resulted from an order.

4. The agency sends a number (counter-plan) R_1 (m) to the premier.
5. The premier sends a number N_2 (m) (the final plan) to the agency.
6. The agency sends numbers (final plans) p_1 (m) and p_2 (m) to the enterprises.
7. The enterprises send performance reports q_1 (m) and q_2 (m) to the agency.
8. The agency sends a performance report Q_1 (m) to the premier.

Some of these elements may be fairly simple. Since the premier needs to know how his information is prepared, statistical and accounting techniques will define fairly precisely the basis of the upward flow of information. Thus, given actual output, an enterprise has precise instructions as to what number to report.[4] So will the agency in reporting its work to the premier.

The downward flow of information is not so simple, however. Given the simple number N_1, the agency must prepare two numbers n_1 and n_2. Given N_2, it must prepare two numbers, p_1 and p_2. Here is where the interesting problem resides. For the set of possible numbers N may be put in one-to-one relation with the points on a line segment, and the set of possible pairs $[(n_1, n_2)]$ may be put in a one-to-one relation with the points in part of one quadrant of a plane. It is not possible, of course, to make a one-to-one relation between the set of points on a line and the set of points on a plane (or segments of these). The agency is able to perform its task because from the points in the quadrant it is able to select a subset, so that given an N_1 or an N_2 it can select a pair (n_1, n_2) or (p_1, p_2). It may be convenient to represent this "admissible" set of pairs as a continuous curve. That is, for any point N^{**} in the vicinity of a given number N^* there exists one pair (p_1^{**}, p_2^{**}) in the vicinity of the pair (p_1^*, p_2^*) into which the agency maps N^{**}. Thus, among all the points in the quadrant, the agency selects one point on some curve as representing possible enterprise plans. It knows which point on the curve to select once the premier has given it his instructions.

It is known, of course, that the Soviet political leadership partly prescribes the way in which agencies select the curves in the multidimensional spaces which they plan. It is also known that

---

[4] These instructions may not be simply to add up totals. For example, tractor output may be valued in conventional fifteen-horsepower units, or fuel output in conventional tons of 7,000-calorie coal. Total output may be valued in fixed prices, such as "1926/27 rubles."

agencies are frequently criticized for "formalistic" or "mechanistic" planning. An agency might, for instance, be criticized if it always assigns production plans for each enterprise as some fixed percentage of total output in the industry, even though some enterprises could expand output more readily than others. In some cases agencies have been criticized for the use (implicit or otherwise) of maximization methods. For example, the discussion on the allocation of investible funds in the period from 1930 to 1955 was marked by very strong Communist party opposition to the use of formulae measuring rates of return on alternative investment choices. Even when such formulae could not be overtly used by the agencies, however, there was some evidence of surreptitious use of the concepts underlying them.

The problem, as stated in the foregoing paragraphs, is static; it could be dynamized: Suppose that there exist lags in the flow of information in the system. Then the government must prepare its instructions on the basis of reports pertaining to some earlier period; the agencies prepare their instructions and their reports on the basis of more or less ancient data; real things happen to the enterprises; and the problem is to determine the way in which output, plans, and government policies change over time, given some pattern of lags in the flow of information through the economy.

The problem may also be stated in terms of games theory. Imagine that the government, the agencies, and the enterprises have pay-off matrices and that their moves consist, variously, in issuing instructions, or producing quantities of goods or reports, as the case may be. In this situation, "coalitions" may exist among among enterprises and agencies, or between the government and agencies, or between the government and enterprises. It is not clear whether these coalitions will be stable, so that changes in the course of events will leave the advantageous coalition intact.

It is known, for instance, that there are advantages for workers who produce more than their norm of output and to enterprises whose output is above plan. Given levels of output, the larger norms and plans are, the worse off are workers and enterprises. In principle, it might be possible for an agency to negotiate with enterprises and to reach bargains which would lead to reduced plans and increased outputs. Whether such bargaining now exists on any large scale can only be conjectured. If there were convincing empirical evidence either way, it would assist the analyst in constructing a theory about planning.

If one admits the possibility of such conflict of interest between different levels of the administrative system, one must also admit the possibility of conflict of interest between agencies at the same level. Press discussion of economic problems abounds with examples of how the day-to-day operations of agencies collide, and with examples of problems where, apparently, no agency is willing to take responsibility for action in matters of concern to the leadership.[5]

Finally, plans may be construed in such a way that they provide genuine forecasts of what the planners think will happen, or in such a way as to provide incentives for people at lower levels to produce more than they otherwise would produce.[6] The Soviet government has always insisted that all its plans were precise forecasts of attainable maxima and, simultaneously, that the achievement of a planned figure was a triumph of the Soviet system. This position leaves the government on both sides of the fence. Foreign observers generally feel that nonfulfilment of some plans is a much more serious matter for enterprises and agencies than is nonfulfilment of others. If so, it must be the case that in some sectors of the economy the response of agencies and of enterprises to instructions from above may differ considerably from the response in other sectors, and also that the response to plans by any given sector may vary considerably over time.

Very little theoretical discussion exists about how the flow of information throughout the Soviet planning and administrative mechanism affects the economy, but certain obvious examples come to mind illustrating the need for such a theory. For example, Soviet railroads have, ever since 1930, been working "under pressure"— that is, there has always been evidence of shortages of equipment and manpower, given the level of traffic they were expected to haul. All statements about railroad policy stated that it was urgently necessary to reduce the average length of haul of freight, and

[5] An extreme case is reported by Soviet defectors concerned in 1945-46 with dismantling German aircraft plants. The machine tools in one of the Messerschmidt aircraft plants are alleged to have been distributed among Soviet food-processing plants despite the efforts of the Soviet Aviation Ministry, because a representative of the Ministry of the Food Industry reached the scene first.

[6] The best discussion I know of concerning actual experience in "forecast" versus "incentive" planning is Ely Devons' *Planning in Practice* (Cambridge University Press, 1950). It relates to British aircraft production during the second world war, but contains much that seems relevant to Soviet experience. A more theoretical discussion is Holland Hunter, "Optimum Tautness in Developmental Planning," *Economic Development and Cultural Change*, Vol. IX, 1961, pp. 561-72.

numerous cases of "unnecessarily" long hauls are cited in railroad literature. Yet the length of haul was always greater than planned, as if operating officials paid as little attention as possible to the plans.

A related problem in the fuel industry has been the question of providing fuel to the area between the Volga and the Urals. Repeated injunctions, both from political leaders and from fuel economists, urged these areas to use local fuel, or at least fuel from the Urals; but consumption data just as regularly indicated the use of large amounts of coal mixed in the very distant Donets and Kuznetsk basins. Once again, the flow of information about the wishes of the leadership seemed not to penetrate the administration.

Discussion of this sort of issue has tended to be political or literary. Thus, Koestler, in *Darkness at Noon*, introduces an engineer who is in prison for designing large submarines rather than small ones. He should have known, it seems, that the slogan "Socialism in one country" meant that wars would be fought near Soviet frontiers and that small submarines would serve better than large ones in the Baltic and Black Seas. It is true, of course, that one of the purposes of the Communist party is indeed to provide another means of transmitting information about government intentions to the lower levels of administration; but nobody can now construct any hypothesis about how Communist party direction affects agencies.

On the face of it, the problem seems silly; but the change in official attitudes represented by the attack on the "cult of personality" (for instance) has had a variety of economic analogs. To return to the formalization, it must be true that with the "cult" an agency supervising two subordinates would have one way of mapping points in the set (N_2) into a curve $[(p_1, p_2)]$ and that after the abandonment of the "cult" it would have a different way.[7] In this sense, Marxist ideology and public economic policy operate as *regulations*, to revert to our earlier terminology. They might appear to be a part of the preference system of the state; however, from what we know of the administrative structure of the Soviet economy, it seems fully as reasonable at present to treat the agencies

---

[7] For example, Soviet attitudes on the use of liquid, as compared to solid, fuel and on the generation of electric power by thermal, as compared to hydroelectric, plants underwent notable changes which seem clearly to have been related to the attack on the "cult."

as separate economic entities, maximizing their own welfare, subject to constraints imposed upon them by superiors and subordinates alike.

Confronted with this thorny set of issues, this book has stopped short in Chapter 12. It has said, in effect, "We shall treat the government and the administration as a single unit; if the two of them make up their minds and produce a plan, then the operations of the actual producers of goods and services are determinate, and equilibrium concepts emerge in a form analogous to (though different from) those in a purely competitive system." The foregoing analysis suggests that this presentation is incomplete. It might be said, in defense of the approach made here, that the omissions are not economic in content but political or sociological. The economic theory of private enterprise economies disregards a great number of social phenomena, in order to concentrate upon a few. Provided that the omissions do not lead to "false predictions," they may be excused.

In private enterprise economies, the phenomenon called *decentralized planning* is very important. Government policy may be discussed separately from business policy, because business is assumed to have profit-maximizing functions, and government in some sense equilibrates the operations of the private sector. The economy does not possess a single set of goals. In a system with centralized planning, however, it is important to try to specify the way in which the small number of economic variables on which the leadership has an opinion are proliferated into instructions for hundreds of thousands of economic units. The concept of a plan as the simultaneous determination of millions of equilibrium conditions by a monolithic state is too simple to convince.

Soviet experience shows that the expression *centralized planning* conceals several distinct problems. The first of these is the question: "How do enterprises respond to the existence of, and changes in, plans?" The second of these is the question: "How do the various macroeconomic instruments of government policy combine (or conflict) in the attainment of a desired objective?" The third of these is the question: "How does the administrative apparatus translate a set of instructions given it by the highest political authorities into a set of instructions upon which individual enterprises base their actions?" The first two of these can be understood in terms of the analysis set forth in this book, but the third cannot.

The fundamental microeconomic results of this book, then, are (*a*) that the operations of Soviet enterprises may be analyzed using constrained maximum techniques; (*b*) that it is possible to give a formal analysis of the role of plans in determining the level of operations of Soviet enterprises; (*c*) that the actions of Soviet enterprises are affected by regulations, including prices, as well as by plans; (*d*) that it is possible to define general equilibrium for the Soviet economy; and (*e*) that conditions under which enterprises may be aggregated into "industries" for analytical purposes may be defined. From the macroeconomic point of view, the principal dichotomizations separate (*a*) the rural from the urban communities, (*b*) current production from consumption, and (*c*) the affairs of the state (the budget and banking sectors) from those of enterprises and households. The center of attention has been on the relation between the state, as issuer of plans and regulations, on the one hand, and planned and regulated economic units on the other. The discussion of these matters produces a theory which differs considerably in detail from the theory of market economies, but one which is based upon methods which should be accessible to economists. On the basis of a theory such as this, it should eventually become possible to develop a theory of how plans and regulations are generated in response to the actual course of events and changes in the wishes of the Soviet leadership.

BIBLIOGRAPHY

This bibliography lists English language works cited obliquely in the text. I also included several papers of mine which amplify topics discussed in this book. "Economic Integration in the Soviet Bloc?" is a first draft of the outline of this book. I have made no attempt to list Russian language material. Readers should note that the volumes edited by Bornstein and Fusfeld, by Holzman and by Grossman contain important articles as well as bibliographical material.

AMES, E. "Banking in the Soviet Union," *Federal Reserve Bulletin* (April, 1952).

_____. "Economic Integration in the Soviet Bloc?" *Proceedings of the American Economic Association* (May, 1959).

_____. "Economic Policy in Eastern Europe 1950-1956," *Annals of the American Academy of Political Science* (May, 1958).

_____. "The Exchange Rate in Soviet-Type Economies," *Review of Economics and Statistics* (1953).

_____. "Soviet Bloc Currency Conversions," *American Economic Review* (1954).

ARROW, K. J. *Social Choice and Individual Values.* New York: John Wiley & Sons, Inc., 1951.

BARONE, E. "The Ministry of Production in the Collectivist State." Reprinted in Hayek, *Collectivist Economic Planning.*

BERGSON, A. *The Real National Product of Soviet Russia since 1928.* Cambridge: Harvard University Press, 1961.

BERGSON, A., and HEYMAN, H. *Soviet National Income and Product Accounting.* New York: Columbia University Press, 1954.

BORNSTEIN, M., and FUSFELD, D. R. (eds.). *The Soviet Economy.* Homewood, Ill.: Richard D. Irwin, Inc., 1962.

BREMS, HANS. *Product Equilibrium under Monopolistic Competition.* Cambridge: Harvard University Press, 1951.

CHAMBERLIN, E. H. *The Theory of Monopolistic Competition.* 7th ed. Cambridge: Harvard University Press, 1958.

CHAPMAN, J. G. *Real Wages in the Soviet Union since 1928.* Cambridge: Cambridge University Press, 1963.

CONDOIDE, M. *The Soviet Financial System.* Bureau of Business Research, College of Commerce and Administration. Columbus: Ohio State University Press, 1951.

DEBREU, G. *Theory of Value.* New York: John Wiley & Sons, Inc., 1959.

GROSSMAN, GREGORY. "Scarce Capital and Soviet Doctrine," *Quarterly Journal of Economics,* LXVII (1953), pp. 311-43. Reprinted in Holzman's *Readings in the Soviet Economy.*

————. *Value and Plan.* Berkeley: University of California Press, 1960.

HAYEK, F. A. VON (ed.). *Collectivist Economic Planning.* London: Routledge and Kegan Paul, 1947.

HICKS, J. R. *Value and Capital.* Oxford: Clarendon Press, 1939.

HOLZMAN, F. D. *Readings in the Soviet Economy.* Chicago: Rand McNally & Co., 1962.

————. *Soviet Taxation: The Fiscal and Monetary Problems of a Planned Economy.* Cambridge: Harvard University Press, 1955.

JASNY, NAUM. *Essays on the Soviet Economy.* Institute for the Study of the U.S.S.R. New York: Frederick A. Präeger, Inc., 1962.

————. *The Socialized Agriculture of the U.S.S.R.* Stanford: Stanford University Press, 1949.

————. *Soviet Industrialization.* Chicago: University of Chicago Press, 1961.

LANGE, O. *Price Flexibility and Employment.* Bloomington, Ind.: The Principia Press, 1944.

MARSHALL, ALFRED. *Principles of Economics,* 8th ed. London: Macmillan, Ltd., 1946.

MONTIAS, J. M. *Central Planning in Poland.* New Haven: Yale University Press, 1962.

VON NEUMANN, J. "A Model of General Economic Equilibrium," *Review of Economic Studies 13* (1945).

NOVE, ALEC. *The Soviet Economy: An Introduction.* New York: Frederick A. Praeger, Inc., 1963.

NUTTER, G. WARREN. *Growth of Industrial Production in the Soviet Union.* Princeton, N.J.: Princeton University Press, 1962.

SAMUELSON, PAUL A. *Foundations of Economic Analysis.* Cambridge: Harvard University Press, 1947.

WALRAS, L. *Elements of Pure Economics.* Translated by William Jaffe. Homewood, Ill.: Richard D. Irwin, Inc., 1954.

INDEX

This book has been set on the Linotype in 11 point Caledonia, leaded 2 points, and 10 point Caledonia, leaded 1 point. Part numbers and titles and chapter numbers and titles are in 18 point Futura Medium. The size of the type page is 27 by 45½ picas.